I Know I'm in There Somewhere

I Know I'm in There Somewhere

A Woman's Guide to Finding Her Inner Voice
and Living a Life of Authenticity

Helene G. Brenner, Ph.D.

with Laurence Letich

GOTHAM BOOKS

GOTHAM BOOKS
Published by Penguin Group (USA) Inc.
375 Hudson Street, New York, New York 10014, U.S.A.
Penguin Books Ltd, Registered Offices: 80 Strand, London WC2R 0RL, England
Penguin Books Australia Ltd, 250 Camberwell Road, Camberwell,
Victoria 3124, Australia
Penguin Books Canada Ltd, 10 Alcorn Avenue, Toronto, Ontario, Canada M4V 3B2
Penguin Books (NZ) Ltd, Cnr Rosedale and Airborne Roads, Albany,
Auckland 1310, New Zealand

Published by Gotham Books, a division of Penguin Group (USA) Inc.

First printing, June 2003
10   9   8   7   6   5   4   3   2   1

This is a work of nonfiction based on the author's treatment of and interviews with
women. The author has changed the names and identifying characteristics of clients included in the work to protect their privacy. Any similarity between the fictitious names
used and those of living persons is entirely coincidental.

Gotham Books and the skyscraper logo are trademarks of Penguin Group (USA) Inc.

LIBRARY OF CONGRESS CATALOGING-IN-PUBLICATION DATA
Brenner, Helene G.
    I know I'm in there somewhere : a woman's guide to finding her inner voice and living
a life of authenticity / by Helene G. Brenner with Laurence Letich.
        p. cm.
Includes bibliographical references.
    ISBN 1-59240-028-0
1. Women—Psychology.   2. Women—Conduct of life.   I. Letich, Laurence.
II. Title.
HQ1150 .B65 2003
158.1'082—dc21   2003002260

Printed in the United States of America
Set in Horley Old Style *with* Wade Sans Light *and* Goudy Sans
Designed by Sabrina Bowers

To Joy and Maya, my greatest teachers, and the light and laughter of my life. May you always be as full of yourselves as you are today.

And to women everywhere.

Contents

Acknowledgments

First and foremost, I want to thank all of my clients and the women who've come to inner-voice workshops for their trust, for the honor of being a part of their personal journeys, and for teaching me what works to nurture their growth. It has been a privilege to know you and to share in your inner lives. I'd like to thank particularly those who allowed me to use their words and experiences to share with the readers of this book. Without your courage and the life-affirming force within you, this book would not have been possible, and I am so grateful for your tremendous contributions.

I am deeply indebted to Ann Weiser Cornell, my dear friend and mentor, and the elegant formulations and practices that compose Inner Relationship Focusing, the emotional self-healing practice that she developed, which has profoundly influenced and contributed to this book. Our work together, and the many discussions we have had over the years, helped to form the concepts embodied in the ABCs of the inner voice, and has shown me the power of directing compassion toward one's inner, exiled parts. I am also indebted to Eugene Gendlin, who first discovered and developed Focusing, and to his work in advancing the experiential approach to psychotherapy. I have also been profoundly influenced by the work of Carl Rogers, by the self-psychology of Hans Kohut, and by Jean Baker Miller and the other pioneers of women's psychology at the Stone Center at Wellesley College. In addition, I was fortunate to have had first-rate teachers and supervisors training me in my profession including Emily Bornstein, Karen Kitchener, Tim Dea, Cindy McRae, Sallie Norquist, Miriam LaTorre, Dan Allen and Mark Kirschhoffer.

I owe a very special debt of gratitude to Dana Crowley Jack, Ed.D., professor at Fairhaven College/Western Washington University, whose book *Silencing the Self* is an unheralded classic in psychology. It stands out as a giant in its crystalline delineation of the intrapsychic experience of women in depression, and in the way it relates women's feelings to the very real circumstances of women's lives. It should be required reading for every person who aspires to be a clinician treating women.

There are many people who helped bring this book into being. Betsy Amster, my literary agent, is a gem of a person who believed in this project, then consistently provided just the right amount of insightful, expert guidance and creative space. Lauren Marino, my editor at Gotham Books, gave her special enthusiasm and keen, professional eye to make the book the best it could be. And Mark Roy competently made sure all the details of the project stayed on track. To Lisa Johnson, Sarah Hall, Haasan Morse, Seta Bedrossian, and Robert Kempe, thank you for your stellar help in bringing this book out into the world. In addition, Susan Page deserves thanks for writing the best book ever written on writing and publishing a book. Mindy Werner helped me bring my voice out onto the page. And Sam Horn gave me astute coaching at just the right moment.

Melanie Choukas-Bradley and Alice McCormick gave me their support and encouragement during the long book-writing process, reading portions of the book, giving me their thoughtful and heartfelt reactions, believing in its message and cheering me on. Laura Davis and Hedy Sladovich lent their considerable editorial talents to make the final manuscript as clear and readable as possible. Thanks also to Linda Alperstein for her expertise on matters of human sexuality; to Myriam Barenbaum, Lisa Breit, Jane and Bill Hodgetts, Danielle Luttenberg and Judith Ann Perlin for their contributions and friendship, and to my good friends in the Shemama women's playback theater. A special thank-you goes to Jamie Harkins for her many contributions to the book.

Very special thanks go to Ernestine Davison, and most especially to Tana, whose love, aid and support went far beyond the call of duty. We could never have done it without you, Tana. You deserve to have all of your dreams come true.

Finally, I am profoundly grateful to my family: My father, Joseph Brenner, encouraged and inspired me to think for myself and believe in my dreams. My mother, Esther Brenner, valued and encouraged compassion and creativity. My sisters, Carol and Linda, two strong, competent women, mothers and professionals, enrich my life. And my two amazing daughters, Joy and Maya, cheer me up and on with their strong inner voices, wild spirits and loving hearts. Thank you both for your patience while this book got written.

Most of all, to my loyal companion, best friend, fellow writer and editor, spirit guide and husband Larry Letich: No words can convey what you have given me through this book and throughout our entire lives together. In our love I feel deeply blessed.

Introduction

I laugh to myself when my clients tell me how calm I am, because, like many women, I am an emotional person. I easily get my feelings hurt. I have deep needs for connection and intimacy. I have always been this way and I still am.

We women constantly get the message that our feelings are something we need to rise above or get over or think differently about or somehow fix. They're fine if we keep them in check and don't let them "affect our thinking." But we have to be on guard to moderate our feelings, and deny our anger or sadness, lest we be called too emotional, or hysterical, or "hormonal." We have to be careful about showing our desire for connection and intimacy, or we could be labeled "needy."

Yet our awareness of our inner selves and our desire for connection are great gifts. I would never for a moment want to give up the incredible richness of my inner life, or the blessings in my outer life, that my emotions and desire for intimacy have brought me. As one of my clients said to her husband after seeing the movie *Pleasantville*, "I live in Technicolor—you live in black and white."

I love helping women find and live from their true selves, which is what I get to do every day in my psychology practice at Women's Counseling and Psychological Services. As a psychologist, I've worked with over a thousand women in one-on-one therapy as well as in workshops on the east and west coasts. Early on in my career, I decided to devote myself to finding the best ways to help women be both as feelingful and as effective in the world as they wish to be, and to claim their own selves yet develop and maintain the intimate connections with others they so deeply desire.

Women have such amazing stores of passion and compassion. Almost all of them, deep down, are motivated not only by what is best for themselves but by what is best for other people, indeed, for all of life. Yet they're twice as likely to be referred for treatment for depression and anxiety disorders, because they've been deprived of the tools they need to make their natural gifts work for them rather than against them.

Almost all women live their lives standing outside themselves, always ready to judge their bodies, their feelings and their thoughts from an external standard, and find themselves wanting. Why do women do this? After all, supposedly we have all won equality with men, and are free to follow our dreams and do anything men do. But, though women's lives have changed dramatically from what they were only a few decades ago—in countless ways, big and small—women do not operate on an equal footing with men. What's more, women's ways of feeling, knowing and being continue to be relegated to second-class status, treated as inappropriate for the "serious" business of the world. Women still are given the message that to succeed in life, they must be more like men, be attractive to men, or be both.

Practically every woman, at some point in her life, has felt that she has lost track of herself and is living according to what other people wanted and expected from her. Part of the reason, of course, is the many real-world pressures affecting women. But women also carry within them an inner legacy, shaped by thousands of years of women's experiences, that tells them to accommodate, adapt and mold themselves to serve others at their own expense.

What causes lasting change? Pursuing the answer to this question has been a passion of mine for nearly thirty years. One thing I've learned is that women don't usually change their lives, or begin to feel permanently better about themselves, by adopting self-improvement regimens or telling themselves to change their thoughts and beliefs. Real change occurs when a woman has a different experience of herself.

I call this a "self-acceptance" book, rather than a "self-improvement" book, because I truly believe that you don't have to change or fix or improve yourself in order to be happy. I believe that living a fulfilled life comes from learning how to listen to your inner voice, to the truth of your inner being in all of the ways that it speaks to you, and to live from it.

Of course, everyone knows that they should love and accept themselves. It may be the most common piece of psychological advice in the world. It sounds good, but if you don't know how to accept yourself, it becomes just another item in that long list of things you "should" do to be a better person.

Self-acceptance is not something you tell yourself to have. It's something you experience when you discover that you can pay attention to your innermost feelings and desires with care and compassion. You can also pay attention in the same way to the feelings you block because they cause you pain, and to the parts of you that you think are unacceptable. Then these aspects of yourself can be welcomed back into your conscious self with the life-giving message they are holding for you. When you do this, you become more spontaneous and alive, quite literally more full of yourself, as you once were as a girl, before you learned that girls and women can't live from their inner selves and follow their own inner lights.

Working with my clients, I found that at some point in therapy, they would have moments when a switch would occur in their consciousness. Sometimes these moments were dramatic, sometimes they were subtle, but always they were meaningful. Women would go from seeing themselves and their lives from the outside to feeling them from the inside. They'd feel a surge of good feeling about who they were, and whatever they thought they had to change about themselves they'd see in an entirely new light.

Until that moment, important aspects of these women's true inner selves were inaccessible to them. Without that access, they had nothing to counter the influence of what I call "outside voices"—the opinions, desires and expectations of other people, or the critical, judgmental voices in their own mind that told them what was wrong with them and what they needed to improve. Once they reconnected to their inner selves, however, they had a new reference point for how they could feel. It became easier for them to understand the signals that came from their inner selves, and so they trusted them more. The outside voices had less of an effect.

I saw these experiences as central to the therapy I was doing. I saw women come more alive as they trusted more and more what their own hearts, minds and souls were telling them. And I looked for ways to help women come to their inner voices more quickly and predictably.

Reconnecting to your inner voice is one thing; staying connected is another. Living from your inner voice is in a great sense a matter of learning what, and what not, to pay attention to within yourself. In the process of doing therapy, I identified five distinct passageways to lead you back to your inner self again and again. I call these the Five Pathways to the Inner Voice. The first four are Knowing, Sensing, Feeling and Wanting. The fifth is the Voice of the Larger Self, the "spiritual guide" within. What comes from the Voice of the Larger Self is something quite remarkable: a quiet, clear message that seems to emanate from deep within your body, accompanied by an extraordinary sense of inner rightness and peace.

The techniques I describe to access these inner pathways are effective because they work with the grain of most women's natures. All the messengers of your inner self—your knowing, your sensing, your feelings, your wanting, and your larger self—are there to help you become more whole and live a life that's most rewarding to you. Once you begin to trust them again and continue to do so, it becomes easier and easier to use them in your life. In every chapter except the first I've provided "innercizes" to access your inner voice based on the work that I do with my women clients. I think you'll find them useful and enjoyable.

I've divided this book into three sections. The first, The Inner Voice Experience, shows how women come to lose themselves and then shows how they reconnect with themselves again, re-experiencing the feeling that they lost of living from their inner voices. After learning what the inner voice is and some of the fundamentals about how to regain it, we then go back to explore in more detail what the outside voices are, how they function to block your inner voice, and what you can do to begin separating yourself from them so as to hear your inner being.

The second section of the book, Aligning with the Inside, teaches you, chapter by chapter, how to use each of the Five Pathways—Knowing, Sensing, Feeling, Wanting and the Voice of the Larger Self—to connect with your inner voice again and again. The third section, Living from Your Inner Voice, goes into more specific detail about how to use these principles to build a life of authenticity from your inner voice, first by being your true self in your intimate relationships, and then by bringing your inner visions into your life. Finally, I'll take a few pages to look at how to relate our inner voices to the larger world around us and the times that we live in.

I've aspired to write this book in a way that will evoke for you this very different way of feeling and being. To do this, I've included many stories from my therapy practice to help make these ideas come alive.

Though the particulars of these women's lives have been changed to protect their privacy, and some stories are composites of several women's experiences, the feelings and words are true. These women have generously allowed me to share their stories and feelings with you so that you can be there with them during the moments when they turned toward their inner voices, in the hope that their stories might awaken the inner voice within you. I invite you to notice as you read their experiences whether they affect the way you see your own.

You might wonder whether, in talking about living from your inner self, I'm suggesting you *only* listen to your inner self. Nothing could be further from the truth. Growing and developing as an adult means increasingly opening to the world around you and letting other people affect and change you. I would be just as concerned about a woman who *never* let other people affect her or change her mind as I would be about one who *always* let other people affect her. The more you feel anchored in your inner being and can validate your own opinions, feelings and desires, the more you can give to others and truly listen to others without fear of losing yourself.

This book can help you if you feel that you're doing more and more with less and less and feeling worse and worse about yourself; if you spend most of your day responding to what your boss, kids and husband want and wonder why you don't seem to know what *you* want; if you have had fleeting feelings of wanting to bring some inner vision or dream to life but immediately tell yourself to be "practical"; or if you yearn to close the gap between who you feel yourself to be on the inside and who you are on the outside. It also can help you if you are already following your own path in life and would like a guide and affirming companion to accompany you on your journey. Though this book deals a great deal with women's issues, much of this book can also help men of heart who'd like guidance on how to live from their authentic selves.

The message of this book is as simple as it is radical for women in any era: You can trust yourself, your feelings, your thoughts and desires, your own goodness and authority. Let the power of your own spirit guide you. The world literally needs you to find and live from your inner voice. Indeed, never has your inner voice been needed more.

I Know I'm in There
Somewhere

PART ONE

THE INNER VOICE EXPERIENCE

CHAPTER ONE

The Forgotten Self

*I believed, at twelve, that I could be a scientist. I read a book a day.
I believed I could be a writer, an actress, a professor of English in
Rome, an acrobat in a purple spangled outfit. Days opened for me
like the pulling apart of curtains at a play you've been dying to see.
    My life was like a wild, beating thing, exotic, capable of
unfolding and enlarging itself, pulling itself higher and higher up
like a kite loved by the wind . . . There in front of me, my own for
the taking. And then, suddenly, lost.*

—Elizabeth Berg, *The Pull of the Moon*

Several years ago, I was on a plane to California to attend a family celebration when I happened to sit next to a very engaging woman in her
thirties. We struck up a conversation, and as women sometimes do, we
told each other about our lives. "Val," as I'll call her, was thirty-four,
had two young children, and was flying to a business convention. She
had also recently separated from her husband. As she told me her story,
I couldn't help but think how much she spoke for so many women I'd
met and worked with over the years. Though her story is her own, so
universal were many of her feelings and conflicts that she seemed almost
to speak for the dilemma of women in our time.

"Until six months ago, I ran *everything* I thought and felt through
the filter of 'What would Richard think?'" She paused and looked at
me, looking to see if I understood.

"Don't get me wrong. I had my opinions. I didn't submerge them
for his. But whatever I thought, whatever I felt, *always*, it went through
my mind: 'What would *Richard* think about this? What would *Richard*
want?'

"I had another filter, too," she continued. "It was 'not good enough.'
I'd worry, 'Is the house clean enough? Is my cooking good enough? Did
I help the kids enough with their homework?' Even though I worked

full-time at my job just like him, I'd think, 'Am I doing a good enough job being a wife and mother?' "

"When I discovered that he was having an affair, after he insisted over and over again that he wasn't, I was permanently freed from ever having to make him happy."

But she wasn't free—not really. "I'm never content or satisfied with myself," she told me. "I reevaluate everything at the end of the day. I'd get together with a friend, for example, and then afterward I'd think, 'Should I have asked her more about her kids, more about her?' I'm always second-guessing myself. And I always think I'm short-changing something or somebody. If it's not my family, it's my job.

"And I keep trying on other people's feelings and opinions for size. I'm glad that I do, in one way," she reflected. "I want to be open, I wouldn't want to be rigid and hardened so that other people don't affect me. But it gets exhausting, to have that much static and so many voices in my head. What a relief it would be if I could listen to others but stand by my own feelings with more conviction!"

We spoke about other things for a while. Then she went back to telling me the rest of her story. "Richard's been seeing a therapist," she said, "and he wants to get back together with me. And if I just follow my heart, I will let him. There is a part of me that still loves him. Also, he is the father of my children. But there is the part of me that says, 'Here is your chance to have something better.' I can feel how exciting that might be, but of course there are no guarantees. So I can feel both of these parts of me, but what I can't get my hands around is the gray in between.

"How does anyone really know what to do? It's so easy for me to lose track of myself," she said in frustration. "Much of the time, I feel like I'm in neutral, ready at a moment's notice to go with the flow of someone with a stronger opinion."

As women we are destined to confront a fundamental challenge that colors practically every day of our lives. On the one hand, we must respond to, notice and be true to who we genuinely are, what we genuinely think and feel in our own unique and inimitable way. For many of us, the pulse of our internal lives beats strongly. We are aware of how we feel— sometimes, perhaps, more than we want to be. Yet this is our gift, one that we must find a way to honor.

At the same time, we are drawn to *connect*. We are drawn to follow that urge inside us, that pull of the tide to respond to others, to take their feelings and needs into account, to reach for that moment of intimacy and communion, to tend the web of relationships that sustains (and sometimes smothers) us, and, if we are responsible for dependent children, to fulfill our responsibility to take care of them to the best of our ability, even when it extracts a great cost from ourselves.

Somehow we must balance these two forces. We must bring them together so that neither one cancels the other out. We must find a way to make them work in tandem so that who we truly are enriches all the people we touch, and so that the connections we have with the important people in our lives mirrors, validates and makes stronger the woman we are inside.

Unfortunately, very few women have been taught how to balance these two forces. Very few have been encouraged as young girls to hold on tightly to who they really are; very few have been told that they have an inner voice that is theirs and theirs alone. Instead, they often learn the intricate arts of developing and maintaining connection at a high cost—at the expense of their true selves.

Tend and Befriend

A few years ago, a group of six psychologists from UCLA announced the results of a study showing that, while each person is an individual, in general men and women react in very different ways to stress. Specifically, the psychologists said that under stress, men's bodies automatically turn to the strategy known as "fight or flight" (gearing up either to fight or to make a hasty retreat), whereas women's bodies automatically prepare them to do what the researchers called "tend and befriend."

That is, when stress mounts, a woman's own hormonal system naturally inclines her first to protect and nurture her children (*tend*) and then to turn to a social network of supportive females (*befriend*). This, the researchers said, was the biggest difference between men and women in their responses to stress.

This finding didn't surprise me. What did surprise me, though perhaps it shouldn't have, was that the research team, headed by a woman, was nervous about publishing the study because they worried that it might be used to stereotype women *negatively*.

"I hope women don't find it offensive," Shelley Taylor, the lead researcher, told a *Washington Post* reporter. "We're trying very hard not to have people say, 'Aha! We always thought that women should be at home taking care of their children.'"

How sad! Here was a study showing that under stress, women are more likely than men to try to make friends instead of enemies, and the researchers still felt the need to worry that it could be used to support keeping women in a circumscribed, traditional role. If only this tendency could be bottled and given to men!

"No man is an island, entire unto himself," wrote the poet John Donne. Rare is the woman who needs to be told this. Most women, in fact, would probably find it laughably self-evident. The human species has survived because of communities of women tending and befriending, protecting and sharing food, resources and information with each other.

Your connections—your relationships—are not separate from your sense of self, as they usually are with men; they are a part of you, included as much in your experience of yourself as your talents and abilities, or even your arms and legs. Chances are, you can feel a tear in the fabric of one of your relationships right in your body. Why can a man go for months without calling his family, or forget to send birthday presents, and not have it bother him? Of course, part of the reason is that less is expected of him because "he's a man." But it's also true that he literally doesn't feel the break in the relationship the same way you do.

This desire for connection and relationship is something our society often puts women down for. Women are labeled "needy" and "dependent," and women who show they care more about connecting than competing frequently get passed over for promotions. It's crazy—in our interconnected world, it's becoming clearer and clearer that even in the business world, success depends more on sustaining good relationships than on ruthlessness and cunning. But old attitudes die hard.

When women don't feel their needs for connection met, they often feel it's their fault, or that something's wrong with them. I can't count the number of women who have told me that maybe they're "too needy" and they want "too much." This is unjust and unfair. It's like a man slowly starving to death thinking he should adjust his caloric needs, that maybe he's being "too hungry."

But the pull toward connection leaves women vulnerable. So vital was connection to sheer survival for our foremothers that most women have trouble disconnecting, even when they want to. If you can feel a tear in the fabric of one of your relationships right in your body, then losing an important relationship, even a bad one, can feel like losing a limb. Doing or saying something that could conceivably cause a break in a relationship can bring up a strong, visceral feeling of fear, as if you were indeed risking injury or death. It doesn't matter if your rational mind tells you you "shouldn't" feel this way. Something within us sets off this powerful reaction. At those times, the need to connect and be connected can become so strong that it overrides all other impulses that arise from the inner self. Because of this, many women—including smart, intelligent, competent women—will let go of their own voices rather than risk losing connection.

We'll talk a lot throughout this book about the "inner voice" and "the inner self." What do I mean by those terms exactly? Your inner voice is the wisdom of your entire self as it makes itself known to you. It expresses itself in many ways; as impulses, as urges, as body feelings, as a sense of knowing what you need and what to do, as a deep desire, and sometimes as a wisdom that can seem to come from beyond your physical body. Your inner voice directs you toward greater fulfillment in your life the way a flower turns toward the sun. But even when you don't listen to your inner voice for years or even decades, it doesn't reject you or disappear completely. It simply goes in the background, becoming softer, ready at any moment to show you a way to take the smallest half-step, if need be, back toward living in a manner truer to yourself. Though you may be afraid of your inner voice, in fact it is always loving and supportive of you. If you are filled with strongly critical, attacking thoughts in your mind, then by definition, no matter how accurate those attacks may seem, what you're "hearing" is not your inner voice.

Your inner *self* is something a little different. By inner self I'm referring to your true inner experience. To begin with, it is the person that you experience yourself to be in your private moments, when no one else is around. It is made up of the things you think and feel and remember, whether or not you express them to anyone else. But your inner self is not limited to what you are consciously aware of. Rather, it includes everything that you know, feel, sense and want, whether you are conscious of these things yet or not. Beyond even that, the inner self includes your connection to what I call the Larger Self, which we'll get to later on.

When we are born, and when we're very young, the inner self is the only self we have. But over time, of course, we naturally develop a public or "outer" self. The outer self is the face you show to the world. It is what you actually say and do, and it includes the various roles you play. When you are in harmony with yourself, your outer self *serves* your inner self. It translates what your inner self wants into a form the outside world will most likely respond to. It helps you find the best way to get what your inner self wants. It does this because your inner self holds the blueprint for how to live the happiest, most fulfilling and most generative life you can have.

What's more, since maintaining the outer self is a tiring job, it's necessary to have places and people in your life where you can relax and pretty much drop the outer, public self and show what's really going on—what you are really thinking and feeling.

When a woman loses touch with her inner self, when she believes her inner self is destructive or untrustworthy or when she feels that it would be "impossible" for her to live according to it, she suffers. Some women feel like they can't remember a time when they were in touch with their inner selves, others feel like they lost it in adolescence, and still others feel like they lost it slowly, gradually, in a relationship with the wrong person or in a lifetime of compromises. No matter when in life it happened, in every case, the easy, natural connection to the self was lost because, time after time, the woman reached out for connection from her inner self and, instead of being mirrored, was deflected.

What is meant by being mirrored? It is to look in another's eyes and know that you've been seen, to listen to another's words and know that you've been heard, to feel another's touch and know that you've been felt. It's in the pleasure of a shared sense of humor or a shared passion for the environment, in the joy of being encouraged by someone who believes in you, in the comfort of arms wrapped around you when you cry. It is a primal need, an essential nutrient, like food, water and oxygen.

Like these other needs, it never truly fades away, though there may be times in your life when you feel you don't need it as much from others, but revel in your own company.

Being deflected is the exact opposite. It is offering the gift of a part of yourself to someone and having that person unwilling or unable to take it. While deflection can sometimes be angry or hostile, more often than not it is done without any conscious intent to harm at all. Mostly, it is expressed in a simple lack of listening or accepting. It can be felt when someone changes the subject when you share your hopes and dreams, or in a silence that says, "You're making me uncomfortable. Don't tell me you're still feeling upset. You should be over it by now."

What's clear is how being deflected makes you feel. It feels like someone is shutting the door on you. Or hanging up the phone. It is a "disconnect," and it doesn't feel good. Depending on the nature of the relationship and the deflection, it can feel like a vague, inexplicable feeling of distance that leaves you thinking, "What happened?" Or it can feel like a real blow, or sting. Yet sometimes it's hard to know what stings, or why. All you may know is that something feels bad, and you may blame yourself for feeling that way. "I'm too sensitive," you may say to yourself, or "I want more than he is willing to give me yet. I should back off."

Since the sting of a deflection is something everyone wants to avoid, you soon learn what will be mirrored and received, and what will be deflected. In many relationships, the inner self is not mirrored. Instead, what gets mirrored are the actions you take to satisfy others' needs and expectations. If those who share your life don't see you, you're in danger of becoming invisible to yourself. If they don't hear you, your desire to connect with others starts to battle with your desire to be true to yourself. If connection wins, you take from yourself the right to know what you know, feel what you feel, sense what you sense and want what you want.

How does this happen? When does it start? Clearly for most of us the foundations start in early childhood.

The First Mirror

> *There were no mirrors in my Nana's house*
> *The beauty I saw in everything*
> *The beauty of everything*
> *Was in her eyes.*
> —Sweet Honey in the Rock, "No Mirrors in My Nana's House"
> (*Still on the Journey*, 1993)

You came into this world already a unique individual, with your own true ways of seeing and being. But you couldn't see yourself. That comes much later—the first inklings at ten or eleven. You first learned who you are from seeing yourself in the eyes of those who cared for you. If they mirrored back who you really were, then you came to know yourself. If they didn't, you may have lost yourself, because they were the source of your life and well-being.

From the moment you were born, you initiated intense interactions—"conversations"—with the people in your life, starting with your mother, and then expanding to the other members of your family and to all the other caretakers, teachers and friends you met. It is through these conversations that you grew up and learned who you were. You brought all the raw energy and exuberance of your inborn nature to these conversations, all of your feelings, your child's perspective, your weaknesses and strengths.

Even before you knew language, you had an enormous amount to "say." And because it was so critical to your flowering as a human being, you had a tremendous drive to be met, to connect and to be heard. But sadly, this may not have happened. While there are exceptions, to the extent that parents do not allow themselves their own feelings, they will not allow their children's feelings. To the extent that they judge and condemn themselves, they will judge and condemn their children. And to the extent that they believe in rigidly controlling themselves, or feel controlled by others, they will attempt to control their children. "I got the feeling," said one client, "that my mother had no power over anything else, but she had power over *me*. So if there was one thing in the world she could make happen, it was that I was going to do her bidding." As another woman expressed it, "The message I got growing up was, 'Don't grow the way you want to grow, grow the way I want you to grow.'"

Judging, controlling, and denying feelings are all forms of deflection. They slowly shut off the flow of who you are. They communicate that huge aspects of you do not deserve love or attention. When people do not know how to listen to their inner selves, and when they don't feel listened to, they tend not to listen to or take seriously the feelings of their children. Then they focus only on the outward behaviors of their children—on whether they are "being good" and "behaving"—and all of their efforts go into correcting what is "wrong" with their children.

Yet the biggest and most common form of deflection, more than all of the judging, controlling and correcting, is simply not responding and mirroring the wonderful sparks of life that announce, "This is who I am."

I saw this happen recently in its purest and most elemental form while stopping to get an ice cream cone.

I was sitting in a nearly empty Dairy Queen when a young couple—they couldn't have been older than twenty-five—came in with an especially cute little two-year-old girl. Rock music from a radio station started playing over the speakers, and this little girl started dancing. And I mean dancing! She twirled, she hopped, she skipped, she bent down to drum her hands on the floor, she spun, she waved her arms and then she started hopping again. There was such sheer joy radiating from her, I felt uplifted just watching her.

"Your daughter is quite a dancer," I said to the father, admiringly.

"Well, she loves goofing around," he replied.

I detected just a tad of disapproval, or at least not real approval, in his voice, so I persisted. "Well, she sure does love to dance, and she's really good at it!"

"She loves attention," said the mother. It wasn't said in an angry or nasty way, but still, she didn't mention her dancing, and there was in her tone a sense that this was something just a bit *wrong* with her.

By this point, the therapist in me wanted to make some small impact on the situation. "Oh, yes, don't they all!" I said. "She's so gifted! I bet she takes after somebody in the family."

"I don't know who," said the father. The mother then pointed at him, and for the first time she had a faint smile on her face. He grinned a little and said, "Well, you know, at home we goof around together, dancing and stuff."

"That's great," I said. Something happened to break our conversation, but I kept watching the girl. When she looked at me, I started moving my head and shoulders in time to the music. Her face exploded into the biggest smile. *She felt understood.* She beat the floor with her hands, and I beat the table a few times with mine. Her whole body shook with delight. She was *thrilled.*

But in the next few minutes, the only response her mother gave her (her father said nothing) was to tell her a few times not to sit down on the "dirty" floor. (It was actually rather clean.)

As I said, the store was nearly empty and she wasn't dancing wildly or bumping into anything. Yet the mother was acting as if she was doing something a little bit wrong.

To their credit, the parents didn't stop her from dancing. I could imagine that the mother may have felt a little uncomfortable at her daughter's "wild" behavior in public. Many mothers feel extremely vulnerable to other people's judgments of their parenting based on their children's behavior. In a recent column, *Washington Post* columnist Jeanne Marie Laskas called this "the Parent Police"—the people who judge how good a mother you are by how groomed, safe and controlled your toddler or preschooler is.

So it was good that they let her dance. Yet they took no pride in the girl's coordination and exuberance, even to an admiring stranger! What's more, there was no *acknowledgment* of her spark. Without that acknowledgment, there's a good chance her spark will dim, and with it some of her aliveness and ability to live according to her inner voice.

I wish I could teach all parents that one of their most important jobs, especially in the early years, is to *fan the sparks,* all the big and little things their child does that make her feel good about herself. You fan them by noticing, responding to and mirroring them, showing the child that those sparks are good and important (without, of course, turning around and exploiting them—by making her perform for grandparents, for example). That is the most powerful thing you can do for the first six years or so to ensure that your child, when she grows up, has the inner strength to face everything life will confront her with.

A child whose sparks are fanned and whose feelings are treated as valid becomes "more." For many people, it is hard to accept a child, especially a girl, who is too "full of herself," one who "knows her own mind." A girl like that will be honest with her feelings, including anger at a parent. She may be "too" loud, "too" exuberant, "too" full of feelings and opinions. She is not held back by fear or by resignation that no one will pay attention to her. She expects to take up space.

This issue of taking up space is important. I'm struck by how often women use the metaphor of *space* to describe whether or not they felt their inner voices were heard and honored. "My mother wouldn't let me have any space for myself," a woman said to me one morning. A few hours later, another woman, talking about an ex-boyfriend, said, "I didn't feel like there was any space for me in the relationship." Women talk about "shrinking" or "contracting" in their lives or with certain people, all metaphors for the amount of space they feel they can take up.

Our inner selves want to be *large*. They want to move. They want to be seen, heard and responded to. A frightening or unapproachable father, a controlling and critical mother stops movement, restricts the space where the inner self feels free. So does a parent who doesn't "hold the space," and who doesn't respond to a call for help, because then the girl's movements can't safely expand into new areas. She either loses her way in a world beyond what she can manage, or she restricts herself to the areas she already knows, where she feels safe.

I sometimes ask my clients if anyone knew them as a child—knew and cared how they really felt, knew what concerned them, knew their likes and dislikes, knew what made them happy. I also sometimes ask what they got applause for. Was it for being alive and exuberant, courageous, showing your budding talents? Or was it for being "nice," compliant and controlled, for helping out, staying quiet and following the rules?

Of course, there are no hard and fast rules to explain why one person loses her inner voice while another holds on to it. There are people who manage to keep their inner voice through the direst of childhoods. Often, it's because they were able to seek what they needed in their environment the way a blade of grass seeks a crack in the pavement. Sometimes it was because of certain books, or a pet, or a teacher who came along at the right moment to mirror and validate who they were. A few had some exceptional talent that brought them recognition and gave them something to organize their inner selves around. Or they simply drew upon some unfathomable inner resource that kept them going.

But generally, to grow up without forgetting your inner voice, you need to have at least one significant person in your life literally listen to your *voice*—to take what you think, feel and want seriously. Too many parents believe with the best of intentions that the parents are the ones who should talk and the children who are supposed to listen, to "mind." But in homes where parents want their children to grow up in possession of their inner voice, the parents know that children have only a limited capacity to listen, and it is the parents who must listen much more, and who must *model listening and empathy,* so the children develop their own minds—and their own selves.

Modeling

All children are affected by whether or not they have been listened to, mirrored and treated as though their feelings are valid. Yet girls often begin to forget themselves for another reason: They begin to believe that keeping their voice is incompatible with being a girl, or a woman. At home, this happens in two ways: by watching how their parents relate to one another, and by seeing how their father relates to them.

Most girls are consummate students of relationships, as keenly observant as any anthropologist studying an aboriginal tribe. And the first and most important relationship a girl will ever study is the one between her parents. Every aspect of that relationship, every interaction, good or bad, gets recorded unconsciously as the model for how men and women "should" relate. How open and outspoken is her mother with her father? Are they equals, or is Dad the "head" of the family? What do her parents expect from, and give to, each other? If a woman subsumes herself to keep peace with her husband or to "serve" the family, that becomes part of the model. If a girl grows up identifying with her mother, she will tend to replicate the patterns of her parents' relationship in her own marriage, even when she thinks she's rejected them.

"I had a very normal, happy childhood," said Faith, a forty-two-year-old mother of four teenagers. "I was close to my mother, I loved my older sister except when we fought, and I tolerated my younger brother." She loved her father as well and thought that he loved her, though "we didn't have much of a relationship."

Until she was an adult, she thought her parents never fought. "I couldn't remember my parents ever having a single argument, or even speaking a harsh word to each other," she said. But as she grew up she started to realize that her father always had the final say. "I tried to talk to my mother about it," she recalled. "When I was a freshman in college, I'd come home on break and argue with her that she shouldn't let Dad get the last word all the time." But she ended up marrying a man every bit as calm, rational and quietly domineering as her father.

Parental modeling is an extraordinarily powerful influence on women's relationships. Researching depressed women, psychologist Dana Crowley Jack found that most of the women grew up in homes where the father was dominant and the mother deferred to his authority, and they continued that pattern in their own marriages. It works the other way as well. Two psychologists, Dorothy Cantor and Toni Bernay, interviewed twenty-five women politicians to find out what features in their history and upbringing made them able to become the national leaders they were. They found that, even though most of their mothers didn't work outside the home, invariably, their fathers *treated their wives as equals.* In their book, *Women In Power,* Cantor and Bernay write:

> It is extremely important that women see their mothers as equal partners to their fathers, not as second-class citizens who can't control their own lives. As children, the women we interviewed constantly received positive messages about women, which contributed to the positive image they developed of themselves as females.

As for conflict, from working with women I believe that girls *need* to see some healthy conflict between their parents. The first times Faith fought with her husband, while they were still engaged, she felt so "ashamed" and embarrassed that she couldn't tell her mother about it in their weekly phone calls. "I felt like our love was now flawed, broken, and that it was my fault," she said. I've heard many women say similar things.

Of course, young lovers are always going to believe that theirs is the one perfect love that will never have conflict. Yet it seems that when the bubble bursts, many young women think it is they who have failed. Somehow they should have been able to maintain the harmony between them. They don't realize that conflict is vital to love. Either they, like Faith, were "protected" from conflict, or, more typically, they saw bruising battles where their mothers were cowed, or endless, pointless battles where they nagged and scolded to no effect while their fathers defended and deflected. In all of these cases, a girl never learns about the power a woman has in her relationship. Without that power, love is *only* surrender, nothing more.

Equally important to a girl's ability to keep her voice is how her father treats her. Girls need a lot of practice being themselves with fathers who follow their lead, who get their own egos out of the way. Unfortunately, fathers like that have been the exception rather than the rule for my women clients. Most had fathers who were well-meaning, but distant. Some didn't think it was their job to be closely involved with their daughters. Others were afraid of doing or saying the "wrong" thing, of feeling overwhelmed and helpless in the face of their daughters' emotions, as they were around their wife's emotions. But without that interaction, girls do not learn that who they are, *as* they are, deserves love, respect and attention from a man.

Some fathers paid attention to them only when they were being cute, pretty and sweet, or joined in what the father was interested in. In other words, only when they behaved in ways that were traditionally feminine and made the *father* feel good. At its most extreme, this included sexual abuse. Getting attention for meeting a father's needs, whether it's to fulfill his "male ego" or worse, sexual gratification, is always terribly damaging to a girl's inner voice, and to her spirit.

A father who sees his daughter as a person, however, who shows he cares by stepping out of his own needs and into her world, who believes in her and lets himself be influenced by her, can have an impact that affects her entire life. "My dad was a Ward Cleaver, woman's-place-is-in-the-home, conservative kind of guy," said one client of mine. "But he wanted me to grow up to do anything I wanted, so he had to change his opinion." The greatest gift that this father gave his daughter, besides his support, was letting her *know* that she had changed him.

Chameleon Training

Once they have reached five or six, there is a new place girls go to learn the art of girlhood: Other girls.

I remember when my older daughter was only five and in kindergarten. She was talking about Chloe, her closest friend in the class. "I like other kids, like Tammy, but I have to sit near Chloe or she feels sad. One time, when Chloe wasn't around, I said to myself, 'The coast is clear. I can play by myself, or do anything I want.' "

I was fascinated—and a little alarmed! This was a girl who'd been encouraged from birth to follow her inner self. How did the feelings of a little girl like her friend Chloe hold such powerful sway over her already?

Think back to your girlhood friends. After your parents, they were probably the most important people in your world. They understood you. They supported you. They were the ones you figured out the world with. And with friends, you developed the skills of caring, empathy and cooperation that you will use your entire life. You learned how to establish and maintain the networks of relationships that women have been relying on from the beginning of time.

Girls teach each other the language of connection, belonging and intimacy. They share secrets and feelings; they tell each other, "you're my best friend." As sociologist and linguist Deborah Tannen has shown, girls as young as in the third grade have already developed the ability to chime in with their friends' feelings, even to the point of exaggerating their similarities. They learn to say in effect, "I know just how you feel; I feel the exact same way!"

But there is a dark side to this education, just as there is a dark side to belonging as a woman. It teaches girls to blend in, to accommodate, to tune into what everyone else thinks and wants—and tune out what they think and want. I call it "chameleon training."

By fifth grade, girls have expanded beyond friendships with one or two girls to form tightly knit "communities" of girls. Where you stand in these communities—based mostly on your social skills—is a very important matter.

Tannen described in her book, *You Just Don't Understand: Men and Women in Conversation*, another researcher's observation of a game fifth-grade girls played called "Doctor Knickerbocker Number Nine." In it, a group of girls formed a circle. One girl would start the game by getting in the center of the circle, twirling around with her eyes closed, stopping and extending her arms. The girl she pointed to had to join her in the circle, who then twirled and pointed to another girl, until nine girls were in the circle.

From the outside, Tannen noted, it looks like a rather strange game. What's the point of it? The researcher, Janet Lever, explains:

> Shouts of glee were heard from the circle's center when a friend had been chosen to join them. Indeed, a girl could gauge her popularity by the loudness of these shouts.

Dr. Tannen points out that the game is "indeed a contest . . . a popularity contest" and that it is an "experiment in shifting alliances." (pp. 180–181).

But these "shifting alliances" are no game. I've been surprised at the number of women who can recall horror stories of being ostracized sometime between fifth and ninth grade, cruelly teased and even hated with a venom by girls who used to be their closest friends. The cruelty often starts with some absurd social faux pas, like wearing the wrong sweater on a certain day or saying the wrong thing to the wrong person.

Or simply saying your true feelings. For Dale, one such incident turned into the most painful experience of her childhood.

> When I was in fifth grade, I was friends with three other girls—Claudia, Cindy and Jenny. For some reason, we made it a rule to rotate who we considered our "best friend." Sometimes it was supposed to be Claudia and me, Cindy and Jenny. Then it would be Claudia and Jenny, Cindy and me.
>
> One day the kids in my classroom passed around a notebook. It was called a "slam book." At the top of each page was a kid's name,

and below it were the comments about that kid from every other kid in the class. That week I was supposed to be Cindy's best friend, but I didn't feel that way. So instead of writing "best friend" on Cindy's page, I just wrote "nice girl."

The next time I saw them, they had all turned on me. From then on, they'd call me at home at night, get me on the phone and say things like "You're ugly" and "We hate you. Everybody hates you" and hang up. In class, they wouldn't look at me. If I looked at them, they'd say, "Take a picture, it will last longer."

This went on for months, all the way until the end of the term. I apologized, over and over, but nothing I did would get them to stop.*

These incidents are devastating to the girls who are its victims. Yet those who are successful at the blending game lose out as well. Like Vivian, a thirty-four-year-old real estate broker and divorced mother of two. "I was very popular as a kid. I always seemed to know ahead of time what other people wanted to hear. I was great at getting with everyone else's program. Right in my high school yearbook, a boy wrote, '*Everyone always feels good when they're around you!*'"

She shook her head ruefully. "I didn't have the slightest clue who I was. I don't think I ever expressed a single opinion of my own to anyone. But I don't think anybody noticed."

Chameleon training teaches girls to be nice, be modest, *belong*. It punishes girls for being smart, honest and outspoken. "Here comes Miss Smarty-pants," a friend of mine was taunted. "She thinks she's so big," another friend recalls. Many women remember "hiding their light" as girls, trying not to speak out in class, concealing their grades, and becoming mortified when their teachers read or drew attention to their papers.

*There is nothing "inevitable" about this. In fact, there is no excuse for such cruelty to occur in public schools. Today, there are programs run in a few American elementary schools, both public and private, where such a concerted effort to ostracize a girl would be discovered and stopped—the "culture" of the school would not allow it. This event happened and lasted as long as it did only because the parents of the girls and the teacher ignored it and allowed it to.

In early adolescence, girls begin to censor not just their actions, but their very thoughts and feelings. As younger children, they *knew* when they were pretending in order to act the way they were supposed to and hold onto their friendships. But now they start to disconnect with what they know inside to be true, rather than risk isolation. Of course, some girls don't. They're willing to be loud and outspoken. But many girls actually start to forget their inner selves—what they know, what they sense, what they feel and what they want. And what they don't forget, they reject. As Lyn Mikel Brown and Carol Gilligan describe in their book *Meeting at the Crossroads: Women's Psychology and Girls' Development*:

> adolescence is a time of disconnection, sometimes of dissociation or repression, so that women often do not remember—tend to forget or to cover over—what as girls they have experienced and known . . . girls come to a place where they feel they cannot *say* or *feel* or *know* what they have experienced. (Italics added.)

Of course, adolescence is a time of enormous change. Even if you do censor yourself, at the same time you are becoming aware of yourself in an entirely new way. And as soon as you are aware of yourself, you become keenly aware of how separate you are, from your parents and everyone else. You're consumed with asking yourself, "Who am I? What am I? How can I be me in this world?" At the same time, you wake up to a loneliness and incompleteness you never felt before, and you wonder, "Will I find love? Who will love me? *Can* anyone love me?"

This fledgling separate self is terribly unreliable, full of painful and perplexing emotions and seemingly irredeemable flaws. It needs more support, and more mirroring, than ever before. Yet most girls don't get it. One reason is that they feel they must reject, or at least keep at arm's length, the mirror their parents hold up for them. They look to their friends, and to the media, to be their mirrors.

What they see reflected there, unfortunately, is a fun-house image that tells them to be obsessed with popularity, social status, their weight and appearance, and boys. Teenage culture, almost totally unanchored to the adult world, takes its cues from the media that feeds off it and exploits it. And that media—the movies, music videos, commercials and magazines pitched to teenage girls—is filled with images of skinny, impossibly pretty girls panting after boys.

It's as if the media is saying to teenage girls, "Remember all those kid TV shows you used to watch that told you you could be any way you want to be and become anything you want to become? We were just kidding. You can be a lawyer, a scientist, or what*ever*, but what's most important is that you look gorgeous, act simpering, and fall in love with a confident, good-looking hunk."

A sane society would create some kind of institution available to all teenage girls (and boys) where they can ask, and answer, the real questions of their lives in order to become autonomous, self-aware women (and men). Today's large middle and high schools don't do this. If anything, these impersonal schools filled with thousands of students, where teachers can't really get to know their students, much less mentor them, where cruel social hierarchies abound and drug cultures easily go unchecked, are perfect examples of what *shouldn't* exist. Many girls, of course, do find places in school where their inner selves are mirrored, especially if they have strong families behind them. But many others don't.

If it becomes too difficult or frightening or painful to feel or trust the self, a girl may abandon the effort and avoid facing herself completely. There are many ways to do this, but the most common is through connection—through relationships. But these kinds of relationships are not in service to the inner self—they're a substitute for it.

Giving Yourself Up, Giving Yourself Away

Of course, of all the relationships women use to define themselves, our intimate relationships are by far the most important. Most women desire intimate contact, and it's not essentially about sex. It's about getting past the barriers to where two people are not hidden from one another. It's about knowing someone and being known in a way that takes the edge off the aloneness of life. And it's intensely satisfying. There is so little opportunity for such intimate contact in our culture, so little space to be safe and undefended. Is it any wonder we want to find that tender place in an often lonely and callous world?

But there is almost always asymmetry in the intimate contact women seek from men. Women yield more of themselves than men do. Women, generally, open themselves more completely, seek to be more vulnerable. They see *changing* themselves for their beloved as a gift of love.

Men change in a relationship, but they don't *offer* change as a gift of love. If a man changes, it must be because he has decided to for himself. Anything else strikes too close a blow to the autonomous self that most men believe they must have to survive and succeed. Men in love offer affection, gifts, and the comfort and protection of their presence. But they don't try to mold themselves for the sake of a relationship. The very idea sounds ludicrous to a man.

Women, on the other hand, use the skills they learned as a girl—to sense the mood of someone close to them, and bend ever so gently to more neatly fit around that person. If it is done well, they do it so seamlessly that not only does the man not notice, neither may the woman herself. From here it's a very slippery slope. How far can a woman go to smooth the edges of her selfhood before she risks losing something vital?

We can't ignore the history and economics behind all this. It hasn't been much more than a single lifetime since wives were effectively the legal property of their husbands. Until the late nineteenth century, if a marriage ended for any reason, the children went automatically to the husband, and it was legal for a man to beat his wife—and, as we know, the laws against wife-beating weren't really taken seriously until the 1970s. Until 1918, contraception of any sort wasn't legal; until 1921 women couldn't vote. Divorce was stigmatized and difficult to get until the late 1960s. Until 1965, classifieds were divided in the paper between jobs "for men" and "for women," and married women were unable to establish credit on their own. Is it any wonder that women learned survival skills based on the husband being far more powerful?

It's amazing to me that the very TV shows I watched as a child showed husbands lording over their wives in ways that today would be considered mentally abusive. In the show *Bewitched*, for example, husband Darrin actually forbade his wife Samantha, and later his baby daughter, from using their witchly powers. Talk about symbolism!

But if relationships have changed greatly on the surface, at the core they're much the same. Fifty years ago men clearly were expected to lead, and women to follow. Today, most men and women still operate from the assumption that men are supposed to lead—just not so obviously or dictatorially.

Of course, there are many more egalitarian relationships today than ever before, where men don't lead and women feel like they are being completely themselves. Yet I'd say the majority of women still hold themselves back with their partners. The major reason for this is the strong, unspoken and culturally pervasive belief that it is a woman's job to take care of a man emotionally. "I didn't dare challenge my first husband, for fear he'd get upset," said Gillian, a fifty-year-old import businesswoman whose work takes her to three continents. "I believed that my worth as a woman depended on how calm my husband was, because that proved I knew how to make a happy home," she recalled. "Deep down I think I believed that men were extremely fragile, that they couldn't handle equality, and if shaken they would break."

What made Gillian fear her husband's fragility? Even though Gillian was childless and fully self-supporting at the time, her actions were embedded in the age-old contract between men and women: that women provide emotional care-taking in exchange for men providing for women and children financially. There is an equation that both men and women believe in without realizing it: that the higher the "quality" of the woman's emotional care-taking, the better and more stable a provider the man will become.

And part of caring for a man in this way traditionally has been to bolster his position as "leader" even at the expense of your self. I have seen many young women do this, innocently setting the pattern for the future of their relationship. Jessica, a client in her twenties, told me recently that she stopped watching *Jeopardy!* around her boyfriend because she knew so many more of the questions than he did!

"I didn't want him to feel like less of a man," she said.

On one level, Jessica is concerned about his feelings, and not "competing," following the girlhood rule that "friends don't make their friends look dumb." But on another level, in this tiny way, she is telling him that she accepts that a man must feel superior to feel and act like a man, and that she is willing to take a secondary role in their relationship; she will not be the star, she will not outshine him. If she doesn't outshine him, then she won't make more money than him. If she doesn't make more money than him, then, should they get married and have kids, his career will be more important than hers.

She's not thinking all these things consciously, of course. She's simply following the patterns and assumptions of our times, based on hundreds of movies and television shows and conversations with friends. It is the cultural sea we all swim in, so ubiquitous that it becomes invisible.

In fact, a great many couples start out with supportive and fairly egalitarian marriages only to run into problems when children come along. In the book, *When Partners Become Parents*, authors Carolyn and Philip Cowan point out that even couples who consider themselves fully equal and modern most of the time fall into sex-role stereotypes after the first child is born: He becomes more serious about his career and works harder to support the family, while she becomes the primary parent and puts her career on hold, or at least de-emphasizes the role of her work in her life. The result is that they start living in very different worlds, at the same time that there is less opportunity to talk about those differences.

There is nothing inherently wrong with following these separate life-paths. American families are responding to a reality that nobody talks about—that in a society that expects most "career-oriented" people to work fifty or more hours a week, it's a colossal challenge for two people to be fully committed to their separate careers and still have time to adequately parent their kids.

But there are two ways this arrangement endangers a woman's ability to hold onto her voice. The first is in her marriage. Only if a woman is very strong in insisting that her contribution is equally important, that her husband be deeply involved in parenting, and that *she have a say* in how he divides his time in work, parenting, housework and other pursuits, and only if her husband validates and respects her contribution, can this arrangement work without subtly eroding her sense of self and her position relative to him.

The second difficulty is inherent in the nature of raising children. Of course, parenthood is one of the most profound opportunities for growth anyone can have. Motherhood offers us a different kind of mirroring: it shows us our capacity to love. We see what we give reflected back in the growth and development of another. The mother-child relationship is intimate and powerful in a way like no other. For many years, our children give us what no one else can: their pure, uninhibited, open-hearted responses to everything and everybody, including us. Our relationships to our children, in all their nuances and ups and downs, become a part of who we are and expand our sense of self.

But motherhood is also one of the hardest jobs on Earth. For all of the validation that motherhood can bring, children place tremendous demands upon us, and they aren't capable of relating to their mother as the woman she truly is; they only relate to "Mommy" or "Mom," that part of her that provides for their needs. And for most women, especially after a second child, there's very little breathing room.

Especially when children are young, motherhood can be so all-encompassing that it may seem easier to merge with the job and forget or ignore any feelings that conflict with it. Yet no matter how devoted you are, being a mother is not the totality of your self. Your more multifaceted adult self needs mirroring somewhere in your life, or you may lose touch with your own spark. I have worked with many women, including many who had full-time jobs, who so fully identified with their role as mothers that they could tell you everything their children needed to develop but nothing about what they themselves felt or wanted.

After a while, many women simply "hear" their husbands' and children's feelings and wants much more loudly than they hear their own. And while they will fight if the *relationship* begins to be in jeopardy, if it's "merely" their own selves that are in danger, they become afraid to rock the boat. Even if they complain loudly and even bitterly about the impositions placed upon them, they don't truly expect anybody or anything to change; they become, in the words of one of my clients, "a loud doormat."

Severed from the Self

> I have such a little self, such a small spark. I'm like a ball—all I
> know how to do is bounce off of things.
> —Faith, thirty-six

When women lose themselves in connection, when they no longer see their selves in the mirror, they begin to reject or ignore who they truly are in favor of who they believe they are supposed to be. Living from an image of who you should be rather than who you are causes a great deal of suffering.

One of the most common ways women lose themselves is by *over-responding*. Believing that they should do everything in their power to take care of everyone else, they begin to live on automatic, consumed by the daily tasks of living and responding to everyone and everything around them. "I was in cruising mode with my family," said Faith. "I wasn't happy, I wasn't unhappy—I wasn't *anything*. I just did what had to be done for everybody else. When I wasn't doing that, I watched TV. My kids were living and growing, but where was I? I wasn't even in the picture."

"I wasn't happy, I wasn't unhappy." I hear about this numbness often. Below that usually is hurt, anger and disappointment, which comes from knowing deep down that they want something more. Yet those feelings are rejected in favor of being adult and "realistic." "This is the way life is," they tell themselves, "so you better get used to it." The hopes and dreams of childhood have been totally forgotten, or dismissed as childhood's chimera, something to grow out of along with Santa Claus, Halloween and Easter egg hunts.

Other women experience a vague yet terribly painful sense of having lost their inner bearings. "For months I felt either weepy or unreal," recalled Alysse, a thirty-six-year-old wife of a very successful advertising executive. It had happened eight years earlier, six months after their son Max was born.

> I loved being home with Max, but I had given up a job I enjoyed, where I was well liked and respected. Tom and I used to meet for lunch and discuss our work. Suddenly I was changing diapers and waking up three times a night. None of my friends were mothers yet; I couldn't explain to them what I was going through. They didn't really understand. It was a tremendous shock, and I was exhausted.

When Max was six months old they moved to Minneapolis, the first of four moves for Tom's career.

I didn't want to move right then, but I knew it was good for his career, and I didn't want to get in his way. I told myself, "I like challenges. Maybe it will be an adventure."

It wasn't. She felt overwhelmed—and found Tom mostly unsympathetic.

I remember this one time when I started to cry, and he really snapped at me. And I felt for the first time in my marriage that I couldn't talk to him about this. I felt as if he was saying, "Shut up and live with this." I didn't feel strong enough to oppose him.

After that, it felt like everything I thought my life was about had shifted under my feet. I didn't know what I wanted, I didn't know what was true for me. Nothing fit together any more. I looked okay on the outside, but inside was a vast void.

Although Tom later became more understanding of Alysse's feelings, the easy camaraderie and equality of their pre-child relationship was broken, and she no longer felt as safe with him. That, combined with all the other stresses of that year, caused a break inside her that affected her for many years afterward.

When women's connection to their inner selves is broken, many women then try to live from the pretense of always being "fine," putting a positive spin on everything, pretending to be feeling and doing better than they really are. A British-born client of mine called this *jolly hopsticking*.

Joan, a client struggling with a severely alcoholic husband, told me this story of going as a family to attend a football game with the family of her son's best friend:

It was fun—sort of. I felt like I wasn't at that game at all. We were all pretending to be okay, but of course, we're not. The truth is, it made me feel very lonely. They had no idea what was going on.

Many women live this "as if" life all the time. Often they sincerely believe that if they look good and pretend to feel the "right" feelings long enough, then everything will be okay. But this just brings them further and further from making the connections that would truly make them feel better.

Actually, feeling the "right" feelings is something many if not most of us have been taught to do all of our lives. From early childhood on, most of us learn that there are parts of us that are "good," and parts of us that are "bad." We're told that we must discipline ourselves to pay attention only to the "good" parts of us, and ignore, deny, imprison or "exile" our "bad" parts.

It doesn't work. All parts of you are you. You can't make the ones you don't like go away—they'll fight just that much harder to live and be accepted. The more you try to shut out parts of your inner self as "unacceptable," the more conflicted and fragmented you feel. But the more you realize that every aspect of you—even those you don't like or aren't "good" enough—deserve care and compassion, the more whole and at peace you become.

I think there is more pressure than ever on women to be practically superhuman. Television constantly bombards us with the illusion of people who look and sound perfect. Some spiritual leaders seem to suggest that if you're having "negative" feelings or thoughts, you must not be "right with God." We're all expected to do so much these days: Make money and excel at our careers. Keep our kids on time, on track, well fed and well adjusted. Have a close marriage. Have great sex. Maintain a gorgeous home. Be responsible for aging parents. Fit into a size eight or smaller. Exercise. Manage our retirement funds. Care about the world. Be active in the community. And—in our free time, of course—relax and have fun!

And on top of all this, we're supposed to manage our *feelings*, never break down, never take things personally, never feel just plain rotten or complain that it's all too much. And if somehow you drop the ball in any one of these areas, you can end up feeling defective, like you need to work on yourself to make yourself better.

It's a recipe for forgetting yourself.

When you live from the forgotten self, a vicious cycle can form. You feel bad, which is a signal that something is happening that doesn't feel good to your inner self. But you think, "What's wrong with me? I *should* be feeling better." So you try to figure out what's wrong, you try to fix and "improve" yourself, you try to live up to other people's standards or expectations, you try to ignore, deny or rise above your feelings. And you may feel better temporarily, but then the bad feelings return, maybe stronger than before. So you criticize yourself even more strongly than the first time, and the cycle continues.

There is a way out. And it doesn't come from fixing, improving or changing a single thing about yourself. We have seen that living from the forgotten self comes from losing connection to our inner selves, to what we know, sense, feel and want. Like the princess in a fairy tale, something essential within us seems asleep and unreachable, locked behind closed doors and blocked passageways.

But those passageways are still there. You just need to know how to open, or reopen, the pathways within and travel their lengths, and listen to what your inner self is trying to tell you. Then you can come back to knowing what you know, sensing what you sense, feeling what you feel and wanting what you want.

CHAPTER TWO

Waking Up to Your Inner Voice

"I want to figure out what's making me unhappy," said the bright young woman sitting in front of me, "because it doesn't make any sense. And I want to learn how not to let things bother me so much."

I was impressed with Amy from the moment I heard her voice on my office answering machine. She sounded forthright, confident, smart, yet friendly. Our first meeting confirmed that impression. Though younger and more petite than I imagined, she greeted me with a self-assured smile and walked into my office with the air of someone about to make a high-powered business presentation. It didn't surprise me to learn that she was a research scientist for a biotech firm.

"My father always said that I was born forty," she continued. "I've always gone after what I want and gotten it, but I can't enjoy what I've done. I'm always on to the next thing."

She started her job, she said, a little over a year ago, and was approaching the third anniversary of her marriage. Work was "very exciting, but very high pressure. We're always under the gun." As for her husband Scott, "He's a great guy, very supportive of me. We love each other a lot."

"The truth is," she said, "I've accomplished all the goals I set out to reach by my thirtieth birthday. Maybe I just need to learn how to relax and enjoy myself more."

But it soon became clear there was a lot more going on than needing to learn stress reduction. The first indication was learning that she loved to travel for pleasure, but wouldn't do it until she lost ten pounds. But she couldn't lose weight because she was unhappy. But she couldn't be happy until she lost the weight.

"Tell me more about being unhappy," I said.

That's when it came out; that she wasn't sleeping very well. That the antidepressants she was taking weren't doing any good. And that she struggled constantly with feeling that she shouldn't feel the way she did. "I've worked so hard to have what I have, and it's what I want. So why am I miserable? Everyone says I'm fine so I should be fine, but I'm not. I'm not at all. I'm starting to wonder if I'm going crazy." The confident young woman suddenly looked frightened, even haunted.

"When did you first start to feel this way?" I asked.

"After I started the job, I think. I don't mind the pressure and the long hours that much. That's just what you have to do. I guess it has to do with my boss. He's brilliant, but not that easy to work for." Actually, he sounded like a tyrant, given to verbal tirades and cold silences that lasted a week with no explanation. He nitpicked her presentations, never once praising them even though they won her company contracts, and twice he stole her work and presented it as his own.

"But it's not like I'm all alone," she explained. "My colleagues are terrific. Everyone knows he's awful. The situation could be a lot worse than what I have. I just want to learn how to not let him get to me."

"We'll see what we can do about that," I said. "Meanwhile, could anything else be bothering you?"

"Well, it's not really important. But we did buy this big old Victorian house that we're fixing up. . . ." Her voice trailed off.

"What's that like for you?"

"I didn't care for it at first. But it's Scott's dream house, and he's so excited about it. It's a ton of work, but it's very creative, in a way. And Scott's right that it's a great investment."

"I understand," I said. I understood more than she knew. Renovating "grand" old houses is one of the most exhausting, time-consuming, often aggravating projects you can undertake. And she was doing it for *him*.

"I imagine that it must be very tiring, after a hard week at work, to come home and work on your house." Her eyes softened a little. "I can really understand why you've been in such distress," I continued. "It seems as if everywhere you go, at work and at home, you have to push past so many of your feelings."

"But that's not true!" she protested. "Everything I have, I've wanted!"

"Are you sure?" I asked.

She thought for a minute. "No, it isn't." Surprised and emboldened by her words, she repeated them. "No, it isn't. It just *looks* like what I wanted."

I let that sink in for a moment. "Can you remember how you felt before you started to feel so bad?" I asked.

"Yes I can," she replied. "I even have a photograph of it on my refrigerator. It's a picture of me and my best friend at her wedding shower. It was right after I got the job offer. I was *so* happy. I thought the whole world was falling into my lap." She smiled broadly at the memory. Then her face darkened. "I never feel like that anymore."

"The person who felt that way is still inside of you. What would *she* feel about your present situation? What would she want?"

She sat thinking. "*She* wouldn't let a boss treat her that way. She never would have wanted to live in a big, broken-down old house. She used to have *fun*. Damn!" she said, "*She* wouldn't have put up with all this!"

The Inner Voice Experience

This was Amy's Inner Voice Experience, a major shift in her consciousness that she would speak of weeks afterward, and which began to turn her life around. One moment she was "outside" herself, seeing herself as defective and filled with feelings and reactions that "made no sense," feelings she should get over and rise above. The next moment she was "inside" herself, totally clear about what she was feeling, her understanding of her situation completely transformed.

This experience happened when she stopped trying to rise above or go over her feelings—to not let them "bother" her—and instead accepted them and listened to what they were trying to tell her. In Amy's case, her feelings were trying so hard to gain her awareness, despite her attempts to push them away, that she started to feel like she was "going crazy." Immediately after this session, her feelings of "craziness" went away. Several weeks later, she could tell her boss (who knew her value to the company) that she wouldn't stand around during his yelling fits. It took a little longer for her to understand what made her "pick up the biggest mountain I can find and put it in my in-box," as she put it, and it took longer after that to sense what she wanted to do instead. The house remained an issue, but at least she no longer pressured herself to enjoy working on it, and she began to insist that she and her husband take some weekends off to have fun.

These may sound like very simple, even obvious realizations and changes, yet they represented a monumental change in the way Amy approached life. "I didn't know it, but I was always trying to force myself to be a certain way," said Amy. "I was afraid that if I listened to myself and stopped ordering myself around, I wouldn't be able to function." She came to me at the point when this approach to life was no longer working. For all of her achievements and confidence, she was beginning to break down. "Now I'm doing just as well, if not better, than I ever have—at what *I* want to do. And I'm starting to listen to myself when I want to stop."

As we learned in the last chapter, what Amy was doing is all too common. The details may be different, but many women try to live their lives according to how they should be, not how they truly are, and suffer endless recriminations of themselves for failing to live up to their own expectations, when in fact it is their expectations that need to be questioned.

But just telling yourself, "I deserve to care for myself better" rarely works for long. It only adds another layer of artificiality over your inner self. What really works is so simple it's hard to believe. It's stopping your efforts to fix. It's getting below all the voices in your mind telling you what's wrong with you and how to change yourself and simply allowing what is truly happening to emerge. And then accepting and being with it, exactly as it is. Time and time again, this has made all the difference in the world.

The Path of Self-Acceptance

The Inner Voice Experience is the very opposite of fixing and improving yourself. It comes from self-acceptance. But accepting yourself doesn't happen by repeating, "I accept myself, I accept myself," over and over. Rather it is a perceptual and emotional shift—a leap from where you are to a new way of being.

The Inner Voice Experience is both the *beginning* of and the *evidence* of an entirely new relationship with your inner self. Your inner self, as you recall, consists of your true inner experience, what you really think, feel, know, sense and want, including what you are not conscious of. The Inner Voice Experience comes when you open your doors and open your ears to your inner self. When you open your heart. It is a reawakening to a different way of living your entire life, creating a life that is in harmony with who you really are.

Sometimes an inner voice experience can occur simply by acknowledging and accepting your smallest urges and impulses, the whispers of your inner self. Such was the case for Claudia, a very quiet and shy woman in her early thirties, who came to me complaining of "not feeling anything for months." She had tried a number of antidepressant medications, but her low mood didn't budge. I had the sense that her life felt a lot like trudging through snow.

One session, we had gotten on the topic of her inner voice. "I don't have an inner voice," she said categorically. "If I do, it doesn't speak to me. I never hear a thing," she said.

"It's not like you have to hear something loud and clear, like through a megaphone," I replied. "Instead of thinking of it as a voice that speaks to you, think of it as inner urges. Have you ever had any inner urges, even small ones?"

"Well, I used to want to be a sign-language interpreter," she said quickly, the words seeming to spill out of her.

"Really? Tell me more," I said.

Then it happened.

"That's right!" she exclaimed, practically jumping out of her chair.

"What?"

"That's right!" Before my eyes, Claudia had undergone perhaps the most sudden transformation I'd ever seen. She was smiling, her eyes were lit up, and her whole body seemed to be filled with an energy that was totally absent a moment before. "I've *always* wanted to be a sign-language interpreter! My closest cousin to me is deaf, and I was a camp counselor to deaf kids for two summers and loved it!"

Her glee filled the room. "Is *this* what you've been trying to tell me about all these weeks?" she continued. "I know what you mean now, because I'm feeling it *right here*," she said, emphatically tapping her chest and heart. "I kept letting it go because I thought it wasn't important, but it *is*."

I nodded in agreement, enjoying her excitement at "striking oil" within herself. "There's a certificate program for becoming an interpreter I know about," she went on. "I've kept a brochure about it in a drawer for *ages*. But it's very difficult. It'll take me years."

She looked out the window. When she turned to look back at me again, her face was filled with determination.

"I'm going to look into that program, I'm going to make that call, I'm going to do it, because I *want* to." And she did. She left the computer job she'd had for nine years, took money out of her retirement fund, and enrolled. Last letter I got from her, she had finished her program, got her first job as an interpreter, and was happy.

Many times you've heard something described as a "breakthrough," and in the case of an inner voice experience, that's often accurate in a very literal sense. People caught in the forgotten self have many psychological layers and barriers between *who* they are and *how* they are. So when they finally experience their inner voice, it is a lot like striking oil. Something breaks through and gushes out.

Yet not all inner voice experiences are this exciting. Sometimes they're not even happy or hopeful. They're just completely and utterly real.

Robin, a minister, came to me because, in her words, she had "stopped enjoying" her work. Soon it became clear to me that she'd stopped enjoying practically everything. But she looked terrific. Her clothes were beautifully tailored, her hair always perfectly in place, and she spoke only in the most mellifluous tones.

And she was meticulously polite, thankful and considerate. It's not uncommon for clients to lose track of time during therapy sessions. But not Robin. I could have set a Swiss watch by her actions. Without fail, a couple of minutes before her session was over, she would rise from her chair and *thank* me. I could very easily imagine her caring for everyone in her large congregation—except herself.

Her inner voice experience came during a week that was even more stressful than usual. A meeting with the governing board of the church had gone badly, and one of her less stable congregants, whom she couldn't turn away, had been calling her at all hours needing support.

She filled me in on all this. And then she fell silent, and I could feel something inside her give way. She sighed. When she spoke again, it was as if a different person was in the room.

"The truth is, I'm exhausted," she said, slowly and heavily. "There's a big, empty space in my heart. I smile, and I smile, and I smile, and nobody ever knows that I don't feel good inside. Nobody. Not even my husband."

She spoke the words half-defiantly, as if she expected me to say, "Oh, it can't be as bad as all that." It was the first time she had ever said anything to me about how she felt without trying to explain it, or fix it, or make it better for herself—or for me.

I just sat there with her, accompanying her in that painful corner of time where there are no answers, and the only comfort is the acknowledgment of the truth. She sat sobbing quietly, tears rolling down her cheeks.

The next week she had tears in her eyes—but for a different reason. "This is the way I used to feel, but I can't even remember when," she said. "I feel alive again. I talk to my congregation all the time about love. But this week, my stepson hugged me and said 'I love you,' and for the first time, for *the first time*, I felt it."

Reconnecting to Your Self

By saying, hearing, and accepting what was true for her, Robin contacted something inside that felt right and real. She had a reference point for being connected to herself, not being out of harmony with herself, a sense of congruence or agreement between her inside and outside. And, like removing a boulder from a stream, it made way for other information to begin flowing smoothly.

This does not mean, of course, that you have one inner voice experience and never again have trouble knowing and following your true self. It is more like an introduction, or a reintroduction, to who you really are. But you must consciously make contact again and again and again. The difference is, it gets easier.

On a physiological level, I believe that when you get back in touch with your inner self, you are reactivating a very important feedback system in your body, one that you were born with but have been trained to override.

You have literally thousands of internal feedback systems, big and small. Touch something too hot and something inside you "gets the message" and instantly jerks your hand away faster than you can think. When you see something startling or frightening, you jump. Taste something that's spoiled and a feedback system gets you to spit it out.

When people lose their connection to their inner selves, many internal messages get completely blocked. That's why Robin couldn't feel her stepson's love. But once you reconnect with your inner selves again, you begin to notice that you can sense many things you couldn't feel before, including when something feels right and when it doesn't.

When it feels right, there is a sense of an inner *resonance*, an inner matching. When a thought or an action doesn't match, it feels "dissonant," discordant, wrong, like something within you disagreeing. I know that people are getting back in touch with their inner self when they stop saying, "Why am I doing this? What's wrong with me? Can you make this bad feeling go away?" and begin checking with themselves and saying, for example, "Gee, I thought I felt this way, but I really don't. *This* is how I feel."

Many people are afraid of reconnecting with their inner selves because they think it will insist they make enormous changes in their lives immediately. It's true that if you listen to your inner voice over time, it will transform your life. But your inner voice is a much gentler and more patient guide and teacher than you think. It doesn't *demand* big changes. Usually it leads you to small, doable ten-degree steps that can add up to big changes if you follow them. There are no endpoints or goals you must reach except the ones you choose for yourself.

Once you have found your way back to your inner voice and begin to trust it more and more, you begin to build neural pathways that allow you to connect with it easily and bring it into your life. As you reestablish these lines of communication, and continue to listen to, accept and trust your inner self at deeper and deeper levels, a qualitative shift begins to happen. You discover you're not just finding or hearing your inner voice, you're living from it. And you begin transforming not only yourself, but the people around you.

Alysse's Story, Continued

It had been seven years since Alysse, whose story I told in the last chapter, moved to Minneapolis and felt her sense of herself get lost in the changes that had happened in her life and marriage. Alysse and Tom had moved three times since for his career. Tom had risen quite far in the process, and for two years they lived in a beautiful old house in one of those pleasant, well-established suburbs where locally owned stores still thrive downtown and old sycamores line the sidewalks. Alysse went back to work part-time when Max went into first grade, and was finally starting to feel at home again. She had even replanted the flower beds. So when Tom came home announcing that he'd gotten the offer to be president of the western regional division of a major national advertising agency, she did not think it was great news.

"I'd just finished putting Max to bed when Tom walked in," recalled the thirty-six-year-old wife and mother. "You'd think I'd be thrilled. For him. For us. This was going to be life at the top. I'd be the envy of everybody, right? We'd have more money than we'd ever know what to do with."

But it also meant moving 3,000 miles to Los Angeles. More important, Alysse knew that it meant a dramatic increase in the time and energy Tom would devote to his job—which meant even less for them as a couple, or for their son, who was seven at the time.

Since his first big promotion that came just before their son's birth, Alysse had always gone along, taking care of Max while Tom worked nights and weekends for months on end. "I felt like I didn't have the right to complain. I would tell myself that this was the price of success, that I couldn't stand in Tom's way, that I was selfish for wanting more."

But not this time. This time was totally different.

"It was as if a door slammed shut inside me. *No*, I thought, *this isn't going to happen again*.

"I told Tom, 'I don't care if this makes you angry, I don't care if this is the job of a lifetime. I'm not going to make this job okay for you, because it is *totally not okay* with me.' "

Tom, for his part, had no trouble recalling that moment. "I was shocked. I think I was too stunned to be angry. I never thought of Alysse as a pushover. We had fights before, and I thought we worked things out. But the look she had in her eyes right then—it scared me!"

Hearing that, Alysse laughed. "I felt fierce. I felt absolutely fierce," said Alysse. "And I didn't stop. 'We're like a garden,' I told him. 'Our family needs to be rooted. Kids need that. *We* need that. And Max *needs you*. This is not a good life for our family. This is not the way we said our marriage was going to be.'"

After that, Alysse and Tom talked, fought, and cried well into the night, airing hopes, dreams and desires that had gotten lost or submerged in the years Tom pursued his career. "We'd never done that before," said Alysse. "I really didn't know what he was going to do. It just kept pouring out of me, what I had to say, yet even as I was talking, it felt like I was holding my breath all night. I had no idea I could talk to anyone the way I talked to Tom that night."

But the next day he turned down the offer.

"I had to admit, she was right," said Tom. "I'd let myself get pushed around. I'm in a 'youth' industry. There's a lot of pressure to climb fast or get out. But there are some things you just don't compromise. I've got a lot of time to make it in my career, but my son's going to be eight only once."

Alysse had been learning to listen to her inner voice for a while. But what had once, in her words, been barely a "whisper" now came through with a roar. And she completely followed what she knew to be true. Even beyond the initial "explosion," she kept going, giving *herself* permission to be fully honest and authentic with Tom in a way she never had been before. Doing so changed the course of their marriage.

It changed Alysse as well. "After that night, I realized much more clearly how I'd been disappearing." After that night, she decided to convert a space in her attic into an art studio and started filling canvasses with her paintings. So far she has had one show at a local art gallery. "I would never have had the guts to do this if I hadn't stood up to Tom."

The Inner Voice and the Larger Self

You needn't have one remarkable breakthrough to begin having inner voice experiences and living from them. Your experiences, like those of many women, may feel more incremental, as you increasingly come to trust and accept who you really are. Yet inner voice experiences, whether big or small, share a number of characteristics.

First, there is a natural *welling-up* of *good feeling*. The Inner Voice Experience feels really good, and it makes you feel good about yourself. You like who you are. You feel comfortable in your skin. What's more, problems that seemed like insurmountable obstacles suddenly seem irrelevant.

Next, there is a sense of *direction*, of "life-forward movement," in the words of psychologist and philosopher Dr. Eugene Gendlin. There is also a sense of *congruence*, of the inner and outer selves matching. Finally, there is a sense of *remembering* something you have always known; at the moment, you can't even quite understand why you had forgotten it.

Some of the gentlest and sweetest inner voice experiences I've heard are "this is who I am" moments. All of a sudden, a person sees herself for who she really is. And what does she see? That, no matter what she was taught, and what she believes, and what she has done, and however she has failed, she is basically good. It's spontaneously entering into a state of grace.

"I had an Oprah 'ah-ha!' moment," said Lydia, a fifty-five-year-old woman who came to see me after her marriage broke up.

I was at a busy intersection in Washington, D.C. The light turned green, and I began walking through the intersection. I noticed an elderly woman, with a walker, stooped over from osteoporosis. I knew she wasn't going to make it across before the light changed. I slowed my pace, not wanting to embarrass her with an obvious offer of help, and had a conversation with her as we crossed the street together. When the light changed, I darted dagger eyes at the cars who had to wait for us.

After we both reached the curb, it suddenly flashed inside of me, "I'm a helpful person, this is who I really am." It brought tears to my eyes, as I remembered my parents, who are now gone, who also went out of their way to help people. I felt them close to me. What's so amazing about this is, I was just on my way to the doctor's office for some tests, and I was extremely frightened about getting the results. Suddenly, I didn't feel so alone anymore, my parents were with me.

As time goes on, the more you live from the awareness these experiences bring, the more natural, comfortable and relaxed you feel about yourself, and the more accepting you are of your faults and vulnerabilities, and other people's.

There is something so pure, true, alive and wondrously unpredictable about a person who is feeling her inner voice. She is fully present in a way that people rarely are. And she is stepping out of the convention of who she should be to be who she *is*.

Where does the inner voice come from? As you recall, the inner voice is the truth of your being as it makes itself known to you. It arises out of your inner self, not from what others say you should be or from what you think you should be.

Yet it is more than just information from your inner self. If that's all it was, then we could say that anyone who always did what she wanted and said what she felt was living from her inner voice. But that's not true. There is clearly another ingredient involved that helps change the sometimes conflicting or overwhelming feelings and sensations of the inner self into the life-affirming direction of the inner voice. That "ingredient," the true source of your inner voice, is something I call the Larger Self. *It is the Larger Self that listens to—that can hear—the inner self.*

The Larger Self is the consciousness, or awareness, that has been with you since birth. It is the *you* behind every breath, the *you* that just "is" whether you're happy or sad, angry or fearful, sick or well, ninety or nine. It is what is beneath all of the ephemeral thoughts and feelings that pass through your mind, in the same way as the ocean is beneath the waves that come and go on its surface.

Your Larger Self contains all of your life-moments up to this time, all of your traits, abilities and potentials, all of your feelings, thoughts, opinions and decisions. And I believe there is even more to it than that, for it also contains your Soul, whatever is in you that's unphysical and eternal, that connects you to everyone and everything else and to God. But even if you don't hold that belief, even if you saw your Larger Self as merely (merely!) the repository of all of your potential and your life-story, you'd have to agree it is very large indeed.

I prefer to call this the Larger Self rather than the "higher self" or "spiritual guidance," because it's not "up there," or even far away. In fact, it is with you all the time, in big ways and small. For example, as every mother knows, sometimes your kids can totally irritate you, yet deep down you know you love them. That "deep down" is your Larger Self.

This Larger Self, however, is easy to miscomprehend, because our minds want to categorize and capture it, when it really can't be categorized or captured. The Larger Self is not a "thing," but the source from which your experience flows. It isn't any part of your mind, separate from the rest, but contains all of it. Many people make the mistake of thinking the Larger Self is the "good" part of them, and then try to live up to it by being perfect. But the inner voice is not judgmental or moralizing. There is only one feeling-quality associated with the Larger Self, and that is *compassion*. In fact, if there is any way at all to "pin down" the Larger Self, it is to say that it is the place inside of us that can listen to each and every part of our selves with acceptance and compassion. As you'll see in this book, if you know how to tap into this Larger Self consciously, it can help you grow and heal in ways you can't even imagine.

This brings us to one of the most important lessons in this book:

> **Your Larger Self is bigger than all of your thoughts, feelings and life problems. Whenever you forget this and make something or someone else bigger than You are, you are out of touch with your Larger Self.**

If you're reading this book, chances are you know your Larger Self is there, but its voice has become fainter than you'd like. It stays in the background, helping you occasionally, becoming "audible" only in matters of great importance or great danger. You've lost the ability to access it whenever you want and make its wisdom and strength a part of your everyday life.

What's wonderful is, you don't have to get over your troublesome or distressing feelings to sense the Larger Self and take advantage of its power. There is nothing you have to cure first. In fact, the exact opposite is true. The more time you spend with your Larger Self, the greater its power becomes. Then you can *use its strength* to begin to heal the sad, hurting or broken parts inside of you.

This is very important. You need your Larger Self as your ally. Otherwise you have no inner resource to heal what feels lost or damaged within you. You will then either be forever dependent on the strength of others, or you will forever defend yourself against these painful parts of your psyche by blocking them out or trying to override them.

How do people reach inner voice experiences, tap into their Larger Self, and change the way they relate to themselves? After all, it's not exactly news that you should "listen to your heart," "follow your bliss," "accept yourself" or "find the answers you need within you." If it was obvious to you how to do this, you'd probably be doing it already.

The rest of this book offers a system for reconnecting with your inner self and Larger Self, and living your life as if your inner voice was your greatest and most trustworthy guide and mentor—which, in fact, it is. It also will show you that it is truly possible to accept yourself, not in an abstract sense, but in the sense of accepting all aspects of who you are, even those aspects that you now consider unacceptable.

Let's take a look next at one woman's experience and see how she comes back to herself after a very difficult and painful year.

Hearing Your Own Story

> Listen, listen, listen
> to my heart's song.
> I will never forget you,
> I will never forsake you.
> —Paramahansa Yogananda

The downturned mouth, the drooped shoulders, the back hunched slightly forward to protect the chest said it all: Loretta was grieving and depressed and terribly angry at herself for it.

"What's come over me? I used to be so strong!" she said. Of this I had no doubt. Loretta was a doer. As a fifty-two-year-old African-American woman who grew up in the South, she remembered segregation and the daily injustices and indignities she and her family suffered. Yet her parents taught her always to respect, and never to pity, herself. She also remembered clearly how hard both her parents worked just to keep her and her brother and sister clothed and fed, and how they insisted on her finishing high school. Now she and her husband were the owners of a local restaurant. In what little free time she had, she tended a vegetable garden behind her place. "They're for my customers," she explained. "My vegetables always taste the best. Besides, it's been my therapy. It keeps me in touch with my roots."

But she had nothing good to say about who she was now. "Look at me! I've got no energy. No self-esteem. No backbone. I've lost my pride," she cried.

In her first session, the week before, I heard about her mother, a matriarch who ruled the family with huge platefuls of food and a voice full of absolute do's and don'ts. "When my mom was happy, the way she sang and laughed and talked would make you feel like honey all over," she said. "But when she was mad, she could cut you to shreds." This continued even after her children were grown. She had fiercely opposed Loretta's relationship with Jeremy, her husband, because he wasn't educated, and successfully prevented it for nine years, until Loretta was twenty-eight. It took a violent assault from an attacker that left Loretta hospitalized for her to go against her mother's will. "I said to myself, if I get out of this hospital alive, I'm going to find out if I really love this man." Even then her mother was furious, saying at one point, "I wish you got killed rather than get stuck with him."

Now I heard the rest of her story. Just one year ago, her mother was discovered to have breast cancer that had already spread to her liver. Helped by a part-time nurse, Loretta took on most of her mother's care, who died three months later. After her death, Loretta took her father, who was in the middle stages of Alzheimer's, to live with her. And then Jeremy, her "lifeline," had a near-fatal stroke from which he was still recovering.

As she told me the story, I noticed something curious. What she had gone through in the past year would have knocked the strongest person off her bearings. But she talked as if she was trying to convince me, as if she were afraid I would come back to her and say, "Oh, that's nothing. What are you so upset about?"

That's clearly what she was telling herself.

"I can't stand myself for falling apart," she said. "I'm not who I used to be. I lost the person I was."

"No, you haven't," I answered. "That strong woman is still there. Your essence never leaves you. It may be buried, or hidden, like the sun behind the clouds, but it's not lost."

I could see something in her glimmering as she heard me say that.

I continued. "Can you *hear* yourself say how much you've been through?"

She looked at me puzzled.

"Can you really *hear* your own story, take it in and listen to it? Like you would a friend?"

I repeated her story back to her, speaking very slowly and deliberately. " 'I took care of my mother, and I handled her funeral, and we went through her possessions, and I sold my parents' house, and Dad came to live with me . . . ' Just slow down and replay for yourself what you just told me. As you hear it, can you begin to have a little compassion for yourself for everything you went through?"

She followed my directions, and as she did, I could see a change crossing her face, a softening, but even more, a sudden recognition. "Yes . . . yes," she said, talking more to herself than to me.

At the end of her session I gave her the assignment to simply take short "awareness" breaks a few times every day, to simply notice herself and how she was feeling, keeping in mind the way she had listened to herself with compassion during the session.

The next week she strode into my office and sat down. "I've been doing what you told me to do all week," she said, a warm smile filling her face.

"You have?"

"Yes! I've been practicing paying attention to what's going on inside me. And I don't feel so upset. I've decided, I'm not going to beat up on myself anymore. NO MORE. I am *not* going to do it.

"I feel so different, one-hundred percent different," she continued. "I can't explain why. But before I had to force myself to go out into the garden. There was no joy. Sunday I was in the garden, and I noticed I was humming to myself, like I used to. Then I brought in some ripe green beans and turnip greens and cooked them up with some stuffed pork chops, just for my husband and me. I even put flowers on the table.

"And yesterday, Jeremy said to me, 'Oh my, I just heard the most beautiful sound in the world.'

"And I said, 'Oh, what's that?'

"And he said, 'Your laughter.'" She beamed. "I didn't realize it, but I could *laugh* again."

The ABCs of the Inner Voice

What caused such a dramatic change, so quickly? I believe it was because Loretta listened to herself in a way she had never listened in her whole life.

Though Loretta was still grieving her mother, that was not the biggest source of her pain. The pain that was sapping her energy was not being able to accept herself, not being able to see herself with compassion.

All of the difficult events of the past year understandably caused her inner self, not to mention her body, to go into distress. Had she known how, she could have acknowledged and felt that distress and remained feeling whole. Instead, her fear of losing her strength made her panic in the face of all that fatigue and turmoil.

This panic triggered a protective mechanism in her brain—an automatic response that tried to clamp down on and get rid of her distressing feelings the way a white blood cell would devour an invading bacterium. But since the distressing feelings were part of her, this "protector" was like an immune system gone amok. Instead of attacking something foreign, it was attacking Loretta.

The protective mechanism was in the form of belittling thoughts so loud and powerful they could actually be thought of as a voice, though obviously Loretta only heard them inside her head. Not coincidentally, this voice said things that sounded a lot like things she imagined her mother would say. "Come on, stop pitying yourself, girl! There's much worse in life than what you're going through! Get out there and do what you gotta do!"

Of course, we can never know what her real mother would have said. But faced with the loss, the stress *and* this constant, harping voice, it's no wonder she felt horrible. And the worse she felt, the more the voice stepped up its attacks. Faced with this much inner conflict, real physiological changes occur, including the release of vast quantities of the stress hormone cortisol, that leave people feeling hypersensitive and exhausted.

This is what Loretta did that broke the cycle: She went from being reflexive to being reflective, and she listened to herself with what I call the ABCs of the Inner Voice—Acknowledging, Being With and Compassion.

From Reflexive to Reflective

Being reflexive is doing all the old, automatic things you do without thinking. It's acting in the ways you're familiar with, even when they don't work for you. Had Loretta listened to her story in the old way, she would have said, "Why bother? I *know* what I've gone through this year!" Or she would have pretended to pay attention to her story, all the while dismissing and minimizing it in her mind. "Big deal. I'm just pitying myself."

The basis of reflecting is the ability to separate from the moment and look at what is happening. As one woman put it, "most people live in a what-you-see-is-what-you-get world." But people whose lives are richer and more fulfilling usually have always known intuitively that there is more to life than what they see. This kind of self-reflection is very different from analyzing yourself, enumerating your faults or making plans for your self-improvement, which is what most of us come to think of as self-reflection.

Being reflective simply means bringing *awareness* to what you're experiencing. You slow down inside yourself a little, "take a step back" from what you're doing and just notice what is happening within you and reflect on it, without any judgment or moralizing.

This is something that often can feel very hard to do—which is odd, because it almost always has a calming effect. When people pause and take a moment to notice what is happening inside of them, their breathing usually becomes deeper and more even, and their muscles relax. It acts as a brake on the runaway train of fearful, critical and blaming thoughts that cause people to feel awful.

Being reflective also means listening to your inner self with new ears. The truth is, we think we've heard our own story so much that we stop listening to it! We become like the people in our lives who we complain don't listen to us. With reflection, we listen freshly to our selves, the way we would like to be listened to.

There are actually three old, reflexive ways that people use to deal with difficult feelings. They either *angrily reject* them, *dismiss* and *minimize* them, or *constantly get immersed* in them. People generally

INNERCIZE I

The Awareness Break

Take a moment to stop what you're doing and simply notice what is happening around you and inside you right now. Not yesterday, not this morning, but right this minute. Slow down, take a breath, and look around. It may help simply to describe what you see or know is happening and then check how you feel inside. "Supper's on the stove, the kids are running around screaming and—that's funny—I'm feeling a little lonely." "It's twelve-fifteen, I'm eating lunch really fast, and I'm nervous about the presentation in two hours."

If you're stressed or in some way not feeling so good, see if you can concentrate, gently, on noticing and describing to yourself the physical sensations of your distressing feelings ("my body is tense and tightened up"), rather than the emotions that are upsetting you ("I'm furious at my boss"). For now, don't do anything with this informa-tion. Just notice, observe and be neutral to your experience. If you choose to do this for more than a few seconds, focus your awareness to notice if the sensations in your body change in any way while you observe them. Do this for no more than a minute or two. If you need to do something other than neutrally describe what's going on inside of you, end your awareness break by saying, ". . . and it's okay that I feel this way."

Do this as often as you like, preferably several times a day.

use all three at different times, but one of them is their predominant "style."

The reflective way of handling feelings is totally different. It involves listening to yourself as you would a friend.

Acknowledging

As Loretta told the story of the past year again, slowly, with full presence in what she was saying, she naturally started to practice the first of the ABCs. Instead of dismissing it, for the first time she truly *acknowledged* what she had lived through.

Acknowledging means acknowledging whatever you discover is true inside, without judgment, even if it's a feeling or want that you don't think you "should" have. When you acknowledge, you are not denying your experience. You are not trying to change, fix or wish it away, and you are not making it smaller or bigger, better or worse than it is. You are simply letting your inner experience be, exactly the way it is.

This isn't easy. It's human nature to want to avoid, fight or change what we don't like or what causes us pain, whether it's something in our lives or something in ourselves. Unfortunately, it doesn't work. Many times, difficult feelings won't change unless they're acknowledged first. Yet you may be afraid of acknowledging "negative" emotions such as fear or anger because you think that such feelings, once acknowledged, will "take over." The opposite is true. By allowing them, they are free to be felt and to pass. By fighting them, they remain with you and you have to continue expending energy to keep them at bay.

At the same time, however, acknowledging is not the same as getting in touch with your feelings and expressing them. A lot of people who are good at knowing what they feel and expressing it are not really Acknowledging, because they're doing these things reflexively. They're not being reflective. Acknowledging is *being aware of* what's going on inside you, *noticing* its presence, *admitting* it's there, and *allowing* it to be there. It's different, however, from *becoming* it. This will become clearer as we talk about the next step, Being With, and it will become even more clear as the book progresses.

Being With

Loretta's acknowledging flowed smoothly into the next step, *Being With*. Being With is magic. Think of Being With this way: imagine you have a friend who's going through a rough time. You've invited her over. You meet her at the door, acknowledge that she's feeling upset, get her a cup of coffee or tea and sit down to listen to her tell her story. That's Being With.

You can actually *be with* and *listen to* a troubled part of yourself the way you would be with and listen to a troubled friend. As strange as it may sound to treat your own feelings as a separate person, this is an amazingly powerful practice.

When Loretta listened to her own story, she stepped out of the pain and distress. Her new vantage point, as the one-who-could-see-Loretta-who-had-gone-through-so-much, gave her mind respite from the chronic state of suffering and self-recrimination that Loretta had fallen into. She literally stepped outside her own mind. And once freed from that painful pain-attack-defend cycle, her psyche could start to heal itself again.

You might think that listening to your inner self and your feelings as if you were listening to someone else would be a distancing, emotionally cold thing to do. In fact, as we'll see in Chapter Six, Being With allows you to feel your feelings more fully, clearly and completely than if you simply plunge into them. Even more importantly, it allows them to resolve. Being With allows your emotions and experience to move *out* of habitual and frozen positions. It is the Houdini key out of the stuck places in your psyche.

Another term for Being With is Keeping It Company, a phrase coined by Ann Weiser Cornell, Ph.D., the creator of Inner Relationship Focusing. This is the healing work of the Larger Self—it can "keep company" with the parts of us that feel cut off, overwhelmed, angry or in pain, much the way you can keep a friend company through a crisis or a parent can keep company with a child in distress. You know what a difference it makes when you can share a painful feeling with someone who truly knows how to listen lovingly and caringly. It can make even a tragedy feel bearable. In the same way, Being With allows you (more accurately, the larger You) to keep company with aspects of yourself in a way that make growth and healing possible.

🍃 INNERCIZE 2 🍃
Listening to Your Own Story

Listening to your story, which Loretta did, is a very powerful technique for practicing the ABCs. I invite you to try it yourself now.

What is the story of your life right now? Maybe, like Loretta, you're in the midst of a series of events you're reeling from. See if you can listen to your own story. Speak it slowly, in front of a mirror or into a tape recorder, or write it out. Then listen to it, or read it aloud, as if it were someone else's—a person in a book, or someone you like but don't know very well, who is telling her story to you for the very first time.

Can you allow yourself to see that person as imperfect and worthy of compassion? See if you can appreciate and understand why this person, in the context of her life, acts and feels the way she does.

Is it the *true* story? If it isn't completely, see if you can go back and make the story more closely match your true experience. Now listen to your story again, and write down how it affects you.

Compassion

Finally, as Loretta listened to her story, I invited her to give herself compassion for what she had gone through. In fact, she was already doing so. By being with her own story in a slow and caring way, she couldn't help but begin to give herself some compassion. But when she truly awakened to the fact that she deserved compassion for what she had lived through, she completed the ABC process—and began to change.

Loretta deserved compassion for what she had gone through. And so do you. I don't know you personally, but I can state with absolute certainty that you do deserve compassion, whether you think you do or not.

And you very well may not think you deserve compassion. One of the most difficult things, I've found, for women—indeed, for all people—is to truly have compassion for themselves. Whether it's anxiety or depression, a job crisis or an affair, women walk into my office braced against the "awful truth" about themselves. Deep down they believe that their distress is their *fault*, that there is something really bad or wrong with them that causes their problem.

I have worked with more than a thousand women in therapy, and if my clients are any indication, most women, far from being self-pitiers, are as tough as nails on themselves. I can't tell you how many women have walked into my office trying to order themselves to get over their suffering. "Snap out of it!" they tell themselves. "Live with it." "Deal with it." "You made your bed, now lie in it." "Count your blessings." But if there's one thing my therapy practice has taught me without a doubt, it is this: The army boot camp approach to yourself does not work. Not in the long run. The only thing that will end your distress and help you make lasting changes is compassion.

Compassion has many names. Gentleness. Empathy. Tenderness. Loving-kindness. Even softness. Compassion, especially self-compassion, is at the very heart of living from your inner voice. Nothing can be accomplished without it; with it, you can bring about miracles. When it is extended to any part of your self that is stuck in suffering, that part begins to heal. Extend compassion toward the hurt, angry and fearful places, the vulnerable places, the foolish places, the clumsy and "defective" places, and even the darkest, most unacceptable places inside of yourself and others, and you'll begin to feel a peace, calm and presence within you that you can barely imagine.

Perhaps you're afraid that if you give yourself compassion, you will never change. You'll continue to be "lazy," or continue to do self-destructive things. I have not found this to be true. Self-acceptance and compassion require discipline, too—the discipline of *paying attention* to yourself and what you feel and do. It's not the same as letting yourself off the hook. Nor do you have to worry that it will make you too "soft." Rather, compassion for yourself will give you strength. It will tell you what you need to sustain you, and keep you in touch with what you're fighting *for*.

There are many pockets of our society, left over from our Puritan history, that are anything but compassionate. Many of my clients grew up in homes like Jeanette's. "I never heard anything good about me from my parents. I only heard about what I was doing wrong. And then I got hit with a belt," she recalled. "My mom, especially. It seemed like all she tried to do was find what was wrong with me, so she could 'correct' it." This is the "hard-eyes" school of child-rearing, the bad-until-proven-good philosophy, and for all the talk of "permissiveness" it's still pervasive. No wonder so many of my clients judge themselves with an iron hand.

Yet even people with caring and gentle parents can have a judgmental voice inside of them—one that lists every one of their defects and is quick to shout, "How can you be so dumb!" the moment something goes wrong. But know this: When you're being hard on yourself, no matter how accurate your attacks may sound, you can be absolutely sure you're not only out of touch with your own inner truth, you're distorting reality itself.

I'm not talking about genuine remorse, which feels very different. I'm talking about the self-berating-bordering-on-self-loathing that almost all of us find ourselves doing sometimes.

One way to counter this is to recognize that everything you do makes sense to, and has a purpose for, some part of you. Even when it is hurtful or self-destructive, some part of you believes it is necessary for survival. That part deserves compassion. Chances are, that part deserves a *lot* of compassion.

Second is to counter it on the physical level. Along with that self-berating comes a physical response. When we are "hard on ourselves" or "beat up on ourselves," that is a very accurate description of what we are doing. The muscles in our neck, arms, forearms, face, stomach and chest all tense up and harden, as we prepare physiologically to fight. But who are we fighting? Ourselves.

What can we do instead? We can, quite literally, soften up. We can approach ourselves with "soft" eyes.

Now, what may happen as you do the following innercize is that you'll have trouble being gentle with yourself—and you'll do the following: You'll get hard on yourself for being hard on yourself! "Oh, I can't be gentle with myself!" you'll think. "I'm screwing up again!"

If you find yourself doing that, what do you do? What you do is to be gentle with yourself—that is, go easy on yourself—for being hard on yourself. Simply notice, with an attitude of compassion, that it's hard for you to give yourself compassion.

It helps to think about how you would be with a friend. Would you talk to a friend the way you talk to yourself? Of course not. You'd be so much more understanding and forgiving. Consciously imagine what you would say to that friend, and then say it to yourself.

For the rest of the time you read this book, and hopefully long after, treat yourself with an abundance of gentleness, more than you've ever given yourself before. As you travel through these pages, you'll realize that everything inside you deserves acceptance and compassion, and the parts of you that you think deserve it the least need and deserve it the most.

INNERCIZE 3

Softening to Yourself

The next time you notice that you're pushing yourself too hard, or having the usual angry, harsh, self-condemning thoughts, do something different: Be *gentle* to *yourself*. Take a long, slow breath, and relax your body. Relax your arms, shoulders and chest. Then relax your face. Soften your eyes. Tell yourself that if you're attacking yourself this hard, it can't be the real truth. If it's something you did that you now regret, tell yourself that a part of you must have had a very good reason for doing it. Think, especially, if a close friend had done what you had done, or made the mistake you made, how you would respond.

Notice if you feel some new feelings (possibly sadness) as you stay gentle to yourself, and if you wish, write them down.

CHAPTER THREE

Outside Voices

"What's wrong with me?"
"Buck up—other people cope, why can't I?"
"I need too much."
"Look at me. I'm too fat."
"I can't say no; it will hurt his feelings."
"I shouldn't care what anyone else thinks."
"Put myself first? That's selfish!"

Outside voices. Everyone has them. And nothing gets in the way of hearing your inner voice more. Outside voices are the feelings, wants and opinions of others that ring so loudly in your ears, you can't hear anymore what's true for yourself. Or they're those voices in your head that shout at you, telling you mostly what's wrong with you and what you have to change. I call these *outside voices* because, even though they're within your own mind, they don't really come from your inner self, from what you know, sense, feel or want, or your Larger Self. Instead, they talk *at* you, causing you to ignore what arises from your inner self in favor of some external standard that you've come to believe is more important or correct.

A Reluctant Green Light

Just to figure out what I personally think about anything, I have to climb over a whole group of people inside me.
—Charlotte, forty-three

"I've decided I can't go to the conference," Charlotte announced.

Charlotte was a forty-three-year-old sales representative whose tough exterior masked an absolutely marshmallow interior. She'd been married for fifteen years to Tony, and together they had three school-aged children. The week before she'd told me how excited she was about attending the annual conference of an organization she belonged to, which was being held in a city about 300 miles away. It would be the first time she had gone to something just for herself, with no family involved, since before her twelve-year-old daughter was born. Something obviously had happened to change her mind.

"You have? How come?" I asked.

"I talked to Tony about it, and he doesn't think it's a very good idea."

"Why?"

"Well, I don't know if I've told you, but he's always been very frightened of me traveling by myself," she explained. "You're not going to believe this, but he's afraid something's going to happen to me.

"We had a big fight about it," she told me with relish. "I said, 'What, are you afraid I'm going to get abducted at a truck stop? Don't you think I've got any judgment and common sense?' But I couldn't convince him. He's like, afraid some nut is going to get me or something. Then he'd have to learn how to get along in life without me. That's what he's *really* afraid of," she said, rolling her eyes.

"So he told you you couldn't go?" I asked.

"No, not exactly." She looked a little uncomfortable. "I told him, 'Well I'm going to go anyway,' and I know he wouldn't try to stop me.

"But I don't want to go anymore. It's not worth it to me. Tony's so against it. And maybe I *am* being selfish. The kids will miss me. And I started having thoughts like, what if something did happen to me? I take the car, I take a risk, something happens and my children grow up without a mother."

This is not an uncommon story. Charlotte didn't want Tony's permission, but for all of her outward bravado, Charlotte wanted, and needed, his affirmation. Her excitement about going to the conference was a spark of her inner self. Instead of cherishing that spark and fanning it, Tony came along and poured a bucket of cold water on it.

So she got angry and they had a fight. But if she then went "anyway," as she told him she would, she'd be the connection-breaker, which would be intolerable for her. Her mind then created a way for her to save face and reestablish her *inner harmony* with him, by taking on *his* irrational fears. "What if something did happen to me?"

I could have tried to talk her out of his fears, but that wouldn't have done much good, when the problem was that she didn't get validation for following her inner self.

"Sounds like he didn't give you much support for what you wanted to do."

"He sure didn't."

"And you wanted him to."

That was harder for her to deal with. "No I didn't! . . . I mean, I shouldn't *have* to have his permission to do what I want to do. Why do I wimp out so much?" Self-reproach crept into her voice.

"Maybe you needed him to realize how tough this was for you to do for yourself? Maybe, because he matters to you, you wanted him to support you, to root for you, even if you yourself had doubts?"

"Yeah. Yeah," she said. "I wanted him to give me the total green light."

"What if you could give yourself the total green light, Charlotte?" I asked softly. "What would you feel?"

She caught her breath. "I . . . I get excited! It's like a free pass. It makes me feel hopeful . . . exhilarated!" She shook her head. "I don't give myself a green light very much. I didn't think I had control over that light."

"The truth is," she continued, "no one ever gave me the total green light to do *any*thing. I've gotten a reluctant green light all my life. My family only cared about what I *had* to do. Anything I *wanted* to do, they said, 'Are you sure? Who's going with you? Did you finish your chores?' No one ever said to me, 'You go, girl.' Not like what my daughter gets from me."

She grinned and leaned forward in her chair. "You know, last week I was watching Katie play soccer. She got the ball from the other team and she started kicking it toward the goal, and running with it, and kicking it, and the girls on the other team were all around her trying to block her, and I don't know where it came from inside of me, but I started jumping up and down in the air hollering and screaming, '*Go for blood, Katie! Go for blood!*'" Charlotte was jumping in her chair, shouting and waving her arms. It was quite a sight. "The other parents must have thought I was absolutely nuts." We were both smiling, thinking about what a different message Katie was getting.

In a moment or two I spoke again. "What if you did that for yourself, Charlotte? What if you went for blood in your life?"

For a long time she couldn't find the words. "I'd feel like . . . running away." She began to cry. "In my mind I see myself running and running and running. All the locked-in schedules and duties and having to always set a good example for my kids. You know, I feel like I can't live life for myself, I have to always share it with them. You know, I learned, if you have a cake, you make sure everyone else has a piece first before you take any. My life's not my own—I always share myself first."

Aligning with the Inside

Charlotte was in the thrall of outside voices, specifically the kind I call *influence*. The word influence, which comes from the Latin *influere*, "to flow in," means the "power to sway or affect based on prestige, wealth, ability or position." Her husband's voice had become so loud to her, and her own inner voice, rarely mirrored in her past, had grown so quiet, that his objections drowned it out.

Influencing outside voices are all the wants, fears, demands and judgments of other people, especially the people most important to you. Sometimes, however, it isn't really what these people think or feel, but what you *think* they feel. They also come from the media, which today surrounds us all with a never-ending flood of images and messages that can cripple our imaginations and drown out the voice of our inner selves.

There's another group of outside voices that I call *internalized* outside voices. These are the voices in your mind that are always telling you "for your own good" what you should and shouldn't do, think, feel and want. They don't literally come from other people in your present life, although they often do echo critical messages you learned growing up. It's as if somewhere inside of you there's a roomful of stern judges with clipboards always ready to correct you, rate your performance and give you demerits whenever you slip up. Not all of them speak harshly, but the bottom line of everything they say is, "You should change. You're not good enough the way you are."

The greatest difficulty of outside voices comes from how much they have become "second nature" to you. But what is your first nature? One way you can tell is by the way you feel. When you're inside yourself, you can feel happy, or angry, or terribly sad, or scared, or at peace. But whatever the feeling is, you feel "present." You feel like your feelings are coming *from* you. When you're caught in outside voices, however, you're most likely feeling awful, enraged, tense, anxious, or numb, though at times they can also make you feel excited or "high." But the difference is, the emotions feel like they're happening *to* you, that they're out of your control.

The trick is to learn how to separate the inside from the outside, to identify what is coming from within you—from what you know, sense, feel and want, or from your Larger Self—and what is coming from what you perceive are other people's needs and expectations, or from the relentless, harping voices within that hold you back or punish you for your supposed faults. Once you do that, you can then begin to turn your attention away from the outside voices and toward your inner truth. I call this "aligning with the inside."

Does this mean you never listen to outside voices? Of course not! We're social creatures. We're affected by other peoples' feelings, opinions, needs and concerns. That's the way it should be. And as you allow yourself to be touched by others, you're changed. Far from being static, your inner self is constantly evolving and incorporating new information from other people and every resource available in your environment.

You can, of course, have positive and helpful outside voices inside you as well. Indeed, good parents spend a lot of time and energy trying to impart them! "You'll succeed if you keep on trying." "Nothing is more important than a good education." "It's going to be all right, you'll see. Tomorrow is another day." Indeed, Charlotte was doing just that when she was shouting to her daughter, "Go for blood!" I tend not to call these outside voices, however, because they serve the inner self, or at least they don't contradict it. They don't *feel* like messages that are overlaid upon who you truly are.

So I'm not saying that you should stop listening to outside voices. I'm suggesting that you begin to identify them for what they are, and learn to listen to your inner self as well. This, of course, is not always a simple task, especially since outside voices can feel like they've been woven into you, so that pulling one thread will cause the entire fabric to unravel. But it isn't true. You can increasingly identify them and experience them as the outer garment that they are, and *choose* which ones you accept and which ones you don't.

Charlotte didn't go to the conference. But coincidentally, three weeks later, she was invited at the last minute to be a part of a panel representing her company at a four-day business convention. She had always passed up these opportunities before, but this time, she chose to go. "Talking about the reluctant green light really helped me," she said. "Tony said all the same old things, but this time I thought, 'I'm *feeling* like he's telling me I can't go, but what did he really say?' The trip turned out to be awesome. But the best moment came when I was eating a late lunch, talking, having fun, and I looked at my watch and suddenly realized—I don't have to be back for the school bus!

"Sure, I want that total green light from him, because that's what I give everyone all the time, so why can't I get it? But if I wait for that, I'll never do what I want."

Under the Influence

Let's look more closely at the "voices" coming at you in your life that get so loud, you can't hear anymore what you yourself think, feel or want. It's hearing your mother say "I haven't seen you in so long" in that *certain voice*, so that you book a flight to her home in Bismarck, North Dakota in mid-February. It's agreeing to go on a camping vacation with your outdoorsy husband while you still have two children in diapers. It's listening to Kenny G with total equanimity with your latest boyfriend even though your taste runs to Guns n' Roses. It's spending eight hours of every waking day chauffeuring your kids to soccer, basketball, gymnastics, music, dance and karate lessons because you're trying to be the best, best mom in the world, and that's what the best, best mom in the world would do. It's feeling bad about yourself because you "can't get along" with the moms on your block when the truth is, you and they have little in common.

And of course, it's the voices we take in from the media. It's just about impossible for any woman not to be affected by constantly seeing the way the media thinks women are "supposed" to be: young, beautiful, glib, perky, living in spacious splendor, surrounded by the latest gadgets and, of course, thin, thin, thin. Body image is one area where women may have actually gone backwards in the last thirty years. The average fashion model has gone in that time from weighing 8 percent less than the average woman to weighing 23 percent less. One study estimated that less than 5 percent of women could *possibly* get as thin as the "beautiful" women shown in magazine photos.

Yet even though we may know that it's all fake, even when we realize that the models and movie stars themselves don't look as beautiful in real life as they do in the photographs, it's no wonder that the constant message that you have to be thin and beautiful to be successful makes women feel bad about themselves. Several studies have shown that spending as little as *three minutes* looking fashion magazines causes as many as 70 percent of women to feel depressed and guilty about their appearance.

There's another kind of outside voice, one that you can hear when Charlotte said, "maybe I *am* being selfish." Thou Shalt Not Be Selfish seems to be number one in the Rulebook of Womanhood, followed by Thou Shalt Not Hurt Anybody, Thou Shalt Always Care about Others, Thou Shalt Strive to Be Perfect, Thou Shalt Try to Please Everyone and Thou Shalt Always Seek Harmony with Other Women. These are the cultural rules, the messages you receive from all around you telling you how you're supposed to be.

The reason all these outside voices have such a powerful effect on us is that until recently, listening to these voices was vital to our physical survival.

This became clearer to me while working with Jolene, a twenty-seven-year-old social worker who grew up on Barbados. "Growing up in a small village," she told me, "is like being in high school. You can't be different. You can't escape your past. You can't do anything or break any connections without everyone knowing about it. And so I learned to constantly worry about what 'they' might think of me."

Until very recently, women could almost never escape the people they grew up with. They had no place else to go. As mothers, they and their children were profoundly dependent on the community for sustenance and protection. What's more, in most cultures around the world, their husband and his family wielded almost total control over their lives.

Under those circumstances, it made sense that women would develop, and pass down to their daughters, a tendency to become very, *very* sensitive about what other people might think of them. And to hold back and automatically blame themselves rather than speak up against being treated unfairly or disrespectfully. It was a matter of sheer survival, for both themselves and their children, to stay on the good side of everybody, no matter what the cost.

Of course, there have always been women who, against all odds, stood up for themselves fearlessly. Just as, to be honest, there have also always been women who, from their own dominant positions in society, used power and aggression every bit as callously as any man, often against other women.

The truth is, women have their own ways to enforce conformity under a veneer of harmony, and to punish one another for stepping out of line. That is why some of women's loudest outside voices are those of other women. I had a client who must have lived on Busybody Street. "I'm worried that if I send my kids to camp this summer, my neighbors will all say, 'There she is, a stay-at-home mom, sending her kids to camp!'" Another client was worried that she'd be judged for enrolling her daughter in only one extracurricular activity a week, when all the other mothers at the school bus stop enrolled their daughters in at least two.

It's women who decide for other women what is acceptable and unacceptable in the social sphere. Women are the arbiters of whether or not you're "selfish," not men, who are generally oblivious to such things. Tragically, women frequently won't tell each other whether they are harboring judgments, resentments or hurt feelings toward one another, even if asked flat out. This forces women to try to imagine what other women think, which may or may not be accurate, without any way to check it out. In the name of "connection," "intimacy," and "friendship," we turn each other into hypersensitive mind-readers, ever afraid that some word or action might damage a relationship or even our entire social network.

It's through interactions with other women that women learn to lis-

ten carefully for what others want, need or expect, and to avoid expressing their desires or opinions directly, lest they be thought "arrogant" or
"bossy." So when women do need to place demands upon one another,
as of course they must at times, they often phrase them in the form of
mild requests. "Will you be coming to our place for the holidays"? coming from your sister-in-law may mean, "You *have to* come to our house
this year." Or it could mean, "You'd better not."

As a result, women have to develop the ability to read the context of
a request to tell what it truly means, and whether it is something minor
or a relationship-threatening emergency. It's often so difficult to discern
this that many women simply end up reacting to every subtle remark or
casual request as if it must be heeded.

Small wonder then, that many women can get truly overwhelmed by
the voices of the men in their lives. Men, at least in the United States,
rarely if ever learn to listen to the unspoken needs and opinions of others. Nor do they learn to couch what they say to make it less assertive.
They learn, if anything, to act louder and more sure of themselves than
they really feel, stating their beliefs and opinions as if they were facts. As
a result, when a woman cares about a man, whenever he expresses his
thoughts, feelings and desires in the way he's learned all his life to do, it
can sound to her as though he were shouting them through a bullhorn.

There is another way that outside voices affect women in their relationships. For many women, the voices of their partner that they produce in their own minds become, in effect, a way of feeling closer to him.
They hold loud and intense inner dialogues with him, imagining what
he thinks and wants and then responding to it. Indeed, if a man becomes
less communicative, a woman is likely for at least a while to spend more
time thinking about him, trying to figure him out to "fill in the gap" in
the relationship.

Selfish or Self-Oriented?

The answer here isn't to deny others' feelings and needs. Obviously
you're going to be affected by other people. You may think, "I shouldn't
care what others think," but if you care, you care! What kind of world

would it be if no one was affected by what anyone else thought, felt or wanted from them? Besides, these voices can serve as "early warning systems," helping you to maintain and repair connections that are truly important to you.

What works is to be *self-oriented*. Self-oriented means becoming oriented *from* yourself, using your self as the point from which to start. I also like to use the term *self-possessed*. Quite literally, do you possess your self? Do you own your own self? Living outside yourself, from other people's expectations or even from the most admirable external standards, puts you off-balance. It doesn't help you to move in your own direction. Becoming self-oriented turns your outside voices into advisors rather than rulers. One way to start doing this is to identify whose outside voices you're listening to, and send them briefly out of the room.

"I don't know what to do," said Barbara, a broad-shouldered woman with a quiet, yet usually decisive manner. Barbara was the oldest in a big, Irish-Catholic family of eight brothers and sisters. While everyone else settled within an hour's drive of one another, Barbara felt that

ૐ INNERCIZE 4 ◕
Time-Out for Outside Voices

Take a situation where some outside voice is causing you to feel dissonant with your inner self. After placing yourself in the reflective mode, name where the outside voice or voices are coming from. (It can be more than one source.) Be as specific about who it is as you can.

Now imagine that you firmly request that person or those people to "wait outside the room" for a while. Now that you can't hear or see them, what do you think, how do you feel or what do you want, for you?

When you've gotten a very firm sense of this, let the outside voices come back in—slowly. See if you still want to take them into account. If you do, see if there's a way you can honor yourself first while including them as well.

such close proximity would stifle her ability to be herself. She moved 2,000 miles away, married and had a family.

Her father was dying. She went to visit him for a week, thinking she was saying good-bye and would be back for the funeral. But he lingered. Two months later, her brothers and sisters were imploring her to return.

She felt them pull at her. *Return, return. Be the big sister we counted on growing up.* But she wasn't that girl or young woman anymore. She had a family, a job and three children of her own. And her siblings were all grown up themselves—why did they still "need" her? Money was an issue as well. Taking unpaid leave now and for his funeral, and the cost of all that airfare, was going to be a real burden.

"If you threw your whole family out of the room," I asked, "and just listened to yourself, what would you want to do?"

She considered it. "I *do* want to see my father again. I want to help my family. I do." She thought some more. "But I can't just stay forever."

"And what about the funeral?"

"I have to go to that, too. No, I *want* to go to that. I can't miss my father's funeral! We'll have to afford it somehow."

When I asked her to "invite" them back into the room in her mind, she decided that she would tell them that she could only come for one week, but for that time she'd help them as much as she could with anything they needed.

After coming to this decision, she felt relieved. "Before, I might have done the exact same thing, but resented it or felt mad at myself for letting myself be pushed around. Now I know I'll be doing the right thing."

Feeding on our Vulnerabilities

Shame is a particular, and particularly painful, kind of outside voice. Shame is the feeling that there's something terribly wrong and unlovable about you, that you're irrevocably defective. It's been called the "master emotion," because human beings will do almost anything to avoid feeling it.

This is how it works: A neighbor acts cold to you, or your boss criticizes your report, or you don't even get interviews for the jobs that you want and are qualified for. At first you feel shock and hurt and maybe anger. Then, without even noticing it happen, you start to contract, feeling *smaller* and *bad about yourself*. "Who do you think you are?" scolds a voice inside your head. Whatever sense of goodness and confidence you had about yourself melts away. I call this "putting on your frog skin." You stop feeling like you're worthy of being a prince(ss). You accept the verdict that you are, and should always remain, a frog.

Inez was a forty-one-year-old freelance writer, happily married with one child, who moved into the area six months earlier for her husband's work. Intellectual and introverted by nature, she didn't "click" with any of the women she met in her neighborhood or the mothers of her son's friends. Though most of the time she didn't think about it, every once in a while the lack of female friendship would bother her.

One day she had a chance meeting with another woman in a bookstore café. She and Judy talked for an hour and a half, sharing similar interests and even life stories. "This was wonderful," said Judy. "Let's do it again." They exchanged phone numbers. "Give me a call and we'll set something up."

Inez was elated about making a friend. She waited a week, so as not to look "too needy," then called Judy back. But her warm greeting— "Hi, Judy, it's Inez! We met at the bookstore last week."—was greeted with "Oh. Hi. How are you?" What followed was an excruciating ten-minute conversation where every attempt to reconnect, such as saying, "I really enjoyed our conversation," was met with a tepid response. No date to get together was set.

Inez came to her session looking shell-shocked. She had trouble at first even explaining what had happened. She had spent the five days since the phone call going over the two conversations in her mind, bouncing between being angry at Judy for acting like she was open to friendship, and thinking that Judy *must* have sent signals that she didn't "really" want Inez to call and wondering how she missed them. She felt far more painfully friendless now than before she met Judy. This awakened desire, coupled with Judy's response, made Inez feel both vulnerable and extremely self-critical.

I spent a good deal of time listening to and validating Inez's hurt feelings and need for friendship. But what was really making Inez loop around and around was the question of what really happened. Did she really do something, she kept wondering, that made Judy not like her?

"Maybe I shouldn't have told her that I was new in town and didn't know that many people. Maybe she thought I was some kind of loser."

"You felt ashamed and humiliated after your phone call with her. Here you showed all this vulnerable desire for friendship and she didn't respond. You thought, she must be thinking something really bad about me, to act like this."

"Yes! Exactly!" A big smile crossed her face. "And ever since, I've been thinking, 'I'm *awful* for needing a friend so much!'"

Needing other people makes us feel vulnerable. And feeling vulnerable causes our outside voices to go into veritable feeding frenzies. Who knows what was really going on in Judy's life? But when Lesley's vulnerable desire for friendship wasn't validated by her, Lesley got wounded, which attracted shame-based outside voices the way blood attracts sharks.

This is true for everyone. In fact, if you're in the midst of an outside-voice attack, there's a good chance you've done, tried to do, or were thinking about doing, something very vulnerable for you. In other words, you were trying to be true to yourself. Good for you! You deserve a hand on your shoulder, and maybe a short break to collect yourself and to look at what has happened with compassion.

One reason needs are so vulnerable is that most of us are accustomed to thinking that if we don't get what we need, or if it seems different from what "everyone else" needs, it must not be legitimate. Poppycock! Every single person is different. Think of all the different species of plants in the world. They're all designed to thrive and bloom in different kinds of environments. They need different temperatures and soils, different amounts of water and shade. An African violet, for example, which needs at least twelve hours of sunlight a day to grow and bloom, certainly doesn't sit around thinking, "I shouldn't need so much sun. I should like living in the shade." I think people have at least as much right to have different and exacting needs as plants do.

One need that's rarely acknowledged and even more rarely validated is the one Lesley had—the need for a good friend. This may be the most vulnerable need of all. The desire for a true friend is something our culture doesn't even have the words for. You can get plenty of commiser-

INNERCIZE 5
Write Your Own Plant Tag

Plants from a garden store come with something that helps the people who buy them: a tag that tells the new plant owner what the plant needs. I invite you to do this for yourself.

Write what you need in order for you to bloom. Write down exactly what you need. Ignore whether you have it in your life. Ignore whether it's realistic to ever hope to get it. If you need a housekeeper to come to your house twice a week, write it down. If you need a loving friend who gives you lots of hugs and encouragement, write it down. If you need five minutes, or forty-five minutes, of quiet solitude every day, write it down.

Take some time with this. Enjoy this and allow yourself to feel whatever feelings this innercize brings up. Above all, see if you can be as truthful to yourself as you possibly can. Keep in mind: What do you need to flourish? What will help you bloom, as all flowers are meant to do?

ation from other women about needing to find a good man, but to whom can you reveal that you need a good friend? Friends are something you supposedly either have or you don't.

In our money-driven culture, there's never any problem finding validation for your material desires. Go to any store, and as long as you have a valid credit card, a smiling salesperson will say, "Of course you need a new outfit! Of course you need a new computer!" But where's the "Of course!" to the statement, "I need a good friend"? It's not there. The cultural answer is more like, "What's wrong with you? Don't you have friends already? Don't *all* women have friends?"

But the desire to have one or more true friends—that is, women (and possibly some men) who validate your inner self, actively support your dreams, aren't afraid to be honest or to hear honesty, and don't hold grudges—is a need as valid as any other in one's life. My observation is that it's not as easy to fulfill or as common as it's made out to be.

Intimidation and Power Shaming

> *We [women] are too ready to accuse ourselves of failure and too reluctant to surrender trust once it is granted, whether to a spouse or an institution. Often, American men learn to project their disappointments outward . . . [while] women tend to internalize their losses. When a proposal gets turned down or a job not offered, women tend to say, I wasn't worthy. Men more often contend that the process was crooked.*
> —Mary Catherine Bateson, *Composing A Life*

Then there are the people who intentionally want to make you feel bad about what you need, feel and think.

Vivian's boss Greta was one of them. She was never satisfied with anything, demanded ridiculous hours while taking time off herself, and cut people down whenever anything went wrong. At one staff meeting, she offhandedly said to the women who worked under her, "Personally, I don't need ego stroking, but I realize some of you do."

Making other people feel bad about themselves and their needs is a very powerful thing to do. Totally immoral, but powerful. That's why people do it.

There are a million and one ways that someone who wants to use power over another person can delegitimize that other person's feelings and wants. People have been doing this to other people since the dawn of time. It always begins with the powerful person conveying some variant of the following message:"I am absolutely right and what you think is absolutely wrong—and besides, what you think doesn't count because *you* don't count as much as I do. You're flawed. There's something wrong with you."

The person with the power has convinced himself or herself of this. But they don't completely succeed until they get you to take on their point of view, to see yourself through their eyes.

Vivian finally got fed up and left. But most times the problem is not so obvious, and women can fall into the pattern of seeing it as their own. This is a loss. There's a difference between understanding your boss's point of view and totally capitulating to it. There is great power in knowing your own perception, goals and truth, and from that stance, looking at the whole situation and deciding what you need to do.

Corinne had a high-level communications job at the U.S. Department of Energy. When her old boss left, a new boss was hired who went from meeting with her weekly, as her old boss had, to monthly, and then stopped meeting with her altogether. She left for a different department. "You're taking it too personally," her new boss told her. "That may be true," she answered. "But I care about my work, so I do take it personally. If I'm not important enough to meet with, then this position no longer fits in with my career goals."

The most pernicious place that such intimidation and shaming occurs is in the home. It's been estimated that twenty percent of American women suffer from either physical or emotional abuse in their marriage. Shame, isolation and genuine fear for the economic survival and physical safety of themselves and their children keep women imprisoned in these abusive relationships.

I've seen this among women who look, on the outside, as if everything is going perfectly. "He belittles me," I was told by Sally, the well-dressed wife of a bank president. "He tells me I'm ignorant, he corrects me constantly. Whenever something goes wrong, he blames me, and I don't know why, but I automatically blame myself.

"He's not bad, just moody," she continued. "When I need to tell him something, I try to catch him at the right time. He goes for a few days without blowing up at me or the kids and I start to feel better. And then it happens again."

If you are in a physically or emotionally abusive or exploitative situation, at home or at work, please let me tell you that nothing you can possibly do can ever justify someone treating you this way. And realize that it's natural if you feel like you can't break out of your situation alone, but that you are not destined to stay where you are. Somewhere there is a hand you can reach out in order to help you get free.

Internalized Outside Voices

Now let's talk about the internalized outside voices, those voices in your head that tell you you are seriously defective and desperately in need of improvement.

Let's take a simple example. Imagine you are waiting to go out on a first date with a guy, and he doesn't show up. At first you might feel surprised, stunned, angry and disappointed. If you checked with yourself at this moment, you'd discover that, surprisingly, you don't actually feel bad—just these other feelings.

But then, as the minutes tick away, something comes over you and you start to feel horrible. What's happened? You don't actually know the guy yet, so you can't be sure you even like him. So what hurts so much?

What's happened is that outside voices have snuck up on you. They might start like this:

"This always happens to me. I'm not attractive enough. Guys aren't interested in someone like me. I'm too _____ (short, skinny, fat, talkative—you fill in your own blank here). I'll never have a relationship."

You turn on the TV. A feeling arises inside you. *I'm sad. I'm lonely. I thought he was cute. I really want a relationship.*

Then come the O.V.s: *That's your problem. Guys can tell you're lonely. It makes them run away. You gotta have more self-esteem. You gotta work out more. You gotta go on a diet. You need more self-confidence. Look at you, you're pathetic.*

After this wonderful inner pep talk, you get on a chair to reach the stash of chocolate chip cookies you've placed at the back of your top cupboard, behind the mixing bowls. As you sit watching an episode of *Gilligan's Island* on cable TV, you think, *God, look at me, all dressed up, eating these cookies in front of the TV. I really am pathetic. What an asshole he is, standing me up like this! But why did I believe him? Why didn't I know he was giving me a line? What is it about me that lets men treat me with such disrespect? Why do I let everyone push me around?*

And on and on. What's certifiably true here? Only this: *I'm sad. I'm lonely. I thought he was cute. I really want a relationship.* And any anger you may feel at him for treating you this way.

How can this have gone differently? Getting out from under outside voices, as I've said, is not always easy. You'll be learning different ways to do it for the next five chapters. But the first step is to identify them for what they are, and then separate from them. Don't argue with them. Don't give them energy. Instead, bring your awareness to what is happening inside you, especially to your feelings, and use the ABCs of Acknowledging, Being With and Compassion.

It might go something like this: You're sitting in front of the TV with the cookies, furiously attacking yourself. And then you say to yourself, "Okay, I'm beating myself up. This has to be outside voices. What's going on?"

You take a slow, deep breath. You stop paying attention to your thoughts, and bring your focus inside you, to somewhere in the center part of your body. You dig down, to what's below all the outside voices, and say what's true.

"All right. The truth is, I'm sad. I'm feeling pretty lonely. I really did think he was cute. I kinda hoped he could be the one."

Now, if you manage to sit through acknowledging those feelings, and letting them just be without judging or trying to fix them, in about thirty seconds you'll realize, from the inside of you out, that this part of you isn't "pathetic"—it's just lonely. It wants a relationship. Is that so bad?

Spend time being with these hurt feelings with compassion. Hey, it hurts to be stood up. Maybe you missed some warning signs that he was a jerk, but then again, some guys are very good at hiding it.

You've just *aligned with the inside*. You've gone from believing the outside voices to anchoring yourself in your inner truth.

I can't promise you you're now going to have a wonderful evening. But if you use the ABCs, listening to your self as you would a friend, with compassion, you may learn things you didn't know about what your inner self has been going through lately regarding finding a relationship. At the very least, you won't spend the evening in misery and self-hatred.

When you're in the thrall of outside voices and believe what they are telling you, I call it *siding with the outside*. In a landmark study of depressed women published in 1991, Dana Crowley Jack, a psychologist and researcher at Harvard, found that they had what she called an "Over-Eye"—what I call "outside voices"—that constantly attacked them. The Over-Eye was filled with the kinds of expectations of goodness and self-denial that have been placed on women through all time, so in effect, it was telling them that they had failed as a woman. By doing so, it silenced their inner selves.

What makes internalized outside voices so insidious is that they can be so darn convincing. "I'm no good." "What's wrong with me." "I can't succeed." "I really blew it that time." "I shouldn't have been so forward." These voices not only can sound like the voice of Authority, but like the voice of Truth itself. Surely you're the defective being they say you are; surely you deserve the admonishment you are receiving! But emphatically they are *not*. When outside voices take over, they keep you from knowing and trusting the best guide you have, your own inner experience.

What can be hard to recognize, but very important to know, is that the crummy, lousy, bad-all-over feeling you get from internalized outside voices is *not* your true feeling. It's a diversion, a decoy, that *masks* your real feelings. You don't want to give it the importance it seems to claim.

This became even clearer to me one day working with Peggy, a very bright and funny woman whose brother and favorite grandmother died in a car crash when she was eleven. She shut down her feelings after that. She came to me after her marriage broke up, in part because she was always pushing her husband away.

In therapy she worked on the grieving she hadn't done as a child, as well as other intimacy issues. But one day she came to a session looking more depressed than I'd ever seen her.

"What's wrong?" I asked.

"I don't think I'll ever marry again," she said in a low, terrible drone. "I don't think I'm really capable of love. Or that anyone could ever love me."

I spent about ten minutes trying to be empathic to this and figure out where it was coming from, but it only kept getting worse. It struck me as so unnatural to the Peggy I'd come to know that I finally said, "These are outside voices. They aren't good for you."

"What?" She was rather shocked.

"You don't need to pay attention to these feelings."

"But I thought you *want* me to pay attention to my feelings!"

I explained the difference between these and her real feelings. "Do you remember when you were truly grieving in here for your grandmother and your brother?"

"Yes." She remembered all too well.

"That was painful, but that was a *cleansing* sadness. Check with your body. Does this feel that way?"

She shook her head no.

"Tearing yourself apart will only make you tear yourself apart more. If you're thinking like this, know that it isn't the truth."

What possible purpose could these nasty little brain-demons serve? Strangely enough, they're trying to protect you. They come up whenever you say or do something, or even think about saying or doing something, that some part of you is convinced is dangerous or would make you "unacceptable" to others. In effect, they yell at you before anyone else does. They also arise when you start to deal with painful memories, thoughts or feelings.

So actually these outside voices aren't "bad" or evil. They simply come from some very scared parts of you that in their own, rather unpleasant way want the best for you. They want to keep the status quo. They're afraid of change. They're afraid of pain. They're afraid of abandonment and exile from the "tribe," which for most of human history was tantamount to a death sentence.

How do these voices originate? Inborn temperament and personality probably have much to do with the degree of your propensity toward them. Your experiences with peers, as a child and adolescent, also can leave you with lasting negative internalized outside voices. But of course, for most people, the nature and severity of these voices is related to what they received and heard from their parents in childhood.

Learning Your Lessons

All parents leave their children a legacy of outside voices.

Ideally this wouldn't happen. Ideally, you would guide your children perfectly toward their inner fulfillment and away from self-destructive tendencies without ever once shaming them, becoming cross with them, or tuning them out. Ideally, your children would never once take your firm but loving attempts to guide them in this manner as an attack upon their very soul. Ideally, you would always mediate the conflicts between your children with the fairness of Solomon, and your children would see the supreme wisdom of your judgment, accept it, and hug each other.

As the kids say, "Yeah, right."

Parents, by their actions, teach their children what brings love and attention and what doesn't. Hopefully not all love and understanding is withdrawn even when the child is at her worst. The inner self of a young child always wants to express itself, and it always wants love and attention for its expression. When the inner self does not get love and attention, it gets hurt. When a certain action, feeling or thought usually results in hurt, it develops a barrier around it, like an electric fence, something painful within that signals, "Back off. Stay away." That painful barricade is made of internalized outside voices.

What is barricaded off is a part of your inner self. If it's not too huge or integral to your ability to live your life, it doesn't matter too much. You compensate for it and go around it. You "don't go there."

If, however, it is a part of you that's shouting, "I must live. I will not be buried," you're in conflict, even in serious psychological pain, as your protective mechanisms fight with your inner self.

Parents don't usually give or withdraw love on a whim. They do it with an agenda, partly conscious and partly not. The agenda is socialization, preparing their children to function in the world *the parents know*.

Parents always impart lessons about the world they themselves believe in. If they believe the world is basically filled with people who are accepting, they will encourage their children to venture forth and meet other people. If they believe that most people are angry, critical or dangerous, they will warn their children not to act too freely or bother the neighbors. If they believe that the world is full of possibilities, their nature will be to foster possibility in their children. If they see it as a place that will punish their children's dreams, they will dampen them.

Despite how it sometimes seems, most people (including most "rebels") remain quite loyal to these parental lessons. Anyone who has ever had to be truly disloyal to their upbringing knows how difficult and even frightening it can be. Parents and other important teachers and caregivers draw the circle of life, the border of safety around their children, that carries forth into the adults they become. Beyond that border, as far or near as it has been drawn, is the Jungle, the Stranger, the Unknown. On the edges of old maps it was written, "Beyond this there be dragons." At the border of the Unknown are some of the fiercest outside voices.

Messages from Our Mothers

> *I learned from my mother that you shouldn't think about yourself first. Over time, I pressed all my needs deeper and deeper in myself thinking that was a good thing. I knew people saw only my outside, saw me as a happy person, though I didn't see myself that way.*
> —Connie, forty-five

While fathers certainly have a powerful impact, for better or worse, your mother is the person whose voice you're most likely to hear inside you. Assuming that your mother was alive and played a major role in your upbringing, it would be amazing if you didn't have her voice resounding somewhere in your head. It's quite possible that, if you added up all the words, no one in your life has talked to you, or *at* you, more than your mother.

Many women have had to cope with mothers who were psychologically or emotionally incapable of handling the tremendous job of being a mother. Women who have had mothers like this have the formidable task of developing a positive identity despite the ways their mothers spoke to or treated them.

Most women's mothers, however, are or were devoted, caring individuals, who loved their daughters and tried to be the best mothers they knew how to be. And that poses a different set of challenges, because a mother's limitations, fears and rigid expectations, which she probably learned from her own mother, frequently get passed down to her daughters.

Mothers, after all, are fiercely invested in their children's survival. That involves not only watching out for their physical safety, but ensuring that they learn the rules of whatever society they're in so that they will be accepted. For girls and women, those rules have always been more stringent and the options more limited than for boys and men. We've already seen how women throughout history have been primed to negate themselves as a matter of sheer survival. Many mothers who've lived this way themselves will then negate their daughter's inner voices as well out of a deep fear of what would happen to their daughter, economically and socially, if she didn't follow the "rules."

One of my clients, Roslyn, gave a most vivid example of this from a conversation she recalled between herself and her mother many years earlier during her first marriage to a demanding and emotionally unavailable husband.

"The first year of my marriage," she recalled, "I tried to tell my mother how I was feeling. 'It doesn't feel right,' I told her. I pointed to my heart and said, 'something doesn't feel right in here.' 'What is it?' she asked me. 'I don't know,' I told her, 'but I'm not happy.' And she said, 'Rozzie, what more do you want? He's a good man, he makes good money and they're hard to find.' "

The bond between mothers and daughters is incredibly powerful, one of the most unbreakable human connections of all. The desire for her mother's approval often can motivate a woman her entire life. Mothers are so influential that their voices can become the background, the "wallpaper" of our psyches, so constantly present that we don't even notice their presence anymore. What's more, so much of what we learned from our mothers has so much value and truth to it that it's hard to tease out what doesn't work for our benefit, while keeping what's good.

"Honey attracts more bees than vinegar," was the lesson Hope, a sixty-year-old college dean, learned best from her mother. "That's what my mother would always say. She was an incredibly charming woman. She taught me that if you never show anger and you smile winningly and say things in just the right way, you can get anything you want from anybody. And all my life it's worked for me very well!

"But somewhere along the way I forgot what it felt like to be angry, to even know what 'No' felt like inside of me."

I have found that women in their twenties are often very conscious of figuring out "what's my mom" and "what's me." But later in life, and especially after having children, women become more reluctant to do so. First, many think that they must have worked through all of that already. And second, women, seeing how hard it is to be a mother, feel a

INNERCIZE 6

Identifying Your "Mother Voices"

Take your mother, or someone else who was very important to you growing up. Conjure her up. Picture her in whatever way—old, young, at home, at the dinner table, picking you up from school, wearing an apron, wearing a suit, riding a broom (just kidding!)—arises in you and feels most powerful to you.

Now imagine the things she said to you or conveyed to you growing up and write them down. Don't write one or two; write as many as you can. Try to write them as quick, declarative sentences or commands (which is the way the emotional centers of the brain stores them). "Eat your vegetables." "You have to soothe men's egos." "Never leave dirty dishes in the sink overnight." "A clean house is important/doesn't matter." Be sure to write whatever positive messages come to your mind as well, such as, "You can be anything you want to be."

After you've written at least ten, notice if you can identify the more subtle messages that you received without words. "Life is suffering" might be one. Or, "Women have to watch their step." Or, "You can't trust anyone but me with your feelings."

Now look over your list. See what messages feel good to your inner self. Mark these "Mine." Take the messages that don't feel good and mark them "Hers."

Now look at the ones you've marked "Hers." Next to the ones that you've let go of, put a check mark. Next to the ones that still have a hold on you, write "O.V.," for "outside voice." These are the mother voices you wish to be conscious of when you hear them inside, so that you can turn your attention away from them and toward what is truly happening within you.

little guilty—they don't want to "bash" their mother. But examining the messages you received from your mother and seeing which ones still affect you unconsciously is helpful at any point in your life.

In a sense, all women today are like first- or second-generation immigrants from another country. We either remember, or our mothers remember, the days when the hopes and expectations of women's lives were much more limited. Most of our mothers unconsciously readied us for a more limited view of our possibilities. Many of us, though our own horizons have widened considerably, still carry those outside voices from the past within us.

Attackers and Defenders

When my older daughter was six, I noticed that it was almost impossible for her to accept the idea that she ever did anything wrong. No matter what the transgression, she'd do anything she could do not to agree with me. She'd say, "I didn't mean to do it!" She'd blame her little sister. If nothing worked, she'd get angry at me for making her feel bad, shouting, "Don't criticize me!" At six years old, she couldn't quite hold on to the two ideas "I'm not perfect" and "I'm still good" at the same time.

I wondered, are adults all that different? We may be better able to hide our real feelings, but how many people are truly able, in most situations where they've done something wrong, to confess, "Yes, I did something hurtful, and I absolutely wanted to, and I have no excuses," and still hold on to the sense of their own goodness?

Internalized outside voices can be very critical, often in fact more critical than anything anyone else might say to you. But no one just accepts them and improves. When those inner criticisms go on for any length of time, the part of you that's under attack defends itself. It blames, it rationalizes, it minimizes, it feels miserable, it rebels, it leads you to scapegoat ("*I'm* really good, but those people over there are horrible!") and to eat *three* boxes of chocolate chip cookies. This simply infuriates the critical voices even more, who step up their attack, which only leads the defenders to defend themselves more.

This is the cycle of suffering. If unchecked it extends the misery beyond the self to everyone in the vicinity and to future generations. No one conquers themselves in this manner. If they think they do, they're deceiving themselves, even deadening themselves.

What's happening here is that the "I," the Larger Self, is not in charge, mediating the conflict between the attacking and defending parts of the psyche. *The slumber of the "I" is at the root of most suffering.* While there definitely are forms of suffering not caused by this—grief at the loss of a loved one is the most obvious—much of the psychological pain and suffering that people endure or seek help for is the result of having some part of the psyche—the attackers, defenders, "rebel," "good girl," "responsible mother," "unfulfilled child" or some other— take over, not allowing the Larger Self to listen to, heal and free the inner self.

Below the attackers and defenders, below the self-recrimination, the shame and suffering, the rebellions and denials, is the inner self. The inner self says, "Look, this is what's going on. This is why I'm doing what I'm doing." But it can't reveal itself while the attack-defend cycle is going on.

The inner voice is the exact opposite of the outside voices. It doesn't sugarcoat you, but it doesn't try to fix what's wrong with you. The out- side voices, with their roaring, are actually afraid for you. Often they're afraid that the truth is too painful for you to feel, or that disaster will strike if you discover it. But they're wrong. The truth can be discovered and felt, with the help of the Larger Self.

The Five Pathways

You've seen how outside voices pull you away from yourself, telling you to follow what other people want or expect, or making you feel that you, or some part of you, is irredeemably bad or defective, unworthy of com- passion or even connection to the rest of humanity.

But as you've learned, in this chapter and the previous one, arguing with outside voices doesn't usually work, and substituting positive self- messages (for example, "I'm an appealing person" or "I deserve to take care of myself") is only partially effective. What's needed is to recognize the outside voices for what they are, and then use the ABCs of the Inner Voice to turn away from them and toward something else.

But what do you turn toward? You turn toward the Five Pathways to the Inner Voice: Knowing, Sensing, Feeling, Wanting and the Voice of the Larger Self. Each one of these pathways brings you back to the experience of being solidly within yourself.

Knowing is the faculty of separation and discrimination; it is learning to know who you are and to claim and hold on to what you know deep down to be true for you. *Sensing* is about learning how to pay attention to the subtle inner senses that can give you enormous information about what is really going on, no matter what your rational mind or other people are saying. *Feeling* is learning how to listen to *all* of your feelings and trusting that every one of them, even the ones you don't think you "should" have, have something important to tell you. *Wanting* is the force that moves you toward what your inner blueprint tells you will be most fulfilling. And the *Voice of the Larger Self*, a voice that emerges when you have fully listened to the other voices within you, is a remarkable source of inner peace and wisdom that can enrich your life and give it a new quality of harmony.

Here's the good news. To find and follow your inner voice, you don't have to get rid of your outside voices. And, as I told you before, you don't have to change yourself. You simply need to shift your focus to something different than what you may be accustomed to—to what you know, what you sense, what you feel and what you want.

PART TWO

ALIGNING WITH THE INSIDE: THE FIVE PATHWAYS TO THE INNER VOICE

CHAPTER FOUR

Just Say Know

"Who cares if you're smart? You're a girl!" That's what Terry's father told her when she was thirteen. Terry, a forty-three-year-old journalist, grew up in a family with few material resources and even less love to go around. What little there was went to her older brother, John. There was no support whatsoever, financial or emotional, for her to go to college.

Though a few teachers praised her along the way, none really reached out to the shy, withdrawn girl whose classroom manner did not reflect the mind it hid. She almost buckled under to her parents' attitudes, until she saw the poster hung on a school bulletin board.

It was a statewide contest that tested knowledge on national and international current events, sponsored by a large metropolitan newspaper. Winners at the county level would compete with one another for a statewide championship. The prizes were scholarships to college.

"I was a junior in high school," Terry recalled. "I was down and depressed. I was taking harder courses and having trouble getting good grades. I didn't feel very smart. It seemed easier to just forget about college, since nobody cared whether I went anyway, go get a job after high school and make money.

"But when I saw the poster, it was like an electric shock went through my whole body. I'd been reading the newspaper since the time I started to read. I *knew*, I just *knew* I was going to win."

The competition called for a test on current events, an essay, and an interview. "I trained like an athlete," she said. "I read three newspapers a day, then went to the library and read every news magazine I could get my hands on. Any important people or events that I didn't know, I looked up in encyclopedia yearbooks. I took notes. I studied." She went on to win the local contest, and in the statewide competition, against challengers from far more affluent and educated families, she placed second, winning a $5,000 scholarship.

After that, "I started applying for scholarships like crazy." And colleges. She got into the school of her choice with her tuition and room and board assured. She proceeded to do well in college, and now writes for a major newspaper.

"I knew who I was from then on," said Terry. "And my life was never the same."

Knowing who you are and what is true for you, and being able to *say* and *act from* what you know, is the first pathway to living from your inner voice. Unfortunately, many of us grew up learning that it wasn't okay to be smart or to show what we knew. We learned to act tentative and measured in the way we speak about our knowledge. In many situations, we simply don't speak at all. "I get quiet, literally silent," is the way Norma, a warm and intelligent businesswoman in her sixties, described it. "I defer my own ideas and go along with others. I give in to my desire to please and get along. I have a fear of being wrong. Also, it seems to take me longer to figure out what I want to say than men, so I stop. When I'm with men, I've noticed that I practically have to force myself to declare my opinions, or I'm literally not heard."

It's easy to see this difficulty as only negative, especially in a culture that idolizes certainty and decisiveness. Yet one reason women may be less apt to categorically state their opinions is their desire to include their listeners and reach consensus. They prefer to avoid polarizing discussions, and they try not to squelch *other* people's voices. That is a very positive thing! As Deborah Tannen pointed out in the book *You Just Don't Understand*, women are more apt to seek and enjoy a conversation that elicits agreement, rather than the "butting heads" style of discussion and debate that many men find enjoyable.

It is indeed a challenge for women to both honor their desire for consensus and inclusivity, and at the same time, value their own opinions, so that their own unique voice doesn't get lost whenever they're in the presence of others.

The faculty of knowing is only partly about intellect. It has to do with being able to access and state *what you perceive as true*. It is also about holding on to that perception, letting yourself be changed and influenced but not getting "talked out of" that knowledge.

The knowing that pertains to the world and the knowing that we have about our inner selves are separate, yet related. As we grow as women, we are meant to combine the knowledge we sense inside with what we learn from the outside world, allowing new input, both from within and without, to affect us, even to change us. The authors of the landmark book, *Women's Ways of Knowing*, called this *constructed knowledge*. Knowledge is not "out there," nor is it "in here." It is in both places together.

Yet if you grew up being told that your perceptions and opinions were wrong and didn't count, it's not surprising if you feel tentative about what you know, whether about yourself, the world around you, or both. How interesting that the most common slang word for unintelligent—"dumb"—literally means "not being able to speak." If someone uses power and authority over you—or "love"—to take away your voice, over time you literally may start to feel "dumb." But women who fight back against their outside voices and *claim* what they know actually begin to feel smarter—not only about themselves, but about everything.

Knowing is the pathway of intention and discrimination. More than any other pathway, it enables you to separate what is you from what is not you. We've talked about how it can be difficult for women to disconnect, even when they want to. This is where knowing comes in. When feelings say, "Wouldn't it be great if we were one?" *Knowing* says, "This is you, and this is me. I want to be with you, but I'm not going to lose me in the process." When feelings pull you in, knowing shows you the way out.

Knowing Yourself

Of all the components of Terry's scholarship contest, the one she remembered most clearly was the interview. "I knew they would ask me who I was, what my values and goals were, why I wanted this scholarship and what I planned to do with my life," she recalled.

No one had ever asked me those questions before. So I thought and thought and thought about them. And the more I thought, the more

I realized that nobody could know me more than me. By the time I went on the interview, I was ready. In fact, I was pumped! I think that interview, preparing for it and going through it, changed me more than anything else.

Every person has a unique inner blueprint for what they need to grow and be healthy, mentally, emotionally, physically, and spiritually. But as we've seen, even if you've had some of your uniqueness recognized and validated, very few of us have been given the support to uncover our full blueprint and live from it. And all of us have learned in our lives that at least some of our blueprint is not okay, it's just not done, it's out of the question.

Historically speaking, women have been free to build a life based on who they really are for only a very short time. While men had at least the possibility that they could strike out on their own, make their fortunes and forge their own destinies,* women were told that the only destiny they were "made" for was to be a mother and a wife, and perhaps a teacher or a nurse. Otherwise you became a *spinster*. An *old maid*. But for the first time we have the choice to say, "This is who I am" and not force ourselves into one mold.

Yet what a challenge this is! It takes asking questions about who you are and trusting your answers enough to base your major life decisions upon them. While this is a good thing to do at any age, I can't emphasize enough how important it is for young women to do. There are so many decisions a woman in her twenties can make that affect the rest of her life. But if you don't know yourself, you basically do what your outside voices tell you to do. Young women today are among the first in history to be truly free to steer the course of their own lives. But without self-knowledge, you can't steer. Knowing is what puts the steering wheel in your hands.

Whatever your age and stage of life, I invite you to take some time to answer a few of the following questions. The first one I think is espe-

---

*Not all men were. African-American men, for example, were not free to forge their own destinies, and were deprived of the basic human right to protect and provide for their families to the best of their abilities until recently.

cially important, but after that one, pick the ones that feel relevant, intriguing or challenging for you. As you do this, see if every once in a while you can bring your awareness down into that place in your center that you go to in the reflective mode. It will bring a greater truth and depth to your answers.

If you're not a "journal kind of person," that's fine. You might want to write these questions on cards and just leaf through them when you're waiting for something or have a few moments. Sometimes when you do it in a few moments, you can feel less pressure to "be creative and think of something." Even reading through them activates a process within that acts on a preconscious level.

- What is *most* precious about yourself? Your artistic talent? Your love for your children? Your intellect? What are three qualities you would not give up no matter how much anyone paid you?

- What are you passionate about? If you have difficulty answering this, then ask yourself what you're passionately *against*, and you'll begin to know what you're passionately for.

- What nourishes you? When times are hard, what feeds your soul and spirit and makes it easier to go on? Do you let yourself get replenished in these ways, or are they a source of conflict for you?

- What is your favorite place in the world? It could be someplace in your present life, or someplace you once were. Write a little about it and what makes it so special for you.

- What is the biggest risk you ever took?

- Think back to when you were a girl. Where was your favorite place to go, your sanctuary where you felt most in touch with yourself? Who were your "special" people, the people who nourished you? These could have been a special teacher, a friend, a librarian, a pet, or even a character in a book. Did you have any interests, any passions that have perhaps fallen by the wayside?

- Can you remember a time when you were "full of yourself"? Being full of yourself is really just loving yourself, feeling confident and comfortable in your skin, and fully enjoying your abilities and interests. If you can remember a time like that, think about it in detail or write it down, and celebrate that moment again.

Wonderful things can happen when you take the time to remember who you are or once were. Michelle was a fifty-four-year-old children's librarian with a grown daughter and two grandchildren. When I asked her if she had any passions, she told me she didn't.

"Did you ever have any passions in your life?" I asked her.

"None," she replied. "There's nothing I ever wanted strongly."

"Think back to what you might have loved when you were a little girl. Think back to when you were reading about girls like Madeline and Pippi Longstocking, before hormones, before relationships. Think back. Create a picture in your mind."

"Well," she began falteringly, "I did like to dance."

With a little encouragement, it began to spill out of her, her love of dance. And remembering her love of dance made her remember her love of weaving, which she said was like a dance, the way the thread and colors wove in and out of each other. I could almost see the swirling colors and swirling circles of her dance as she talked about them.

"Boy," she said after describing these things vividly for fifteen minutes, "I never thought to call my enjoyment of dance a passion, but I guess it was, since I didn't want to do anything but dance.

"And you know," she continued, "I wasn't always so wishy-washy. I have an old photo of myself as a little girl with my hands on my hips. My mom said I was a feisty thing. What happened to me?

"You know what?" she continued. "I'm going to hang that photo up on my mirror."

Going Further

There are several other very powerful questions you can ask yourself.

1. **What abilities do you pretend to yourself that you have less of than you really do?** Put aside, for a moment, the ways you pretend to be different from who you are with other people, and think about how

you pretend to *yourself* to be different from the person you deep down know yourself to be. Practically all of us have areas of our lives where we pretend to ourselves that we are less than who we are. It may be out of a false sense of modesty, or it may come from a real fear of what would happen if we admitted to ourselves just how smart, or talented, or caring, or capable we truly are. Then we'd have to come out of our comfort zone. But imagine what would happen if you really *did* live up to what you yourself know is possible for you!

2. **What weaknesses, vulnerabilities and genuine limitations do you deny that you really have?** Many people, especially if they grew up with neglectful or irresponsible parents, learn to deny their weaknesses, vulnerabilities and genuine limitations and to never ask for help. This is an important coping mechanism and can be a great strength. But it has its costs. You may look very strong on the outside, but important parts of you can't grow because you can't get the help and nourishment you need. Admitting your weaknesses, limitations and vulnerabilities, even just to yourself and your own inner voice, opens the door to a much more authentic and solid strength.

3. **What is the Big Problem, the area of your life you most want to grow in?** You've come to this book for a very particular reason. This is the time to write down what you want help with most, as clearly as you can possibly state it. "Ask and ye shall receive" is one of the most famous quotations from the New Testament. I've found this to be exactly true with inner-voice questions, as long as you are patient and really willing to listen to the answers.

Just Say "I Know"

Deena, a petite, attractive thirty-two-year-old fashion designer, divorced her first husband, a domineering and mercurial artist, and now, several years later, had fallen in love with someone "totally different." At first she was gloriously happy. But after dating six months, she started to notice that, though she still loved him, she felt more drained than energized by their relationship. He never wanted to talk things out, only to have a good time. When she gave him a copy of *Men Are From Mars,*

Women Are From Venus, he threw a fit and threatened to break up with her. And he was beginning to pressure her to move to Florida where he lived.

"He's like a drug affecting my brain," she sighed. "When I'm with him, I feel so good. We have so much fun together. But in between the times with him, I don't think he's right for me. I don't know what to do."

I asked, "What are the things you *do* know?"

She took a deep breath. "Okay. I know that I love him. He's good to me. He would do anything for me . . ."

I gave her a quizzical look. "Really?"

"No, because he's not willing to talk over any of our differences." She paused, thinking things over. "I know he has a naive view of love. He says, 'We love each other, it'll all work out.'"

Then something clicked. "And I know," she said, her voice getting stronger, "that that's not enough. Because I've been married before. I've been there. I know what the end result will be and I don't want it. I know that I love being with him, but I also love my job and my life, and I don't see myself moving to Florida."

Realizing she couldn't imagine making a permanent commitment to him, she soon told him she wanted to start dating other people.

So often, women tell me they are "confused." But confusion usually isn't all that confusing. Most of the time, it happens when someone you care about directly contradicts or invalidates what you know deep down to be true. Rather than risk losing the relationship, you give up your clarity—and get confused.

Interestingly, men who take away women's knowing often use women's emotions against them. For example, there was Derek, the very persistent ex-boyfriend of Hillary, an attractive young client of mine. "I know you still love me," he'd tell her, after she told him for the umpteenth time that their relationship was over. "I'm changing . . . you're throwing away the best thing you ever had . . . you haven't given me a chance."

Sentences like these are emotion trigger words. Derek was simply very good at getting Hillary to think and feel things that were against what she knew. "Yes, I do still love him," she'd find herself thinking when he did this. And it was true—a part of her still did. "Maybe I won't find a better love. Maybe he really is changing." But deep down her own knowing knew *exactly* how (in)sincere his words were. When she switched her attention, and said, "Wait a minute—what do I know to be true right now?" she knew immediately what was going on.

Women frequently resist paying attention to their knowing. Generally speaking (and with a great many exceptions), they're more apt to see themselves as "feel-it-alls" than "know-it-alls." Knowing might seem "heartless" or "selfish." Women are also under a lot of pressure from others to *feel* and *care* and *connect* whether they want to or not. A friend of mine who's an executive coach tells me that executive- and managerial-level women who aren't emotional and nurturing inspire far more anger and upset in their underlings than male bosses who act exactly the same way.

But just as most men would benefit if they allowed themselves to be more aware of their feelings, so most women benefit by becoming more aware of their knowing. In fact, there are times when it's absolutely critical. "I must have used that knowing exercise twenty times this past week," said one woman who was breaking up with her domineering husband. "It's the only way I kept him from bulldozing me."

When you want to access your knowing, ask yourself, "What do I know to be true right now"? Another way to phrase it is, "What do I know to be true in my bones?" Then *keep going*. Let one thing that you know to be true lead you to other things that you know to be true, and then to still more. Most women are amazed by how much they really do know, in that deep-down way.

This kind of knowing is different from the kind of analyzing that most of us fall into at times. We've all had the experience of analyzing a situation to death, only to feel just as confused as when we started. That is because most of the analysis we do only involves our "head," whereas knowing involves our whole selves.

Another reason this happens is that you've gone from what you do know to what you don't *yet* know. Instead of trying to come up with an answer prematurely, recognize that you still know something—you know what you don't know. For example, you can say, "I *know* that I want to change jobs. I know that I *don't know* what my options are." Saying that keeps you crystal clear. From there, you can continue to say everything you know about your work situation, from what your needs and wants are in a new job to what you're afraid will happen if you make a change.

One thing that is not true knowing, however, is "I know I should." "I know I should leave him/get more organized/lose ten pounds." No matter how accurate those statements may be, very rarely does change come from them, because you're talking *at* yourself. You're not coming from your inner experience—from what you truly know, sense, feel or want.

Every time you find yourself saying to yourself or a friend, "I don't know. I don't know what to do," think of it as a cue to yourself to think, "Okay—what *do* I know? What *do* I know to be true?" Be scrupulously honest with yourself. You may also need to put some physical distance between yourself and the situation so the outside voices aren't so loud.

Confusion doesn't only occur in relationships. It can occur in a situation involving your job, or volunteer commitments, or wherever your knowing puts you in conflict with what others want or expect from you.

Libby had made up her mind not to renew her teaching contract in order to devote herself to starting a home-based business. When she made her decision, she was elated. "I was miserable as a teacher," she said. "It never was for me. I only did it because I was listening to my mother." But the week before the deadline for renewing her contract, all the reasons for quitting seemed to disappear from her mind. "It's not so bad," she said. "I must be crazy to leave such a secure job. I'm putting all this pressure on Brian to support us all for a while, and it's not fair. Maybe I shouldn't do it."

I asked her to check with her knowing.

She sighed heavily. "I know . . . that I don't really like teaching. I know that I don't want to be in a classroom anymore. I know that I'm excited about my business. I know that I want to do something different. A lot."

I encouraged her to keep going.

"I know that we won't starve. I know that Brian's nervous . . . I know he likes the way things are." That's when she started putting things together. "He *likes* what he's got. He likes the money I make, *and* the dinner on the table, *and* most of the housework done for him. And I'm tired of doing it all, *and* not liking my job, *and* reading homework and grading papers every night. I've supported him in his career, it's about time he supported me."

Now she was on a roll. "I know we can swing it financially. And if we can't, I've *always* worked. I've *always* been able to make money. If I have to, I'll find a way. But I deserve a chance to try and do something for my-self."

By the time she finished talking, there was no question in her mind that she was going to go through with her decision. Later in the session, she said, "You know, it really is tough to change the way things are. I never had any role models for doing what you want to do. But when push comes to shove, you just gotta know it for yourself, and then do it." She did.

Libby was ready to make a change. But—let me make this very clear—*you don't have to be!* Just because you know something, doesn't mean you have to do something about it right away. You're always free to choose. In fact, you may have very good reasons not to rush into action immediately. Be very gentle with the fact that your life may not be in accordance with what you know. It's an achievement in and of itself to acknowledge, or "know-tice," what you know and not deny it.

INNERCIZE 7
What Do I Know to Be True?

Pick a situation in your life where you feel confused and overwhelmed, or where you often find yourself feeling conflicted or guilty. It may be with your spouse or partner, or a family member, or a friendship, a job, a volunteer commitment you've made or an organization you be-long to.

Now ask yourself, "What do I know to be true about this situa-tion?" If you feel stuck, start with the simplest absolute truths that you can say, think of—for example, "I know I have this job," or "I know I'm married to Bob." Then either say out loud or write down everything you know as it comes to you. Let each knowing come to you, one after another, until you can't think of anything else you know. Afterwards, just take in and notice what you know.

Connecting through Knowing

Knowing helped Deena separate from her boyfriend, but it helped Rita connect with hers. Rita had a history of abusive relationships. After a great deal of personal work, she met a man who was loving, kind and caring, very different from any man she'd ever been with. After a couple of months of dating him, she came to a session very agitated.

"I have to break up with Matt," she said.

"Why? What happened?"

"We had a couple of fights."

"Was he abusive to you?"

"No! But—I don't know. How can I trust that he won't be? How do I know that he's not going to be like the rest?"

After we talked a bit, I invited her to check with what she knew inside.

"All right, I know he respects me. I know that he's kind, and gentle. I know that we really talk through our differences and I couldn't do that with any other guy I've been with. I know that we argued and he got mad, but he never threatened me. I know that I'm not afraid of him. I know he's gentle . . . I already said that. I know that he's different." She stopped and took a deep breath, then continued. "I know that I'm scared. This is so new to me. I'm not used to it. I'm afraid to love a man again. But I know that I want to love him. I *do* love him."

In this way, Rita used her knowing to discriminate between her present situation and a painful past. By doing so, she was able to see what was new and wonderful in her latest relationship.

You can check with your knowing to help you in those everyday moments when other people's desires tug at you and threaten to make you lose yourself. This is good to keep in mind, because we don't just lose ourselves in big ways. We lose ourselves in little ways, a minute here, an hour there. You can get yourself back in the same exact way, a minute or an hour at a time. As a very wise woman who happens to be my manicurist recently said to me, "Life is mostly a series of small events." Listening to your knowing can help you keep the small events of your life aligned with your inner self.

One recent Saturday morning, I was torn between going with my husband and two daughters to an event at my older daughter's school and spending some time alone to replenish myself. My older daughter expected me to go. My husband said, "Do you really want to be alone? You'll probably only end up working."

It would have been very easy for me to just go along. Instead, I went to another room and asked myself what I knew to be true. In response, I said to myself, "I know I'm exhausted, and I have a very busy week coming up. I know that the moment she gets there, my daughter will be off with her friends, and it won't matter so much to her that I'm there. *This time,* I really need to be alone." As I said that, I actually felt myself grow stronger, and I knew it was right. A few hours later, I felt rested and refreshed, and was far more available to my daughters than I would have been had I gone.

That was only a small matter. But trusting what you know can have huge ramifications. It can make you powerfully clear about yourself and the world around you and give you a strength you didn't know you have. Whenever people have stood up for what is right and against what is wrong, whether it was the fight to end slavery, women's right to vote, or the civil rights movement, they met with ferocious opposition, yet ordinary women joined those battles and often led them. How could they take such hatred spewed at them and still hold on to their vision? I believe it was because of their ability to align with what they knew to be true. When you have that, you can be temporarily set back, but you can't be knocked down. It's an ability every woman has inside her, whether she is marching against segregation or presenting in front of a roomful of executives and a jealous and demeaning boss, as Natalie did.

It was our company's annual convention. There were a ton of people there—about thirty salespeople, representatives from our major clients, the president, the division vice president, and three or four directors. I had prepared the report for our division, and was slated to present it. Without telling me first, my boss began presenting my report, going through about half of it before handing it to me, saying, "Now I'm turning it over to the 'fun person.'"

Before I would have been devastated if someone did that to me. I wouldn't have been able to perform. This time, I said to myself, "Wait a second. *I* know what I'm doing. My boss was the one who had to take over half my presentation to make herself look good."

My presentation went very smoothly. Later, some key people made it clear to me that they knew who was responsible for the presentation. More important, *I* knew it. That's something my boss can't take from me.

As powerful as knowing is, there are still those times when, no matter how much you know, you find yourself doing things and repeating patterns that cause you pain, but for some reason you can't seem to make a change. At those times there is something operating below your conscious awareness, something that hasn't yet been put into words, that still needs to be discovered.

That is where *sensing* comes in.

CHAPTER FIVE

Developing Your Sense-Ability: The Wisdom of the Body

It was a late Saturday afternoon in April, 1988. My father was in a hospital in New Jersey for three days undergoing chemotherapy because his cancer, which had been in remission for two years, had recurred.

I was living in Denver at the time. That morning, when I'd last spoken to him, he told me he was feeling okay. "Don't book a flight right away to see me," he told me cheerfully. "Wait until you can clear your schedule." "Is there anything I can send you?" I asked. "Oh, some music from the great masters," he replied.

So there I was, standing in the CDs and tapes section of a Target department store looking for some classical music cassettes, when suddenly my heart started beating fast, and I felt a piercing pressure in my gut. "What am I doing in a store?" I thought. "I've got to call him."

I rushed out of the store to my car. It was about 6:30 in the evening— the sun was just beginning to go down. I thought about the two-hour time-zone difference. My father was an early sleeper anyway, and now he was sick. I had to call him very soon.

I got home in fifteen minutes and gave him a call. We had a wonderful talk. I told him I was worried about him, that I wanted to come see him. I told him again just how much I loved him, and how much I wished him to live to see the child I would have one day. "Don't worry," he replied. "I will have all your babies on my lap." We exchanged a few more words. I told him again that I loved him and wished him good night. "Good night, dear," he said, and hung up.

When the phone rang at 3:30 the next morning, I didn't need to answer it to know he was gone.

I will forever be grateful to my body for sensing that something was far more wrong with my father than what I had heard, and for letting me know with such urgency in the middle of a noisy, crowded department store. Somehow—who can tell how?—it had picked up the imminence of his death, below the level of reason, logic and intellect, below even the slightest signal of conscious awareness, using sensors more sophisticated and acute than the grandest instruments of modern medical technology.

This is the bedrock of our being, the wisdom of the body. It is from our bodies that we sense our lives. You can see this reflected in our language. Phrases like *moved by the music, scared stiff* or *shaken to the core* show how, when we deeply experience something, we involve not just our minds and our emotions, but our bodies as well.

Think of your body. Not your proportions, not your weight, but the amazing miracle that your body is. Your heart beats. Your blood flows. Your cells divide. Your muscles expand and contract. Your cuts and bruises, most of them, heal. And you grew from a single cell, to a baby, to a child to an adult. All without a single conscious thought to direct any of it.

As a woman, you even have the ability to create a human life where there was none before. But not with your conscious mind. Later, when I did get pregnant, this took some getting used to. I was someone who was used to making things happen in her life. At first I found it hard to accept that, aside from eating a healthy diet and taking basically good care of myself, there was nothing I could "do" to help make the baby.

For centuries, Western civilization had a very low opinion of the body. Science thought of it mainly as a machine, amazingly intricate but essentially dumb, not much more than a vehicle to carry around and feed the brain. Religion saw it as the source of evil and temptation, the home of destructive emotions and impulses, something that must be transcended to enter the kingdom of God.

But scientists have recently begun to understand that the body is "intelligent" in its own right. And it *speaks* to us all the time in the language of inner senses. We're all very familiar with our outer senses— sight, hearing, touch, taste and smell. But we spend much less time noticing, interpreting and, most important of all, trusting the subtle body sensations that signal what's happening *within* us: the catch in the throat, the throbbing around the heart, the knot in the stomach, the vague sense of tension or uneasiness. This is the way the body communicates to us.

Sometimes the body fairly shouts at us, as when it tries to alert us to danger in a stranger's too-friendly smile. Other times it's whispering, using subtle signals called *felt senses* that, when properly deciphered, are filled with extraordinarily rich information about ourselves and our lives, including the answers to many of our problems.

I call the ability to sense, interpret and trust what your body is telling you *sense-ability*. Like any other skill, it's something you can develop. Developing your sense-ability sets in motion a wonderful synergy: The more you trust what your body tells you, the more easily it offers its wisdom to you. The more easily you can hear it, the more its message will seem trustworthy to you.

While many still believe that it is only through transcending the body and its feelings that one reaches a more spiritual state of being, I believe the very opposite is true. Predominantly, the inner voice *speaks through the body*. Your path and purpose in life and the steps you need to take become much clearer when you open up the pathway that leads to your inner senses. Sensing the body, far from drawing you away from your mind or your spirit, actually leads you to an expanded sense of self.

The Language of the Body

Imagine for a moment that you never learned to talk. You grew up, you became physically and emotionally mature, yet for some reason, the whole universe of words and language that starts to unfold around the age of eighteen months simply never happened for you. How would you think? How would you experience the world?

You'd live from moment to moment, constantly awash in a sea of sensory information. You wouldn't know what *grief* meant, but you'd still experience *heartache*. There'd be no word for *joy*, but there would be the same glorious physical and emotional sensation that comes when your child runs across a room and jumps into your arms. Excitement, boredom, fear, anger, indeed every shade of your emotional palette would still exist, just as they clearly exist in any healthy normal preverbal toddler. But how do they exist, if you have no words for them? They exist as *body senses*, or *inner bodily states*. In fact, you'd probably notice your inner states much more, and much more accurately, than you do now because without the mind's chatter they would occupy a much greater proportion of your consciousness.

Of course, you did learn to talk, just like everyone else. And when you learned to talk, you learned to think in words. Words give human beings an extraordinary flexibility and control over their experience that no other animal has. With words, you no longer have to have your awareness be where your body is. You can read a novel and be transported to a totally different reality. You can recall in detail what you did last summer or plan next summer's vacation. You can learn economics, entering levels of abstract thought that would be absolutely impossible without the power of our complex language abilities. Yet when we gain the gift of language, something is lost as well. With our thoughts, we can override our body signals, or they can simply be drowned out, the way sunlight blocks out the light of the stars.

But body senses are still our most elemental and direct experience. Everything else is an overlay. Our emotions, in particular, are attempts to translate our body experience into a language we can understand.

Say you woke up one morning with a jumpy, jittery feeling that made you feel like yelling at anyone who so much as said "hello." This is a body experience, one that your body is experiencing for some reason. How you interpret it and what you do with it is up to you. You could try to ignore it and rise above it completely. You could label it "bad." You could dismiss it as hormonal. You could translate it as being furious with your husband for getting home late last night.

But the truth is, there is a specific meaning to that sensation, and your body is trying to communicate it to you. Let's say the real reason you're jittery and cross is the presentation you're scheduled to make at three that afternoon; you don't feel prepared, and you resent having to make it at all. If you hit upon this reason, and said, "Oh! This has to do with the presentation!" you would immediately notice the difference. You'd experience a small feeling of relief in your body, a sense of something easing. It's as if something in your body said, "Ah! You understand me!" And most likely you'd stop feeling bothered by other people for unrelated reasons.

But most of us grow up to be very poor interpreters of our body senses. No one told us that it was something worth learning to do. So we settle for a very rough approximation of what we're truly sensing, accepting what we *think* we feel. When we misinterpret the meaning of our body senses, there is often the feeling of repeating the same patterns of feelings over and over again, without any relief.

Flora, for example, came to therapy in part because of what she called "a problem with anger," especially at her husband. One afternoon, she came to a session furious at him after he had taken their son to a baseball game the night before. "He *always* does this to me," she said. "He didn't tell me ahead of time. I could have planned to do something else. He didn't ask me if *I* wanted to go. How could he be so inconsiderate?"

Now, it was certainly inconsiderate of him not to consult her or give her prior warning, and for many women it might have been good to express their anger about that. But expressing anger did not make Flora feel better. It did not bring any sense of easing. So after acknowledging her anger, I suggested that she go just a little deeper and take a moment to sense the feeling in her body right in the present moment.

She was quiet for a few seconds. "Oh!" she exclaimed. "This is kind of embarrassing, but I'm just feeling . . . *left out*. And"—she paused again for a moment—*"jealous*. And now that I've said that," she continued, with a surprised laugh, "I don't feel angry anymore!"

Flora was accustomed to "translating" all negative or upset body senses as anger. And once she *labeled* her sense as anger, it was easy for her mind to support the emotion by developing a line of thinking to support it. ("Of course I'm angry at him. He's a rude and inconsiderate man, and he always has been.") This is something people do all the time—we *think* we know what we feel, based on habitual reactions, on thoughts about how we "should" feel, and on memories of how we felt in similar situations.

But when Flora let go of what she was thinking, and even of what she thought she was feeling, and went straight to what was happening in her body in the present moment, she was surprised to discover something else. When she named it correctly, it stopped bothering her.

This is the magic of sensing. When feelings and sensations remain unnamed and mysterious, they stay stuck. All the "I shouldn't feel this way" thoughts in the world aren't going to make them change. But paradoxically, when they are named properly and allowed to *be*, without trying to argue them out of existence, *that* is when they are free to change, even to release completely.

Making Sense of What You Sense

This is the basic first step of a gentle but very powerful mind-body technique called *Focusing*. It is the most powerful method I know of to develop sense-ability and use it for personal growth and healing. What makes Focusing so remarkable is that it is a method for making *direct contact* with who you are and what is happening inside you.

Focusing helps you to get in touch with and understand what your body is trying to tell you. In the 1970s, University of Chicago psychologist Eugene Gendlin, Ph.D., the originator of the Focusing process, discovered that when people paid attention to subtle inner body states in therapy sessions, the way Flora did, they made rapid progress. They more quickly untangled the problems that brought them to therapy. Dr. Gendlin called these subtle inner body states *felt senses*, and realized that people could learn to get in touch with them and work with them by themselves or with the help of a friend, outside the confines of therapy.

For many women, Focusing has a special value. So many times, women are called "too sensitive." It's a ridiculous put-down, because sensitivity is an extraordinarily valuable trait. Think of scientific instruments. The most sensitive ones are always the most expensive, and the most useful. I've noticed that when women use their sensitivity to help others, by understanding how they feel and knowing what they need, it's considered an asset. But the moment their sensitivity causes them to get angry or upset about something done to *them*, it becomes a liability. This is not exactly fair.

But it *is* true that's there's nothing in our culture that teaches women how to understand and process all the sensory information coming from within and without. It's like having a very sensitive instrument without the software to guide it, and as a result it continually goes on overload. Focusing is like a program that allows you to make sense out of all that you sense.

I invite you to try the following Innercize, which in fact is the first step of Focusing. It may sound difficult and complicated, but it's actually a naturally unfolding process. Read the Innercize all the way through once or twice, and then try it. The whole Innercize should take less than five minutes.

⋧ INNERCIZE 8 ⋦
The First Step of Focusing

Bring yourself into the reflective mode that you learned about on page 48. Make yourself comfortable in a chair, take a few deep breaths and close or at least lower your eyes. This helps you to bring your attention inward.

Now bring your awareness into the center of your body, especially your throat, chest, stomach and abdomen, and gently ask yourself, "How am I inside?" or "What wants my attention right now?" Then wait, for a few moments to about a minute, until you start to become aware of a body sense forming somewhere in those areas.

It may start out as a sensation—like a fluttering in your stomach, or a feeling of a tight band across your chest. It may start out as a feeling-word, such as "left out" or "fear." Or it may start out as an image.

Whatever it is, it is likely to be subtle, vague, fuzzy and unclear. That's because it is still in its "native language"—it has not yet been put fully into words. If you feel like you're "groping" to get a handle on it, and you can't quite put your finger on what it is, you're doing exactly the right thing! Focusing is slower than thinking or ordinary feeling. Avoid the temptation to rush to "figure it out." If you begin to feel frustrated, just acknowledge the frustration and return to the body sense that's forming. Allow yourself to remain in a state of uncertainty and let it unfold at its own pace.

Once you become aware of a body sense, try to describe *exactly* what you are sensing. Let's say you're sensing a tightness in your chest. Say out loud, "There's a tightness in my chest." Now check with your body to see if that matches the sense.

Notice if you can *feel* if there's a "yes," "no" or "not quite" to that statement. If you don't get a clear enough response, repeat the words again. This is critical to the process. If it is a "yes," you will feel a small easing, as though something inside you said, "you got that right." You may sigh unconsciously. If it's a "no" or a "not quite," keep sensing inside. What's going on inside you right now? Stay with it until you can describe what you are sensing inside you in a way that elicits a "yes."

So now you have a body sensation, such as "it feels tight in my chest," or an image, such as "it feels like there's a heavy steel ball in my stomach." You've checked that description and gotten a "yes." But what does it mean? It can be rather baffling. You may be tempted to blame it on what you ate for lunch.

Keep doing exactly what you're doing, paying attention to what's going on inside you. Because the sense is going to change—either by getting noticeably stronger, or changing to a different sense altogether. When you become aware of the new sense, repeat what you have just done—name it by describing it, and check with your body to see if the description fits.

As you do this, the process will unfold. Chances are you will then sense the emotional quality and possibly the meaning or reason behind the sensations that have just arisen in your body. Again, check with the description that comes to your mind and see if something within you seems to answer, "Yes, that's what I'm saying."

If you have gotten this far, you will probably feel a sense of relief, an easing in your body. A few tears may even come out of your eyes. Unless you feel like continuing, this would be a good time to begin slowly opening your eyes.

Here I can only give you an introduction to the principles and techniques of Focusing, which I hope will be enough to get you to begin using it in your life. If you are interested in learning more about Focusing, I recommend you pick up a copy of Gendlin's classic, *Focusing*, which is still in print, and read it. For the most comprehensive, step-by-step manual written so far on how to Focus, alone or with a partner, I recommend *The Power of Focusing* by Ann Weiser Cornell.

The ABCs of Sensing

What you've done in the preceding Innercize is to begin a dialogue with the deepest portion of your psyche, the part that experiences everything in the form of wordless body states. You've asked it, "How are you?" and it's answered, "This is what's really going on with me right now." And if you've accepted it and not begun to argue with it, you've probably sensed an easing, a small sigh of relief.

The most important thing to remember is that body senses are usually slower and fuzzier than what goes on in your head. To utilize them, you need to pay attention to them in a relaxed and patient way, without pushing. It's a lot like going from broad daylight into a very dark room. At first, you can't see a thing. Then slowly your eyes become accustomed to the darkness and you begin to see shadowy shapes. Little by little you become aware of the contents of the room. You step into it tentatively, cautiously, and explore. Eventually you are fully aware of everything in the room and can comfortably move within it.

Ordinary consciousness is like that broad daylight—and your inner truths are often in that dark room. But you can't *force* yourself to see in there. You just have to wait, pay attention, and get accustomed to a different, less sharp kind of vision.

Eva began therapy in an emotional stir. Married with two small children, she had met a man at work, fallen in love, and had an affair. I invited her to go below all the surface upset and sense what was happening deep inside.

"I'm sensing a wooden spool of thread inside me," she said. "That's pretty strange, isn't it?" she asked me, opening her eyes.

"Not necessarily. See if you can stay with it," I answered.

She closed her eyes again. "Yup—It's a wooden spool of thread, and it's red, covered in red thread . . . and it's full of knots . . . knots everywhere. There's no place to grab that string and pull . . ." I sat silently, waiting.

"That's it," she continued, "that's what I'm feeling—a lot of knots, and no starting place, no place to start unraveling the string!"

Her body sense gave her an exact picture of what she was feeling right then—that she couldn't figure out where to start to unravel the emotional knots she was in. Just sensing this first dilemma—that she didn't know where to start—*gave* her the place to start.

At some point—sometimes with the very first felt sense or sometimes with the third or fourth—the "tight feeling in my chest" reveals itself to mean "lonely" or "angry" or "overwhelmed at how much I have to do." The temptation at this moment will be to start to *think* about the feeling in order to make it better. For example, if you realized you were feeling "overwhelmed at how much I have to do," you might start thinking about rejuggling your schedule. If you noticed a feeling of anger inside, you might immediately say to yourself, "I'm not really that angry, just a little annoyed." Or, you might instead start thinking about why you're angry and what you're going to do about it, or *should* do about it.

However, there is a *far* more healing thing to do at that moment. Instead of trying to fix it, let that feeling know you hear it exactly the way it is. As strange as this is probably going to sound to you, this sense or feeling is a *part* of you that needs to be heard by you—that is, by your fully conscious Self. And hard as this may be to believe, when you encounter something inside you that is angry, hurting, or in any other form of distress, you don't have to try to change it, or fix it, or nurture it, or heal it, or pray for it, or convince it to face reality, or do anything to make it better. Simply giving it the kind of open, nonjudgmental understanding that you'd want from your best friend is so profoundly new that the sense, once heard, is never the same. Hearing it in this way, in the reflective mode, is bringing the energy of the Larger Self to your inner self. That's why hearing is *enough*.

Remarkably, by listening to it in this fashion, you can almost *watch* as your inner self starts to work toward its own resolution. Have you ever had the experience of "talking out" a problem with someone who listened nonjudgmentally and gave practically no advice, and found that you were able to come up with your own solution? The same principle applies when you listen to your inner senses. The resolution may surprise you, since it doesn't come from thinking it through, but rather, from *sensing* it through.

It had been eighteen months since Toni's thirty-year marriage had broken up. The divorce was mostly amicable, and she surprised herself by how quickly she seemed to move on. But her early progress seemed to have ended, and for a number of months her life had gotten stuck in a holding pattern. "I wonder if there are issues I have to resolve about Phil before I can move on," she said in a session one day. "I'm not even sure they're resolvable. What should I do?"

I invited her to ask her body for the answers.

After guiding her into a relaxed and reflective state, I asked her, "So how is the whole issue with Phil? Sense it in your body."

She sat with it for about a minute or so. "This is surprising—I sense a little fear there."

"So you're noticing fear there. Really acknowledge the fear. See if you can be with it for a while."

"It's kind of vague. . . . It's anxiousness."

I acknowledged the "anxiousness" she felt and waited while she sat, paying attention to her inner senses.

"It's not moving," she said finally, a little worried.

I reflected that back to her in a reassuring voice, and told her she didn't have to "make it" move, but just to keep company with it, as though she was sitting over a cup of tea with a friend.

She followed my instructions. After a while, she spoke again. "What I'm getting is, there isn't a safety net. If anything goes wrong, I'm on my own. Before, if things got screwed up, at least we were in it together. There was a comfort zone." She sighed, and nodded her head. "This feels true," she continued. "I feel a little better."

This exercise took only ten minutes, yet it powerfully clarified for her the issues affecting her and helped her to move on. "I was worried that my main issues were anger, jealousy and humiliation," she said a week later. "But my body told me that my biggest issue was being on my own. There was such a certainty about it, I didn't have to think about it anymore. I know that my biggest fears about being on my own are all financial. Now I know that's what I really have to deal with."

Sense-Ability, Compassion and Transformation

Who in the world doesn't sometimes do things that later make them feel angry at or even ashamed of themselves? Who has never said to herself, "Now, why do I do that?" or conversely, "Why don't I do what I know I should do?" The reason, many times, is that, to some part of you inside, doing what you think is "wrong" is the right thing to do. This part may even be trying to protect you from harm. You may put yourself down, you may make a hundred resolutions to fix this bad glitch in your personality, but you probably have never tried to do the one thing that would work, which is spending time sensing deeply into what may be behind your actions.

How do you handle a part of yourself that has feelings that you don't like, or that leads you to do things that are against your values or desires? Aren't there *some* parts of yourself that you just have to "straighten out" somehow? No. All aspects of yourself deserve to be listened to with compassion by you. They have a purpose and some good reason for being there and feeling the way they do. They're hurting in some fashion. *You don't have to agree with them*—nor, obviously, do their bidding—*to extend to them the compassionate understanding they need.* But if you want these aspects of yourself to transform, give them the listening that they've never received.

You can silently say to whatever felt sense you've become aware of, "so you're angry—or sad—or afraid," whatever it is experiencing, and then pay attention to see if you can feel a response inside, as though something within you feels better understood and cared for.

When you do this in Focusing, you discover with every fiber of your being that no part of you deserves to be condemned, and that acceptance and compassion lead to change. This is what makes Focusing so amazing and gives it so much power to cause transformation.

Carolyn was one of the most brilliant women I had ever worked with. She was a pioneer in the field of telecommunication technology and one of the original architects of the Internet. But decades of working sixteen-hour days and constantly pleasing other people both at work and at home finally took their toll. In her fiftieth year, after her partner suddenly ended their relationship, she had a complete physical and emotional breakdown.

She was hospitalized, her health deteriorated and for eighteen months she couldn't work—she could barely get out of bed to eat. She was forced to move from her beautiful mountain chalet in Utah, finally ending up in a tiny four-room apartment in a building a few miles from where she grew up to be near her parents, who were ailing.

For months she lived with packed boxes covering almost every inch of her floor space. Little by little she put away her clothes and other essentials and stored what wouldn't fit. But the second bedroom, the room that was to be her study, remained stacked from floor to ceiling with boxes. There were twenty-three boxes of computer books and technical papers, and her computer, her mainstay and source of employment for twenty-five years, was also still boxed.

She criticized herself relentlessly for not unpacking. Every week or so she'd resolve to empty the boxes, but the boxes remained. She decided to try Focusing in my office, to see if it would shed light on the problem.

After she closed her eyes and focused her awareness inside, she gently and silently asked her inner self, "What is it about getting my study unpacked that's causing me so much trouble?"

In about a minute, a body sense formed, vague at first and then slowly becoming clearer, like a Polaroid picture developing in her hand. "It's hollow," she said. "No, not exactly—more like *empty*."

She sat with that a while longer. "And it feels huge—it feels like it fills the entire inside of my body." She nodded her head—yes, that felt right.

After a few more moments, she said, "Now I'm noticing something else. It feels like . . . *fear*." Silently she spoke to that inner place, saying "Oh, you're afraid," and she felt like she got a "yes." A tear gathered in the corner of her eye.

"Now the huge, empty feeling is back—and it feels even stronger," she said. "And at the same time, I keep hearing that line from the Peggy Lee song—you know, 'Is that all there is?'"

A minute went by, as she sat across from me, very intently paying attention to what was going on inside her. Then suddenly it fell into place.

"Oh! I'm living in a box full of boxes," she said. "I'm afraid I'll have to live forever in a box full of boxes." Silently she said to the fearful place inside her, "I really hear you. I hear that's what you're afraid of." Huge tears ran down her cheeks, ending the strain of constantly criticizing and attacking herself.

Something within her was convinced that if she unpacked those boxes, she would be stuck in her "boxy" little apartment forever. It saw unpacking not as a step in the right direction, but as a resignation, an endpoint. No amount of coaxing or arguing with herself made a difference. Only when she *heard* and *acknowledged* what was going on inside herself after *sensing* what was true for her, could change occur.

And change did occur—rapidly. In a week, she had unpacked and plugged in her computer. Within a month she was back at work at a job she loved. "I can't believe how different I am!" she told me. "My office mate called me an extrovert. Me! But I guess I am one now. I talk to everyone, easily. I'm having fun. I'm blossoming." She also decided to take a break from intimate relationships, or even to stay away from them permanently, because she knew how easy it was for her to give herself away, and she wanted to take care of herself and savor her own company.

Focusing with a Friend

You might have noticed that I didn't seem to have to do very much in the above example. It's true. Carolyn did almost all the work. But Carolyn still felt helped by my presence. That's true for most people. While it definitely can be done alone, there's something helpful about talking to someone who's paying warm, respectful attention, rather than talking to yourself, or to your dog—although, actually, a pet might be a very good listener!

So, if you can arrange it, try Focusing with a friend. But the ground rule has to be this: Whoever is being the Listener can't start advising, or fixing, or in any other way sticking her two cents in. Not even a little bit. The most helpful thing she can do is to silently give her best attention and presence to the one who's Focusing. At most, she can help the process along by repeating back the felt-sense words, with the words "you're noticing" or "you're sensing" in front of them. As in, "You're sensing a tight feeling in your stomach," or "you're noticing it's sad."

This is a great way to support a friend and to get to know her in a deeper way.

The Sense of Your Self

The examples here may sound easy and clear, but the first few times you take the time to listen to your inner senses, you may have a hard time really trusting them. After you end the Focusing session, and later in the day, your outside voices may come barging in to discount what your inner senses said. "Oh big deal!" they'll shout. "What's so new and important about that?" Listening to your inner self runs so counter to the cultural message of changing yourself, don't be surprised if you start thinking "this can't work." This will happen whether your first attempt doesn't produce very much—a distinct possibility—or even if you get something amazing on your first try. I do invite you to stick with it. Eventually you will have an entirely different relationship with your inner senses, and with your inner self.

Charlene had been Focusing for about fifteen minutes on the problems between her and her husband when she came to this moment: "It's small. There's a sense of 'small' there," she said. "It feels like I'm fading away."

She spent a long time sitting silently, just staying with the sense. "It's . . . a deep-down feeling of being small. It's been with me a long, long time. It's like a child who's been all alone."

She opened her eyes and looked at me. "Does this mean that I have to nurture my inner child?" she asked.

"No," I replied. "You don't have to fix it, nurture it, or make it feel any different. All you do is hear whatever's there as it changes."

Something about hearing me say that made her almost jump, as if I had startled her. "You mean I *don't* have to nurture it?" she said. Rolling her hands in front of her, she continued, "You mean, I just hear the next thing, and the next thing, and the next?" I nodded. She closed her eyes again. "Oh. This is scary. Well, actually," she reconsidered, checking with her body again, "it's not. It just *feels* like it could be." A smile was playing on the edge of her lips.

"That's right," I said. "It seems like it could be scary to listen to these voices inside, but in fact it's not. Because they don't want to hurt you. Sometimes they change just from having you care that they feel the way they do."

She nodded her head again. Then she opened her eyes and looked at me, amazed. "I get it! You mean I'm learning how to communicate with myself!"

It was a moment of sheer revelation for her. "You hear all the time," she said, "how you have to love yourself and have a good relationship with yourself. It sounds right, but the truth is, I had no idea what it really meant! Just the other day, I was telling my daughter the same stuff, you know, 'you've got to love yourself, you've got to be your own best friend.'" She smiled and shook her head at the thought. "Honestly, you know what? It *repulsed* me," she laughed. "Like, what in the world does that *mean?*"

What Charlene said is true. If you haven't been in touch with yourself for a long time, how can you love yourself? It's like loving a relative you haven't seen or spoken to since 1983. If you want to truly start loving yourself, do what you'd do with any other estranged relationship—make yourself available for a warm, nonjudgmental conversation.

Sensible or Sense-Able?

Practically anyone who has ever gone hunting for a new house or apartment has used sensing. You know the feeling of walking into a place and feeling your whole self go, "This is the place!" You also know the body-sense that says, "I definitely can't live here" or "I don't know what it is, it looks nice, but I don't like it enough." In matters like where they live, most women allow themselves to pay attention to what their senses tell them, but in other, possibly more important decisions such as men and careers, they often do not.

This happens because, with men and careers, we're telling ourselves to be "sensible"—that is, rational—rather than *sense-able*. We're looking at the surface of things and what we imagine others would think about our situation, rather than what's true for us. Mercedes, a young scientist at a government agency, described this succinctly. "I had a wonderful job. All my friends were jealous of me. The only problem was, it wasn't for me." She didn't acknowledge that this was true until she started waking up every night at three in the morning because of work stress. "That literally was my 'wake-up call' to change jobs."

As for men, you may talk yourself into staying in a relationship with the wrong man by allowing what a man seems to be, or what you think you *should* be feeling, to cloud over what your senses are telling you. You may forget that most men deliberately strive to present a good surface, no matter what is true underneath, and that some men consciously try to deceive and manipulate women. Your inner self, however, is rarely really fooled—just ignored. This will be covered in more depth in Chapter Nine. But Dory Hollander said it well in the book *101 Lies Men Tell Women and Why Women Believe Them:*

> Most of us sense what feels safe and what doesn't. We intuit who's trustworthy and who's feeding us a line. But as time passes we forget. We train ourselves to disregard the early cues, to be ever so reasonable, to be relentlessly polite. We end up smiling, no matter what we're actually feeling, papering over our best hunches and reassuring ourselves that we're just fine, thank you.
>
> But the funny thing is that we don't truly forget our hunches. We remember them *after* the hurt, *after* the betrayal. . . .
>
> In the pursuit of connectedness, we forget that being nice or polite is usually far less critical than taking care of ourselves and avoiding or surviving threatening situations.

I'm not saying that you should dismiss your rational mind when it comes to making decisions about your career—or for that matter, about love. But make a point of listening to what your body is telling you as well. And if you find yourself deliberately going against the signals from your body—for example, staying in a relationship that you sense isn't good for you—at this point, just acknowledge to yourself that you're doing that, without judging yourself. Remember that *acknowledging* doesn't have to mean *agreeing*, and *listening* to your body doesn't mean you have to always *follow* what it says. Your inner self wants most of all to be heard, to be given a place at the table. It doesn't require that it dictate your life.

At the very least, learn to notice your gut responses, your inner "nos" and "yesses," and to trust them more. Notice when your body recoils, your shoulders tense, your breath feels like it's caught, when you get a sinking feeling. Notice the situations where your body relaxes, your breath eases, and you feel an urge to do something or move toward something. Many women have had childhoods where they were deprived of the human right to feel and express a strong *"NO!"* and where their natural "yesses" were not paid attention to. As a result, they have trouble believing in the basic correctness of their gut responses. But your body is very smart. It will pull you away from what will hurt you and move you toward what will help you, if you let it.

Make yourself comfortable with a wonderful word: *something.* You don't have to know what you're sensing. If you're sensing *something,* that's a clear signal that *something's* going on either within or around you that you have to pay extra special attention to. You're like a doe in the field who has just noticed the tiniest flicker of motion in the distant tall grasses, and who has become totally alert, waiting to see what her next action must be. The secret of sensing is knowing that you don't have to know for certain, you don't have to prove it with evidence, and you don't have to have all the data to take seriously what you perceive.

Finally, some women may never sense into their bodies simply because their lives feel too painful. They may be single mothers working two jobs just to survive and support their children, or they may be married to an alcoholic and don't know how they can make it alone. If that describes you, sometime during the day when you're by yourself, see if you can sense into your body just a little bit, and then give your inner self all the gentleness and compassion you can muster. You may feel that your situation is unfixable, but even then you don't have to lose yourself. If you can remember to notice what's going on inside you and be gentle and compassionate to those feelings, you are still holding on to who you are. Deep down, your Larger Self will begin working to bring you toward a solution.

CHAPTER SIX

Having Your Feelings
without Them Having You

Mira started crying even before she sat down in my office for her first session.

"It's my fault the marriage didn't last," she sobbed. "My depression ruined it. I'm so lost."

She told me her story, crying quietly most of the time. Eleven years earlier, she met and married Cal in a whirlwind, six-month courtship. She was twenty-three and he was thirty. Within a year she had Luke, and two years later, Katie.

A couple of years ago, she became severely depressed. At first Cal was kind and attentive, but when none of the drugs the psychiatrist gave her helped, he began to grow cold and distant from her. About six months after the depression began, he told her he wanted a divorce. "I can't blame him," she said. "I mean, I couldn't—you know—*love* him anymore. I didn't *want* him."

She didn't contest it, and agreed to joint custody. Having not worked outside the home for almost ten years, and feeling the way she did, she took a series of low-paying retail sales jobs. Meanwhile, Cal remarried, and recently, he told her he was contemplating asking the court for sole custody.

"He says the kids would be better off if they spent more time with him and Sharon (his new wife). And maybe he's right." She looked terribly defeated, and I remember thinking, *It's like she was beaten up from the inside.*

"That sounds like a lot of outside voices—all the ways you tell yourself what's wrong with you and what you have to improve," I said.

She nodded slightly. "People are always giving me advice about what I can do to feel better. I'm in sales and I have to look good all the time."

"I know how much you have to hold it up out there. You don't have to do that here. Here you can look within your heart and feel what you really feel."

Hearing me say this, she hid her face in her hands and her body racked with sobs. "I'm so *tired* of being no good for anybody! I'm so *tired* of it!" Her crying took on an entirely different tone. The pain and outrage of being told for so long that she was "no good for anybody," and believing it, ripped through her.

In a few minutes her crying calmed. This was the opportunity I was hoping for. I didn't want to be the only compassionate listener in the room. If she was ever going to heal, she needed to know how to give *herself* the compassion, strength and wisdom she needed to grow.

"What words would describe how it feels inside?" I asked her. "If it helps to concentrate, you might want to close your eyes."

She closed her eyes and paused for a few moments, searching. "It feels heavy and tight and a lot of pressure."

"Where do you feel it in your body?"

She put her hand on her heart. "Right there."

"See if you can stay right there with it."

A look of deep, intense concentration came over her. I had the feeling of a door opening, and a part of Mira inside reaching out to be heard and understood.

"It feels afraid . . . lonely . . . unloved."

"Does it feel understood by those words?" I continued.

She nodded slowly, her hand still on her heart. "Yes," she said quietly.

"It needs so much for you to hear it," I said gently, "instead of you joining in with all of the criticisms. It needs a lot of protection."

She nodded slowly. "It says it's afraid . . . of living alone. Of being left alone. And it's afraid . . . it's afraid of Cal. Afraid it could lose the kids if it doesn't say yes to him." She wiped a tear from the corner of her eye.

"Let it know you hear it's afraid." I replied. "See if it wants to say more."

"There *is* more. It's . . . it says it's *angry*. It's angry that he'd try to take away my babies. It's angry at the way he's always bulldozing me." She opened her eyes. "I'd forgotten that I felt that way. It's hard for me to say no to him. To anybody, really."

I noticed that she could say that now without the tone of self-condemnation that had filled her speech before. "Maybe you can check how that place inside you feels now?"

"It's a little calmer. It's not as muffled or squashed."

"What does it need?"

She paused again for a few moments, took a deep breath and let it out. "To be heard without judgment, just to be heard as it is. Oh!" she said with a sudden gasp of recognition. "*TO NOT BE MUTE!* To not be afraid! Just to be loved and accepted and free."

The tortured woman who had come to my office was gone for now; in her place was a woman who, while still a little afraid, had an inkling of what she needed to do, and a feeling that somewhere inside her, she had the strength to do it.

A week later Mira reported, "I talked to Cal this week. I told him that I didn't want to give up custody—that they're my kids, too." She'd also called her lawyer to see if she could get more child support.

In this session, Mira realigned with her inside. She did this by separating from the outside voices, then listening to what her feelings and inner senses were telling her. She also used *disidentification*—listening to her feelings rather than *being* her feelings.

Mira was caught in an overwhelming flood of emotion, but what freed her from it was not pushing away her feelings or "making" herself into a stronger person. Instead, she found a way to connect with her feelings in a manner that allowed them to be heard and their message assimilated. Mira's inner self, though stifled by a lifetime of being dominated by others, was still there, trying to communicate to her through what she was sensing and feeling. All it needed was for Mira to learn how to listen to it.

Mira kept joint custody of her two children. Eighteen months later, she accomplished a triumph she never imagined could happen: Though she had declared bankruptcy around the time of her divorce, she bought a house of her own.

I get to have my own house! And brand new! And I get to pick the carpets and appliances and everything. And it's right in the area I want to live. I never thought it would be possible!

I was so scared when I went to the realtor's office. What a

moment when the mortgage banker called and went over my bank-ruptcy details and my job history and said, "Well, I'm convinced, I'm going to tell the broker she can write a contract today." The broker asked me, "Do you want to do it today or wait?" I said, "Oh, let's do it *now*."

I have so much to do! I have all of these new goals to work to-ward. Neither of my children have been to the dentist in years. And I'm standing up to my ex. I told him, "We're getting rid of some things around here, and I expect your participation in getting rid of your junk, because we can't function in this mess." And he said, "Aye, aye, sir." I'm awake now. I've gotten my head out of the sand. I've been asleep for *too* long.

Mira's life was turning around.

In general, women have more access to their feelings than most men. They have an easier time experiencing and naming what they are. Yet identifying your feelings is one thing, and truly *honoring* them is quite another. I've found that women spend a lot of time talking *about* their feelings, and talking *around* their feelings, yet still have a lot of trouble accepting and trusting their feelings and allowing themselves to feel them. Many times, women try to change what they feel, or tell them-selves that they "shouldn't" feel what they do.

This chapter is about learning to honor *all* of your feelings, includ-ing the ones you or others feel are "unreasonable" or "unacceptable." Honoring your feelings means welcoming them, listening to them and treating them with the attention, care and respect they deserve. When you let your feelings be, and listen to them openly and deeply, you be-come freer. You're more in harmony with yourself, more spontaneous, calmer and more flexible, kinder to yourself and others. At the same time, you become stronger, more able to know and stand up for what you need and want, and more able to marshal your energies to create a life that reflects your inner voice.

Three Myths about Feelings

Most of us have learned three very destructive myths about feelings.

Feelings aren't intelligent. The biggest myth is that feelings are "primitive," irrational, inferior to thought and intellect, instead of the vital and profoundly intelligent faculties that they are. This is just as true for difficult and unpleasant feelings as for the pleasant ones. Typically, people divide their feelings into "good" feelings and "bad" feelings, and spend a lot of energy trying to control their "bad" feelings or change them into "good" ones. The idea that a "bad" feeling might have a good reason for being—might even have something *very important and valuable* to say—is rarely entertained.

This myth is rather entrenched in Western civilization, going back as it does at least twenty-four centuries to Aristotle. Aristotle saw human feelings as essentially the same thing that animals have; only reason, characterized by logic and intellect, separated human beings from animals, and the only ones who had it were . . . free men. Feelings were needed, feelings were not to be denied, but feelings were to be ruled, kindly and benevolently if possible, just as men were "by nature" meant to rule women and slaves. He could not imagine any kind of viable relationship with feelings other than "wise" ruler and "dumb" subject.

Feelings are self-indulgent. It's self-indulgent, says this myth, to treat your feelings as if they're important, real and worthy of attention. This goes especially for feelings such as sadness, fatigue, fear or doubt. Those who believe this myth think it's weak to heed feelings, and stronger not to. And they think that if they or anyone else is "overreacting," then they could, and should, stop.

These first two myths are more typical of the way men experience themselves than women. Many men believe, like their fathers and their father's fathers did before them, that the only way to act responsibly is to rigidly control their feelings, which they associate with sexual and aggressive impulses that they don't want to act upon.

In general, men tend to negate and minimize their feelings. There's some evidence to suggest that, to a degree, this is "natural" for many men. It certainly can be a wonderful trait if it helps you to think clearly in terrible situations, or if it enables you to risk your own life in order to save others. But it does have a cost. Negate, minimize and suppress your feelings long enough, and you begin to lose yourself. Your ability to feel fully alive slips away, bit by bit.

It also causes problems when it causes men to negate not only their own feelings, but their wives' or partners' as well. Some men do this because they sincerely believe that saying, "Aww, it's not so bad" is supportive, since that is the way they manage their own distressing feelings. But to most women, "it's not so bad" does not feel supportive. Far from it.

Women often suffer most not from the original source of pain, but from being told that it shouldn't upset them so much. This leaves them fighting an exhausting inner battle to hide and "manage" their feelings around other people who want them to pretend to feel better, often because *they* can't cope with seeing them in pain.

Feelings are permanent. People often react as if "negative" feelings must be ignored or denied at all costs, because deep down, they believe that feelings are permanent and can't change! Many people don't realize that expressing feelings can change them into something different, that "something's wrong" does not mean "something has always been wrong and will always be wrong," or that upset feelings don't always mean that something needs fixing.

Families and Feelings

> Growing up, I thought there was something wrong with me for being so "sensitive." My parents didn't want me to be angry or sad. "Anger doesn't serve any purpose," is what they'd say. Now I realize that I was just naturally full of feeling. Good God, there's so much information that comes from my feelings, including my anger. I never knew how essential my feelings really were.
> —Tracy, forty-year-old married mother of two

In addition to the cultural myths, most of us spent our entire childhood learning not to trust or value our feelings.

Very few of us grew up in families where the whole range of our feelings was mirrored, accepted and honored. More likely, you grew up in a family where some feelings were okay and others weren't. In some families, anger is okay and wanting to be close isn't. In other families, happiness is okay and sadness isn't. I've also had clients whose families were the exact opposite: When they felt sad, they received comfort and support, but when they felt happy they were ignored. There are families where feeling brave and strong is always encouraged, and feeling weak or frightened is positively taboo.

Family rules about feelings can also be more specific, such as, "It's okay to be angry at Mom but not at Dad," or, "It's okay for parents to be angry at children but not for children to be angry at parents." A great many women grew up in families where they had to pretend that all the fear, embarrassment, anger, loneliness and sorrow they felt living with an alcoholic parent didn't exist.

Children's feelings are often so raw and uncontrolled, and parents' feelings are usually so worn down and overcontrolled, that there's bound to be a clash. It takes a lot of effort, self-awareness and understanding of children to be able to accept, nurture and guide their feelings.

If a feeling doesn't get a response for long enough, eventually a child will stop showing it, or show it much less often. But all the feelings that you learned were not okay to feel are too vital to your very being to simply die or disappear. So instead they get banished, "exiled" from your conscious awareness. They become a part of you that you don't know.

Your inner self never wanted you to lose your anger, your sadness or your excitement. It never really wanted to live pretending not to feel what it felt. It only hid those rejected and "unacceptable" feelings because that was the only way you could grow up without getting continuously hurt.

As an adult, however, it's possible for you to create a life where all of your feelings are allowed. The feelings that have been exiled haven't been lost—they've just been kept in safekeeping. As soon as you begin listening with an open and compassionate heart to what your inner self is trying to tell you, what was locked away will start returning to you.

The Lowdown on Feelings

Here are the facts about feelings, as opposed to the myths.

Feelings are real and enormously valuable. In our hearts, women know this; we have always known this. Strong feelings don't mean we're "unbalanced," and they certainly don't make us weak. The truth is, we are never more powerful than when we stand up for our feelings and act from them.

Feelings are a highly concentrated form of information from your inner self. Yes, the information needs some decoding at times. But first you have to receive it. So the basic rule is: What you feel is simply what you feel. If you're angry, you're angry. If you're hurt, you're hurt. No person or authority in the world can tell you what "should be" going on in your heart, nor do you have to prove, to yourself or to anyone else, that you have a "right" to feel whatever it is you're feeling. In fact, all the arguing in the world against what you feel is not going to help as much as simply *letting your feelings be.*

Marguerite, a thin, nervous, blond-haired woman in her thirties, came to me because she had been feeling down and depressed for three or four months, and she had no idea what was causing it. I began by asking her if there was anything troubling her in her life. "Not really," she said. Her marriage was good. Her kids were "the best thing in her life." There were no particular problems she was having with either her parents or his.

Her job? "It's okay. I don't mind it. It's not as interesting as it used to be. . . ." But her face registered a feeling very different from "it's okay."

It turned out that she worked as the editor of a trade magazine in a rather unglamorous industry. For a number of years, the job had become routine to the point of boring, but she hadn't minded because it was close to home, it paid well, and she could do her job and still have plenty of energy left for mothering.

She hadn't minded, that is, until four months ago. That's when, at a local writers' gathering, she heard about a job opening. More money, just as close to home, working for a much more interesting industry with a boss she knew and liked. Just when she thought she was going to get the offer, the company decided to hire from within.

"But it's only a job," she said. "I tell myself, 'You're so lucky to have the life you have and a job that supports you so well. What's your problem? Buck up! Your kids are doing great, everyone is healthy, you're married to a great guy. Deal with it.' "

The truth was she was *disappointed*, and bitterly so. She was trying to rise above her feeling of disappointment and be "strong," but in reality her outside voices and her harshness to herself were crushing her.

She was, in fact, *afraid* to feel how disappointed she was because she could think of no real-world solution. There were no equivalent jobs in the area, and moving the family, or commuting a long distance to work at a similar job elsewhere, were "not options," as she saw it. The outside voices in her mind told her harshly to accept what they imagined couldn't be changed.

When she simply allowed herself to feel her deep disappointment and frustration with her work life, she came back to herself. Her energy returned and she began to enjoy her life again. And once she faced her situation, she was able to find a solution. She realized that she had been holding herself back—that her old job was not utilizing half of her abilities. She found a much more interesting job forty-five minutes away, and because of her skills was able to negotiate the right to telecommute three days a week.

So often, women are afraid to feel their unhappiness because they don't believe they have the power or the right to change what's making them unhappy. Then they put themselves down for feeling that way. But the truth is, a great many women are unhappy, usually for very good reasons. Being unhappy doesn't mean that there's something "wrong" with you or that you're a failure. It just indicates that something in your psyche or your life is in distress and needs healing attention.

In many cases, unhappiness is a signal from your inner self the way pain is from your body. It can keep you from talking yourself into what is in fact unacceptable to your being. Your mind can spin all these interpretations of why you should accept what is making you miserable or why you can't have anything better. But your inner self doesn't accept them.

American culture adulates people who project an unflaggingly positive, cheerful, "can-do" spirit. But mental health doesn't mean being happy all the time. It's about being resilient, knowing how to heal and recover from losses and difficulties, being flexible rather than brittle. Allowing your feelings, not suppressing them, helps you to do this.

In fact, ceaseless positivity cuts you off from a lot of important information. "When I was in my twenties, I was Miss Positive," said Candace, a forty-five-year-old divorced television producer. "I thought 'winners' could never have negative feelings. Because of that, I didn't learn a lot of things I needed to find out, like that I don't like *this* kind of man or *that* kind of job. If I wasn't trying so hard to be so *good* all the time, I think I would have avoided a lot of problems!"

Feelings are not facts. They're not permanent, like a chair or a table. Feelings have their validity *as feelings*, but they may or may not be accurate statements about reality. Just because a woman, for example, is angry at the way her husband did the dishes doesn't necessarily mean that he did them improperly. Just because a mother is mad at her toddler's twenty-fifth "no" of the day doesn't mean the boy is doing it to "sass" her. Just because somebody feels a strong prejudice against another group of people doesn't mean that the traits she attributes to them are really true.

Feelings change when you're willing to explore them as *feelings*. When you believe them as immutable facts, you get trapped in them. A person might say, for example, "I am scared *because* the world is a dangerous place" and therefore never stop being afraid, because the world's not going to change. Feelings are always a mix of internal and external reality. If this person fully listened to her fear as a *feeling inside her*, not as a fact about the world, she'd become much clearer about what she was afraid of, and why, and what she could do about the fear. Then her feeling wouldn't be static, but would change into something that helps her live more fully.

This brings us to the third fact about feelings, which is:

Feelings are temporal. Arguing, debating and denying your "incorrect" feelings rarely works. It usually just pushes them underground. But feelings that are accepted and validated as feelings actually change. There's an alchemy that occurs when the whole self is brought to bear to create a more harmonious internal and external reality.

The tragedy is that people generally do not know how to acknowledge and be with their feelings, allowing their full selves to work them through. Feelings that are not felt, acknowledged and accepted exactly as they are often get stuck. You can see this all around you, in people who have become afraid of dealing with how angry they are, and who then stay angry, sometimes even holding grudges for years while congratulating themselves on their self-control. Or people who avoid feeling their sadness and lose all joy in life. Or those who avoid feeling fear and live their lives as fear's captive.

As Eugene Gendlin, who originated and developed Focusing, described it:

> What is split off, not felt, remains the same. When it is felt, it changes. Most people don't know this. They think that by not permitting the feeling of their negative ways they make themselves good. On the contrary, that keeps these negatives static, the same from year to year. A few moments of *feeling it in your body* allows it to change. If there is in you something bad or sick or unsound, let it inwardly be, and breathe. That's the only way it can evolve and change into the form it needs. [Italics added.]

Sitting with Your Feelings

But wait, you may think. Letting my feelings be sounds good, but it doesn't work. Concentrating on my feelings just makes them worse. If I just gave in to feeling sad, or angry, or disappointed, and I didn't try to make myself feel better, I wouldn't be able to function.

Your objection is understandable. You want to pay attention to your feelings in ways that make them work *for* you, not against you.

So how do you do that? More than any other pathway, the ABCs of Acknowledging, Being With and Compassion apply to your feelings. In the Pathway of Feelings, these translate into using specific skills. Acknowledging and Being With become the skills of *sitting with* your feelings and *listening to* your feelings. Compassion becomes *validating* your feelings, or *giving them empathy*.

Let's begin with the skill of sitting with. There's something in human beings that makes us wired to run from difficult, frightening or uncomfortable feelings inside us. The running takes many forms. It can be in the form of intellectualizing, minimizing or spacing out. It can also be in the form of panicking, blowing up or "going to pieces." Yet what actually helps—sometimes with astonishing speed—is to stop running and to simply sit with them.

Start by going into reflective mode. You stop what's going on, breathe deeply once or twice, "take a step back" from what you're doing and notice what is going on inside you, without any judgment. Giving it a simple, preliminary name, such as "I'm feeling upset right now," will give you a place to start.

Then you let yourself feel the feeling and the sensations that go along with it as it's experienced in your body. Just take a *minute*, and I really mean a minute, sometimes a little more, sometimes a bit less, and let yourself *have* that feeling. Let it course through your body. Don't impede its flow by thinking about it or trying to change it or immediately trying to figure out the solution to your problem.

This is something people don't seem to do naturally for some reason. Which is a shame, because simply by paying attention to the pure feeling, an answer—often a very surprising one—frequently presents itself.

Jo had been a freelance graphic artist for two years. She came to me, in part, because she was having a terrible time getting any of her work done during the day. She was missing deadlines, frequently having to work all night, and was dropping the ball on her share of family matters as well. Her husband was hinting that maybe she wasn't "made for" freelance work. She felt like a failure.

Her third session, she came in feeling especially ashamed of herself, she reported, because she wasted almost the whole day before playing solitaire on the computer and surfing the Web.

She was all ready to tell me how awful she was, and all the ramifications of her terrible lack of self-discipline on every aspect of her life, when I stopped her. "Would you be willing to try something?" I said.

"Sure. Anything's better than this," she replied.

"Close your eyes, and imagine that you're in your home office at the beginning of the day, and you're getting ready to sit down at your computer. What's happening in your body right now? What sensations are you feeling?"

She was a quick learner. She closed her eyes, breathed deeply and concentrated, scanning within her body. "I'm getting a nervous, uncomfortable feeling. Fluttery, jittery. I want to get up, or space out."

"Just sit with that feeling a little longer. Just let it be there and feel it."

Just twenty seconds later, she let out a big laugh. "Ha! What I got was, *I don't like feeling alone!*

"That's so funny!" she continued, opening her eyes and looking at me. "I mean, it's so obvious, but it's so true! That's also why I don't ever, ever take thirty-minute exercise walks, even though I'm always telling myself to. I don't like the feeling of being alone!"

She marveled at this realization for a few minutes. It wasn't as if she never thought that she didn't like feeling alone before, but it was the first time she really *felt* it. It hit her with the force of a revelation. But she still was in a quandary.

"I don't think getting a regular job is the answer," she said. "The truth is, I've set up my life so I can work this way. I don't want to *not* be alone, exactly."

"Maybe you can go back inside, and see what it is that makes being alone so uncomfortable."

Again, she closed her eyes and paid attention to her inner sensations. "Yeah, uncomfortable really fits. I'm very uncomfortable being alone. What *is* that?" she wondered aloud. "It feels like, I'm afraid that I'm going to come apart when I'm alone. Not that I'm going to start crying or anything. More like, I won't be able to think, because no one's around to help me figure out what to pay attention to."

Actually, this is a pretty common problem. Many people have an easier time responding to other people's wants and needs than figuring out what to do when they're alone.

She continued to puzzle over it while sitting with it. She had a great deal of motivation for finding some solution to this problem, so she stayed with the feeling and gently asked inside if there was something she could do about it.

All of a sudden, her inner self gave her a solution: "I got the words, '*collect myself.*' That's what I'm supposed to do when I feel this way. I can really see that," she said, smiling and nodding her head. She started moving her arms in front of her as if she was gathering a bunch of bulky items. "I'll just collect myself—you know, pull myself together."

The next time I saw her, three weeks later, she told me that her productivity had *tripled*. "I hardly space out at all anymore!" she exulted. "Whenever I start to feel scattered or like I want to avoid my work, I just pay attention to that uncomfortable feeling inside of me for about a minute, and then I know what I want to do. I'm enjoying being alone for the first time. I put on music that I like. I even took a few walks!"

Jo had experienced many painful emotions in the past two years, but they were caused by avoiding a very simple, and not even very painful, uncomfortable feeling! I've seen this over and over—all of the surface emotions and outside voices are far more painful than the deeper body feelings below them. It's positively amazing what a few minutes of sitting with and through a feeling can often do.

This same principle can apply to many things that people procrastinate about. A phone call you're avoiding making, for example, starts with a simple uncomfortable feeling that's over in seconds. If the feeling's allowed to flow, it's nowhere near as unpleasant as the hours of agonizing that result from not doing it.

Naming the Elemental Feelings

At times, sitting with may not seem to be working. It takes a little more. If you've been going over and over something bothering you, but feel like you're "going in circles," this is a signal to sink deeper into yourself, to check with your body more, to see if what you think you're feeling is indeed what you feel, until you finally do connect with your inner self. Maybe, like Flora in the last chapter, you're not angry, you're jealous. Maybe you're not sad, you're relieved he's leaving. When you tell the truth, the whole truth and the *exact* truth about what you feel to yourself or to someone you trust, your inner self feels heard, and you feel better.

This is going as close to the bone as you can, down to your *elemental* feelings. When you reach the "bone truth," you know it.

This was brought home to me by Shannon, a pretty, spunky twenty-nine-year-old whose marriage of seven years ended a year earlier in divorce after she discovered that Keith, her husband, was having an affair. She was trying to sort out her feelings about Roger, her current boyfriend.

"I love Roger," she said, "but I told him if he betrays me, or ever lies to me, I'm out of here."

"Is that really how you feel?" I replied.

"No, but I wouldn't be surprised either if it happened. A part of me's become very cynical. I just don't trust anybody completely, after what Keith did to me. Roger will probably ask me to marry him before the year is over, but I told him I'm not selling my condo just in case."

"You're labeling your feeling as 'I don't trust anyone,' but that's just a label. What if you sat with that feeling, and felt what was underneath it?"

"Oh, I can't sit with my feelings. I can't contemplate them without wanting to take action right away to fix them."

"Just try to for a moment." She sighed and her shoulders relaxed. An instant later she teared up.

"I feel hurt, betrayed, unsafe. That's what it is. Not that I don't trust, but I feel so unsafe inside. I've been feeling unsafe ever since what happened with Keith."

Shannon was a "doer" who tended to barrel past her feelings. Immediately after she broke up with Keith, she had a series of short-lived relationships. But the feeling of unsafe *needed to be heard first*, so none of those men made her feel safe inside. Once she reconnected to that feeling of unsafety, she was free to feel whether she feels safe with Roger. Not feeling unsafe kept her locked in the past. Feeling unsafe gave her the possibility of a new present and future.

❧ INNERCIZE 9 ❧

Sitting with a Feeling

Take a moment when a feeling is bothering you, or has been bothering you for a long time. Take a deep breath, let go of thinking about the "problem," and draw your attention to the way the feeling feels in your body. Is there a tightness in your throat, a tension in your chest, a pain in your heart, a sinking feeling in your stomach? Name the feeling as accurately and precisely as you can. Is it a little sad, very sad, worried, frightened, furious (to name a few)? Notice when you get an inner "yes." Now sit with the feeling for at least a minute, letting yourself experience the *whole* way it is in your body, exactly as it is, and see if it has more to tell you. Let it change, disappear or run its course as it flows through you.

Friendly Advice

Obviously, you may not always feel like working out your feelings alone. Talking it out with friends, sharing feelings and problems, is for most women a major indoor sport. And besides, most of the time it helps.

But sometimes sharing a problem feels like it impedes a solution as much as it facilitates one. Some friends can be too quick with advice. You can also get caught up in the surface emotions or the external aspects of the problem and not attend to your inner self. If you find this happening, a different way of talking about the problem with a friend can make all the difference in the world.

When you share your feelings in the manner below, you'll find that your pace will be slower and you'll say fewer words. The feeling may get

INNERCIZE 10
Sitting with your Feelings with a Friend

Choose a friend who you consider to be a good listener. If you notice that you're talking about something bothering you without feeling any better, tell her that you'd like to do something a little different, that you don't want to talk so much about the problem, you want to work on it a little more deeply.

Ask her just to listen and offer silent company for a while. Then make contact with the feeling in your body and start talking from the feeling. "I know Mike's not right for me, but I can't make myself break up with him . . . I get this really empty feeling in the pit of my stomach thinking of breaking up. Just terrifically sad." See if you can only say things that ring honest and true inside you, and if you realize that something you said doesn't ring true, correct yourself: "No, not sad, exactly—*lonely*. The truth is, I'm afraid I'll be lonely without him." Go for the elemental feelings, especially for the feelings that you didn't know were there, and say them until they feel complete.

a little more intense, but most likely not extremely so. You may, for example, shed a few tears. But the difference is, the feeling will either abate or change. Thoughts are infinite. People can talk about their feelings for a very long time. But almost all feelings, when they're felt for what they are, are quite finite. They take only minutes to run their course.

Listening to All Parts of You

> *Might we not say to the confused voices which sometimes arise from the depths of our being: "Ladies, be so kind as to speak only four at a time?"*
> —Anne-Sophie Swetchine, *The Writings of Madame Swetchine,*
> c. 1869

Many times you can't just sit with a feeling and have it resolve. Sometimes this is because you have more than one feeling, and you need to sort them out. Other times, your feelings may be so intense or involved that they feel overwhelming. At these times, you need more than to sit with your feelings. You need to *listen* to them.

All feelings have their life-affirming story to tell. As you've learned, there are no bad feelings—only ways that they get "stuck." And there are no "bad" or "unacceptable" thoughts or parts of you—only parts of yourself that you have exiled from your consciousness and no longer listen to. Once you have listened to them and welcomed them back into the "family" of the self, they become sources of knowledge, creativity and strength.

Think back to Mira, the woman in so much pain who began this chapter. Her healing began when she noticed and described her feeling in her body. But that's not all she did. Intuitively, she did one more interesting thing. She *objectified* it. She said, "*it* feels heavy and tight and a lot of pressure," and half a minute later, "*it* feels afraid . . . lonely . . . unloved." In her consciousness, there was now *the feeling*, and there was *her, noticing, observing and describing it*. The feeling now had a reality *separate* from her. It was now a *part* of her—an "*it*"—that she could communicate with and care for.

This process is called disidentification. It's what you do when you *listen to* a feeling. It was developed by Ann Weiser Cornell, the creator of Inner Relationship Focusing, and it's one of the most powerful techniques I know for emotional healing, and for "having your feelings without them having you."

Let's talk theory for just a minute. As you know, in a single day, or even a single morning, you can go from being happy, to excited, to angry, to scared, to loving, to frightened and back to happy again. You can feel confident one minute and lack all confidence the next. All of these states of being can be very different from one another—and can even be quite contradictory in their thinking. For example, have you ever felt lonely, picked up the phone to call a friend and then changed your mind, thinking, "I'd rather have time to myself"?

So you're not just one single, consistent self, the way you may think you are, or the way you may think you "should" be. Instead you are a whole constellation of "selves," held together and given continuity by a central identity (what you refer to when you use the word "I"), which itself is part of the Larger Self. Technically these "selves" are called *ego states*, but let's just refer to them as "parts" of you.

There's any number of "parts" within you, and they keep changing. They're like the instruments of an orchestra, led by the "conductor" that is your central identity. You could have a "scared" part, a "shy" part, a "maternal" part, a "gutsy, risk-taking" part—each of whom may "solo," or may play with several other instruments, or may stay silent and wait, depending on the "music" being played and what the conductor desires.

These parts have their own unique perspectives and different things to "say" about situations and decisions. This, after all, is what *ambivalence* is all about. Imagine you've gotten a job offer working for an exciting but struggling new company. One part of you may say, "Yeah, go for it!" while another part says, "I don't know. It's a lot more work. And the company could go under." The first part then says, "I want the adventure!" But the other part says, "I want the security. And the better benefits!" While there may be outside-voice aspects to these two parts, neither one is actually an outside voice. They're two genuine inner-body states, or inner "selves," that happen to disagree with each other.

It isn't necessary to think about this business of parts in those areas of your life that are going well. But the broken, hurting, sad, scared or angry parts within you need listening and healing. This is where the objectifying process comes in.

When Mira observed her feelings the way she did, she was no longer *identifying* with them. That's why she didn't say *"I* feel lonely, afraid, and unloved." Now something very profound could happen. The feeling-state was free to tell Mira its "story" and tell her what it needed. She could listen to this hurting part of her the way a mother can listen to a child's tearful story about something that happened at school.

When you use disidentification, two very remarkable things occur. First, you are free to listen to your feelings and learn about them without *becoming* them. With disidentification, no matter what the feeling—anger, fear, rage or grief you thought you got over twenty-five years ago—you can let it be and be with it without worrying about getting overwhelmed or having the feeling become the totality of who you are. Because of this, you gain a freedom to explore your feelings more fully than you ever had before.

Second, *because* you are not becoming your feelings, but are separate from them, your feelings have a listener, which is what they want and need the most. Disidentification allows those feelings to be heard, released—and *healed.*

⤳ INNERCIZE 11 ⤳
Listening to Your Feelings, Using Disidentification

The next time you feel a strong, upsetting emotion, bring yourself into Reflective Mode. Then, instead of saying to yourself, for example, "I'm feeling very sad," try saying, "a part of me is feeling very sad" or "there's a lot of sadness there." Yes, it sounds odd—but notice if you (and the feeling!) both don't breathe a small sigh of relief. Then put the feeling beside you and let it tell you how it's feeling, reflecting back to it now and again to show it that you're listening. Notice what happens to the feeling. Let it continue until it feels complete.

Molly, a forty-one-year-old account manager, was having trouble at her job. Her workload had increased, and she was having to work longer hours and come in on weekends for a boss whom she couldn't seem to please.

Molly could have tried to rise above how she felt, which wouldn't have helped much, or she could have spent her whole session telling me how awful her job and her boss were. Instead Molly chose to listen to her feelings as if she were listening to a friend.

"So what's going on inside?" I asked.

She smiled, picking up on my cue, and closed her eyes.

She breathed deeply and slowly a few times, paying calm, careful attention to the sensations in her body. "There's this really sad feeling filling me," she began.

She was silent for a while. "It's . . . exhaustion. It's sheer, utter exhaustion. I've just been pushing myself, and pushing myself, and pushing myself."

She paused again. "And there's a tightness in my chest . . . I've just been so angry. It feels like I'm being hit by huge waves and I can't stop them or get out of the way.

"I'm really feeling just how angry I've been inside. This isn't what I wanted. . . ."

For the next few minutes she kept acknowledging and feeling all the exhausted, angry and helpless feelings she'd been keeping tied up inside. Yet despite the intensity of what she was feeling, she never *acted* as though she was furious or helpless. Disidentification moderated the feelings. Suddenly she relaxed and laughed. "God!" she said. "I haven't felt this human in ages!"

Listening to the Unheard Voice

Within all of us there are many parts that do not get heard. Most of these are simply the "minority voices," the parts of us that we don't wish to identify with. If you're striving with all your might to become a partner in a law firm, you're not going to be listening very much to the part of you that would much rather move to a Caribbean island and open a crafts kiosk. That's natural. But as we all know, if you totally ignore and reject a strong part of you long enough, eventually it will find some way to make you notice it.

That's what parts do. They push to be heard. They want you to include as much of your whole inner self into your life as you can. But there are other parts of you that almost never get heard, instruments in your orchestra that never play because at some time in your life, playing that instrument caused you a tremendous amount of pain. Locking away these instruments allows the orchestra to function, but at a steep price—the price of traits and feelings lost, as well as a general "disharmony" in the system. So a conflict ensues. There is a drive inside you to reclaim what has been lost and to become whole again. Yet at the same time, your outside voices will try hard to keep those unheard parts walled away, because of the pain associated with them. The way to reach and include them again is to be willing to listen to them, and listen to what they feel.

Molly's job situation was the latest in a series of jobs where she would exhaust herself seeking the approval of her cold and demanding woman supervisor, and get repeatedly hurt when she didn't get it. After nearly a year of turmoil, she finally started to look for a new job, and soon found one. Though her new boss seemed totally different, she worried that her old pattern would repeat itself.

So I guided her into her body. She started with her ambivalence, discovering that there was a part of her that would just as soon have stayed in the old job, because as bad as it was, all its problems were already known. After acknowledging this, she started to sense there were deeper issues beyond this common human tendency to stay with what is familiar. Listening closely, she realized that "this part of me knows how to handle the negative and answer it, but it doesn't know how to handle the positive. It doesn't believe that anything positive is sincere."

She sat with it longer. "I'm getting that it feels angry and mistrustful. . . ." Then she heaved a huge sigh. "Oh, I know what this is! This has to do with my mother leaving my father and me and moving to France when I was twelve." She was quiet for a moment. "That's why it's so mistrustful of what people say. She said she loved me, and then she moved five thousand miles away."

This wasn't an intellectual insight on Molly's part. Nor was she "analyzing" herself. This was a fresh, deeply felt awareness, coming directly from the part of her that she was making contact with.

I suggested that she sense what this angry and mistrustful part of her needed to tell her. At first she couldn't—a strong feeling of fear stopped her. So she listened to what "the fear" was afraid of—that she'd be overwhelmed by the feelings of that time in her life and not able to function—and it subsided. Once the fear was heard, it became clear that the "mistrustful" part of her had more to say.

"It feels betrayed, abandoned, and lost. It tried to pretend to be okay, that it didn't need my mother, but it wasn't true."

"So it feels lost and bereft. It couldn't tell your mother how much it needed her. Let it know you hear that's how it feels."

She nodded. "I'm beginning to get a visual image of it now. It looks like me, around thirteen or so." She was silent again. "She said she feels unworthy. If she was worthy then she would have been loved. She thinks that maybe if she wasn't born, her mom wouldn't be so miserable." As she said this, huge tears fell from Molly's eyes.

The session continued another ten minutes, as Molly listened and validated the anger and pain this part of her felt. Finally she said, "I really felt how hard she tried to act older, to act like she didn't need a mother because my mother was such a wreck at that time in my life. She tried to be so tough. She didn't want anyone to see how needy and little she really felt inside."

I believe there is something within us that seeks out analogous situations in our lives to tell us what we haven't yet healed. It's as if each bad work situation, and even more, the *pain* that they triggered, were notes from the walled-off part of her inner self, saying, "Remember when we were twelve and Mom left? I'm still hurting about that. Listen to me!"

This began a new relationship that Molly had with herself. She began to feel lighter. She didn't need to intellectualize her feelings as much to keep them at bay. And she was able to build a better relationship with her new boss, who turned out to be a wonderful person.

It didn't take hypnosis or any analytic interpretation on my part for Molly to reach this. Molly just spent time noticing and observing what was going on inside her, and then allowed herself to see these feelings as *parts* of her. Then she chose to be with the fear and to allow what was just below the surface to arise. By doing these two things, she created "room" in her consciousness for the feelings to reveal and explain themselves. While in this case, it led to Molly relating to a "child" part of her, it doesn't need to happen this way, and most times it doesn't. Unheard places reveal themselves and get healed in many ways. There are no literal "inner children" inside. There are just feelings and patterns that get suppressed, that are still stored within our system and need to be listened to.

Validation Is Invaluable

> *The doctor who did the D&C said, "Don't worry, hon. We'll get you past this and within a year you'll have a healthy baby and forget this ever happened." After he left, the nurse snorted in disgust. "What a crock of horse manure," she'd said, crossing her large arms. "Losing a baby is a heartbreak that you never forget." Nurse Phyllis Burkey was a woman Joyce remembered with fierce affection. "It sucks," Phyllis Burkey said, "and don't let anyone try to tell you different."*
> —Anita Diamant, *Good Harbor*

Validation. It's like water to the inner self. When life gives you lemons, the last thing you need is for some doofus to throw sugar on them and pretend it's lemonade. Maybe tomorrow you'll decide to launch the lemonade franchise equivalent of Starbucks, but let that idea first come from *your* mouth, not from the mouth of a member of the Happy Brigade. Today, while the wound is still hurting, or while the fury is still seething, such happy talk only makes you feel alienated from the rest of humanity. Today, what you want is for others to respect, or even better, echo resoundingly with the truth of your present experience.

One of the great things about "parts" is that it is far, far easier to accept and validate aspects you don't like about yourself if you don't identify with them. Then you don't even have to agree with them! For example, you can't say, "I'm so angry at my husband I could kill him!" with any conviction, without having at least two or three "voices" inside you rising up immediately to object. (At least, I hope you can't!) But if you said, "A *part* of me is so angry at my husband, it wants to kill him!" well, that's certainly something you could sit with and listen to. For another example, you could be a division vice president with 500 people working under you, and still discover a part of you that feels weak and small, one that would benefit from your support, comfort and validation.

Wholehearted validation is something people almost never get for their most difficult feelings. It seems that in our culture at least, anytime someone goes beyond "reasonable" feelings and levels of expression, everyone around them gets afraid that a little validation will cause that person to go crazy or fall apart. But feelings don't shift unless they're accepted *exactly* the way they are, neither more nor less. If they're intense, they're intense! Once they're accepted, they'll change into another form. But until then, they'll stick around.

Bonnie, a twenty-one-year-old junior in college, came to me saying she "had to" get over her relationship with her ex-boyfriend Mark, which ended eighteen months earlier. She said that everyone in her life told her she was pitying herself and had to move on.

They had been together for a year when Mark decided to break up with her. One day he told her it was "over," and then never wanted to talk about it again. Since they went to the same school, she had to see him almost every day, and no amount of pleading could get him to tell her what happened.

At first her friends sympathized, but he was part of their social circle, too, and after about four months, as if by consensus, they all decided she should get over it. She tried to take their advice, but it didn't work. In fact, her mental state grew worse, though she pretended to feel better. Her self-esteem plummeted, and she contracted mononucleosis. She was in deep distress, which was made worse by trying to push her distress away. "It's crazy for me to still be upset about him. He's already had two girlfriends since me!"

"Oh, I don't know if it's so crazy," I said. "He was your first love, wasn't he?"

She turned and looked right at me. "Yes, he was!" she cried. It took only a little validation and encouragement from me for all of her feelings to come out—the love she had for him, the misery and frustration of never getting any explanation for his change of heart, her shame for still wanting him, her fear that she would never again find anyone else she would love as much and the pain of feeling cut off from all of her friends, not being supported by them.

It took just *one* session of exposing and examining together all these different elements, and wholeheartedly accepting their presence within her, for her to begin letting go of Mark. This didn't mean that Bonnie didn't have more to talk about and resolve, or that Bonnie never again felt sad about losing Mark. But at this point, her *acute suffering* was coming from having her distress constantly shoved aside by herself and others. Caught in a social network that never fully validated just how cruel his silent treatment was to her, her pain had nowhere to go.

When you begin to listen to parts of you that haven't been heard, it would make sense that they would want quite a bit of validation from you. Imagine if *you* hadn't felt safe to speak for many years, and finally found a listening ear, but that person didn't say anything that made you know they were really with you. You'd stop speaking pretty quickly, too.

So there are a few basic validation techniques that you can use. You can let it know you hear it by silently saying, "I hear that you . . ." or "I understand that you . . ." and empathically repeating back to it exactly what it said. You can *give it a lot of empathy*, by directing empathy toward that part of you and saying, *"Of course* you would feel that way" or *"Naturally* you would feel the way you do." If you feel you can't give some part of you empathy, that's okay. Don't try to force it. Instead, direct your attention to that part of you that *can't give that empathy*, and listen to what *it's* feeling.

If a feeling feels huge, intense or overpowering—if it feels like it's going to overtake you—then accept that as part of its message, by saying, for example, "you feel *that* urgent, you want to overpower me." That will put you back in control. Very strong feelings of sadness and anger can be helped by naming their size. Is it as big as a house, a lake, an ocean? Finding its size, no matter how big that size might be, still contains it and makes it finite.

Feelings of hatred, fear or envy can damage your life if they permeate your being. But the truth is, you can have *parts* of you that feel intense rage or fear or deprivation. They too, deserve to be listened to and welcomed home, though this may be difficult to do alone.

Aside from this deep inner work, it helps simply to remember in your daily life that you have a right to feel what you feel. It may also help to acknowledge, at least to yourself, just how much during the day you have to act a whole lot nicer and more reasonable than you feel inside. If this is true for you, Heaven knows you deserve a *break*. There are times when you might just want to get in the car and yell, or write out the nastiest things you're feeling, or go with a friend to the beach and shout whatever you want to the waves! Claim as loudly as you must what you need, what you want, what you didn't get or aren't getting—and hopefully have a friend there saying, "Yeah! You go, girl!" Tomorrow you can be reasonable again, but for now you can give yourself permission to be unreasonable for a change. Be just for you.

Becoming Adept at Anger

Now let's deal with the emotion most people have the hardest time with: Anger. *Anger is the emotion of personal power*, the one that lets you feel that you can affect your world.

When my youngest daughter was two, one of the very first phrases she spoke was "Heyyyy—don't *do* that!" With the brevity of a poet—or a toddler—she managed to say *What you're doing is upsetting my feeling good in the world, and I want you to stop*. In four little words, she captured the essence of anger, the emotion that marshals your energy to set the world right.

Anger is an absolutely vital human emotion. Anger motivates you to protect yourself, and in many cases your loved ones as well. Anger pushes you to fight for what you need and tells you when your being has been violated. Anger attempts to restore the balance of your personal power when you feel powerless, to establish that you have certain core requirements of physical and emotional sustenance and human dignity that *cannot* be denied by the world or other people. If you *can't* feel angry, if you say to yourself it's always wrong or useless to feel angry, then you can't feel the basic sense of personal integrity, power and "space" that every single creature on earth has as their natural birthright.

At the same time, anger can at times be nothing more than a defensive, reflexive reaction to a threat that may or may not be real. Anger frequently gets used by those with more power to intimidate and control those who have less. Anger upsets applecarts and threatens the status quo, which often can be a very good thing, but it's also the emotion most likely to create discord between people.

I know of no culture that teaches people to handle anger well. Traditionally, societies have tried to forbid even the feeling of anger against authorities and those in power, from the king on down to the "master" of the house. They also try to deny or paper over conflict between members of the group, while allowing or even encouraging open aggression against the weak and powerless, targeted scapegoats within the society, and outside enemies.

Strong feelings of anger cannot simply be forcefully squelched. They have to be dealt with somehow, even if that means displacing them onto the wrong person. The worst-case scenario, which unfortunately happens all too often, goes something like this: The boss humiliates the husband, the husband screams at his wife, the wife takes it out on the oldest kid, and the oldest kid hits his younger brother. In each case the horrible sense of utter powerlessness is alleviated, temporarily, by exerting power over someone less powerful.

Everyone desperately wants to feel that they can exert influence over their environment, especially over the people who affect them the most. If you can't influence those people—whether it's your partner or, if you're a child, your parents—you're going to feel angry. If this continues over time, you're going to feel powerless. Then, if you're ignored or punished for being angry, you're going to feel even more powerless—and angrier.

Anger is a fluid and empowering emotion. But if a person's sense of personal power is thwarted long enough, her feelings may "solidify" into chronic anger or into permanent states of resentment or bitterness. When anger, resentment and bitterness become states of being, they become defenses against feeling the sadness, powerlessness, fear and longing below them.

Practically all women have heard that it's not nice or "womanly" to be angry, and most of us grew up in homes where our anger was frequently either dismissed or harshly treated. What's more, women are affected by all the ways that we were given less power than men for so many centuries.

And let's face it—it simply can be scary to feel angry and express it to anyone who is big and powerful enough to respond by hurting you back. In every confrontation with another adult, there's always that risk. But never risking conflict is an even greater risk. It means living your life in the shadows, always being the moon reflecting other people's sun, never shining your own light.

Because anger can easily be triggered "thoughtlessly"—that is, as a quick, reflexive fight-or-flight response from the oldest portions of our brain—it's the emotion you want, more than any other, to bring *awareness* to. If you have a tendency toward reflexive outbursts of anger, take some time, when you're not angry, to get to know this part of yourself. Get in the reflective mode, conjure up a recent incident, and replay it, this time observing and noticing each thing you feel. *Slow down*, and even *stop* the action at certain points, and sense everything happening within you, especially the small and subtle feelings and thoughts that get hidden or overridden by the outburst. You might want to try befriending the angry part of yourself and listening to its story—though, if it goes into tirades of blame and self-justification, be careful to listen to those as *feelings*, without accepting its reasoning as *facts*. I'm not saying you're wrong to feel the way you do. You may be perfectly justified in your anger. But if you get caught up in being angry rather than being the anger's listener, you won't get relief from the anger, nor will you get any clearer.

Most angry feelings are fleeting. But anger, when it's not heard, can build, especially in close relationships. The following is a three-step approach to dealing with anger that's getting "stuck."

1. Put the anger next to you and give it permission to express itself. If you're feeling a great deal of anger, first let yourself hear it. This is hard to do without expressing it out loud in some way, so you may need to share it with a friend, or say it out loud into a tape recorder, or write it down in a journal. But see if you can get the feel of the anger in your body and lay out all the aspects of your anger.

2. Find out what your anger needs and wants. Behind anger is a desire for something—something that you're not getting, something you may not think you *can* get. But anger that doesn't express the want behind it becomes powerless. It doesn't lead to anything.

3. *Bridge* with your anger. Remember that your goal is not just to *express* your anger, but to have your anger and your wants be *heard*. So you want to bridge between how you feel inside and what you say to the other person that will increase the probability of what you want happening.

Expressing anger, after all, is one of the very first communication skills you had. When you weren't happy as a baby, you cried or howled. You didn't worry about whether anyone understood you! This kind of unmoderated "protest behavior" works for babies. As adults, we don't usually cry or howl when we're angry, but we have our own forms of unmoderated protest behavior—we complain, yell, scream or nag. Unmoderated protest behavior is healthier than giving up and becoming resigned, and it can feel like a relief to do. But it doesn't usually get you what you really want, because the people it's directed at get distant, angry and defensive—which only confirms your belief that "it's useless to get angry."

Part of bridging is looking at whether what's making you angry was actually done *against* you. Most of the time, people do upsetting and annoying things for reasons that have absolutely nothing to do with us. Usually, they're not tuned in to the impact they make. For example, your boyfriend may do incredibly insensitive things that justifiably make you angry, but out of obliviousness, not lack of love, which changes how you may want to respond to it.

The basic skill for conflict is to express your anger, then express what you want and need without attacking the other person's character or motivations. And then *stop!* Let the other person answer! See if you can listen and respond to—not attack—what the other person says, and keep moving toward what you want.

Conflict is a messy process. You don't have to do it perfectly. On the other hand, barbed verbal assaults—words chosen for no other purpose but to wound—need to be kept out of all conflicts, the same way physical assaults would be. There's a feeling behind those assaults that you need to hear within yourself, not act upon. Remember, the aim is to be heard and understood, and perhaps to motivate the other person to make a few changes. It's not to defeat the other person. Such a victory, even if you could achieve it, would always be self-defeat.

Listening to Others' Feelings

True listening is love in action.
—M. Scott Peck

So much of the suffering in the world is caused by the harshness with which we treat feelings, both our own and others'. When you realize that you don't need to oppose your own feelings, but can listen to and accept them, it's a short step to realize that it's just as counterproductive, if not more so, to oppose or try to *change* other people's feelings. If you actually want to have an *impact* on other people's feelings and behavior, there is absolutely nothing more powerful, paradoxically, than fully listening to and accepting how they feel, and letting them know it. Then they are much more likely to hear and value what you have to say.

Audrey, a forty-eight-year-old teacher and mother of three, was at her wit's end because her mother, who was suffering from complications from a previous surgery, was refusing to go back to the hospital. She told Audrey that she just wanted "to stay home to die." Even after several long, exhausting arguments between the two of them, the older woman showed no signs of changing her mind.

Audrey first had to give her own feelings some attention: her grief that her mother was so sick, her fear that she would insist on staying home and thus seal her death, her anxiety that her mother might become incapable of taking care of herself for a protracted period of time, her sadness to see her ill and in pain.

Once she took care of her own feelings, we focused on her mother's. I suggested that, instead of arguing with her mother about going back to the hospital, she give a lot of empathy to how her mother felt—by saying things like, "I can really understand how you feel, you are so sick and tired of being in that hospital, you don't want to be there another day. Hospitals are rotten places to have to be in." I then suggested that instead of getting angry at her, she express the caring behind her anger that she expressed in my office—telling her, "Mom, I love you, and I'm not ready to lose you yet, not without a fight."

Audrey tried my suggestion, and by the next week her mother had gone back to the hospital. What's more, the two women had grown closer.

Everyone wants to be heard. And almost no one takes the time or attention to listen to other people in a way that makes them *feel* fully heard. Usually, like Audrey and her mother, when others oppose us, we oppose them back immediately. For some reason, it seems counterintuitive simply to listen to others—we think that by listening with an open mind and heart, without argument, they will get stronger and "win," and we will lose. But the opposite is actually true. When people feel that what they think and feel is truly being taken to heart and accepted as real and valid for them, even when they're being "difficult," they almost always relax and feel relieved, and will be more open at least to hearing your point of view.

When you accept and begin to honor your own feelings, you can also teach others to accept and honor theirs. Tracy, the woman who grew up being labeled "sensitive" by her family, found herself teaching an unlikely student—her father.

My father always held back his feelings. "You can't let your guard down for a minute," he'd always say. Recently he told me that he could never let himself cry when he takes me to the airport at the end of my visits, because it would just make me feel bad for leaving, and there would be no point to it. I told him the point is, you cry for two minutes and then it's over, and you feel better.

Last week, we were together in his toolshed and he came across his father's old hammer. "I get real emotional holding my father's hammer," he said. And I said, "Well, you still miss him." And he started crying—for a minute. Then he caught himself. He was half-crying, half-laughing, saying, "I can't believe I'm crying over a hammer." Then he stopped, and he looked *terrific* to me, and I said, "Hey! Guess what! You're okay, we're all still here, it's still Saturday and we can still go to the hardware store." He just shook his head and laughed.

CHAPTER SEVEN

The Lost Art of Wanting

"Don't want too much," the voices warned.

No. Want. Want life.
Want this fragile oasis of the galaxy to flourish.
Want fertility, want seasons, want this spectacular array of
creatures,
this brilliant balance of need.

Want it. Want it all.
Desire. Welcome her raging power.
May her strength course through us.
Desire, she is life. Desire life.
Allow ourselves to desire life, to want this sweetness
so passionately, that we live for it.

—Ellen Bass, "Live For It"

"What do I want for myself?" exclaimed Michelle. "*Please* don't ask me that! Ask me something a little smaller, like what do I want for dinner!"

You first met Michelle back in Chapter Four. She was the fifty-four-year-old, recently divorced children's librarian who remembered her passion for dance and weaving.

We laughed together, and she continued. "It's almost . . . repellent to me, to think about wanting for myself. Immediately I think, 'Good mothers and good wives don't ask that question.'"

"Whose voice is that?" I asked her.

She paused. "I'd have to say it's my mother's. But that's a funny thing, because I always remember my mother saying I can do whatever I want. But I watched her, and I could see she always put herself last."

She went back to the question of her wanting. "Asking what I want for myself makes me feel insecure. Like if I ask this question, my whole life is going to get unglued and I'll fly off into the ozone.

"I let myself take little forays," she explained. "I've taken classes here and there. But I've never taken them very seriously, like they're important or should have any effect on my 'real life.' "

That's when she brought up weaving again.

"For example, I took this weaving class a number of years ago. It was so delightful. But the whole time I had this feeling of unreality, as if this wasn't really me. Like, I'm not a weaver!

"Oh, this is so strange," she suddenly said. "Just today I was thinking that maybe I'll take my loom out of storage and move it near the window. But then I got embarrassed, like what would my neighbors think if they saw it!

"But maybe I can move it somewhere more private, like my breakfast nook."

Many women, like Michelle, have trouble wanting for themselves. This isn't surprising, since we're in fact the first generation of women who have been given any societal permission to want for ourselves, much less to go after what we want. Few of us grew up with any models for doing this. Like Michelle, wanting for ourselves, for many of us, triggers outside voices telling us that we're being "selfish," "unspiritual," not the way a woman should be.

This is a terrible shame. For the truth is, *wanting is good.*

Wanting, in fact, may be the one absolutely essential ingredient to following your inner voice and becoming who you truly are. Only wanting has the energy, the power, the force to bring about change.

Wanting is the psychological vehicle, the motor, the muscle, that moves you from where you are to where you are going. Before you could walk, you had to want to walk, perhaps to get a toy at the other end of the room. Your wanting literally propelled you upward and forward. Wanting more independence from your parents made you *want* to learn to drive. Without wanting, there simply wouldn't be any reason to grow past your present limitations. Wanting is the impetus of the Universe acting within you, expanding Creation.

Your true wants are at the very core of you, expressing your individuality, because they are as unique and individual as your fingerprint. And it's what you do about your true wants—the straight or convoluted path you take to get them or avoid them, embrace them or deny them, pursue or sneak around or compromise them—that in fact becomes the story of your life. Indeed, it determines in the end whether your life story was happy or sad.

One thing is for sure: No matter what anyone has ever told you, trying to deny or transcend your wants doesn't get rid of them for even a moment. But it does make life a lot less fun!

The philosopher and Zen monk Allan Watts once said, "The most revolutionary question anyone can ask themselves is, 'What do I want?'" But allowing yourself to spend time with the question, "What do I really want, for me?" is very difficult. Even after you get past the concern that it's "selfish," the moment you ask that question and answer it, almost inevitably you will start to wonder, "Can I get that? Do I deserve it? Will other people approve of me wanting that?" In most people, if a want feels impossible to get or unacceptable for some reason, it gets buried, labeled "foolish," "childish," a "pipe dream." Only safe and easy wants are allowed through.

There's nothing wrong with these safer wants. Buying a dress, for example, because it looks great on you and makes you feel good, is also an expression of your inner self. But it expresses only a small measure of your true wanting. If your deeper and more vital wants are always denied, no amount of shopping will satisfy. What truly increases your life energy is asking yourself, "What would fulfill me? What would excite me? What gives me pleasure and joy?" and then listening to the answers. This opens another pathway to your inner voice.

Walls around Wanting

Children start out filled with the energy of pure wanting. I want a candy bar. I want a doll. I want to grow up to be an actress, a ballerina, a doctor and an astronaut. I want. I want. I want.

But as with feelings, children soon learn that there are good wants and bad wants, wants that are acceptable and "reasonable" and wants that are unacceptable, "unrealistic" or "impossible," wants that parents approve of and wants that make them mad. And they may learn that they make their parents really mad if they want "too much."

On their part, parents react to their children's wanting based on what they themselves have learned about wanting in their own lives. As adults, they've been exposed to the harsh realities of life. Most have known the pain of shattered dreams, and most, probably, have given up on many of their own wants, in part to raise their children. It's difficult, then, for most parents to openheartedly accept and support all of their children's wants and dreams. The more that parents have given up hope that their lives can reflect what they truly want, the more they may feel

⅋ INNERCIZE 12 🍃
What Limits Were Placed on Your Wanting?

Take a moment now to think about when you were a child. You may find yourself drawn to a specific age, maybe eight, or four, or thirteen. Whatever age you choose is fine. Imagine the house you lived in at the time. How did you feel then?

Now think about the people who took care of you or were most important to you—your parents, maybe your grandparents, perhaps a very special teacher. What wants did you have that you were told, or simply sensed, were not okay to ask for from them?

These could be material objects, but it could have been other things as well—more hugs and affection, for example, or help with schoolwork or support for your unique talents.

Take a little time to sense this. How did you feel? Maybe you re-member a specific incident. Were certain things "acceptable" but other things that mattered even more to you not?

What did you do with those feelings of wanting?

Give yourself an opportunity to write down what you've found.

anger and resentment at these little beings who seem to want and expect so much out of life without appreciating "how tough life really is."

When your wants as a child bumped up against something your parents couldn't give, either material or emotional, you may have gotten shamed, put down, made to feel that what you wanted is bad. In this way, the limitations of your parents become the limits of your own wanting.

When I have offered the preceding innercize to groups of women in workshops and asked them to share what they wrote, it is always a very moving experience. So many stories are shared of wanting more closeness and affection with a father or a mother, wanting a talent to be seen and appreciated, or wanting parents to get along and be happy together. The tragedy is that these wants were not heard and mirrored when they were children. When wanting is not heard and mirrored, the process of feeling and expressing your wants becomes inhibited. Your wants become part of the unexpressed background of your childhood, the painful lack that nobody ever talks about.

Other stories participants have shared usually involve a dream deferred, not out of lack of money, but out of a lack of caring or openness of heart. "I wanted a piano, but my father considered wanting a weakness," said Dale, a fifty-year-old high school teacher sadly. "If I wanted something very badly, I almost had to act as if it didn't matter to me anymore in order for me to get it. It took five years before he got one for me, and then it was obviously as old and cheap a piano as he could find. And it wasn't because we couldn't afford it. It was because he couldn't give me something that big that I wanted."

What the heart wants most as a child, just as it does as an adult, is to be seen and heard, to feel connected, and to express itself. All true wanting traces back to two fundamental needs—to be who you really are, and to be seen and heard and valued for who you are, for your own unique self. Even the small, "childish" wants of little children should be treated with care, seriousness and respect, though of course not always granted, because those little wants are the training ground for experiencing more important wants later on and believing in the possibility of getting them.

It's very helpful to become aware of the wants that were not met in your childhood. If acknowledged and accepted with compassion, they can become powerful impetuses to the expression of your deepest being. But if not acknowledged, wants can become the stoppers that tell you that you can never get what you really want in life. Or they can lead you to try to fill that empty space with some substitute that doesn't work. You could end up feeling like the "hungry ghosts" of Buddhist lore—creatures with enormous bellies and tiny, pin-like mouths, wandering the earth and never being able to feel full and satisfied.

Evoking the Power of Wanting

Penny, a thirty-four-year-old systems analyst, had worked very hard for several years to work through a traumatic childhood and young adulthood. Now she was basking in the pleasure of reclaiming herself.

"I feel reconnected to the person I used to be—to my other self—before it went underground. It's like getting back together with someone I used to be very fond of. I'm back in touch with the person who did have wants, did have passion, who had more personality than could be contained," she said, smiling.

"That's so wonderful!" I said. "Tell me more about that person you were."

"Everything interested me," she said. "I talked a lot. I soaked things up like a sponge. I was always curious, always making connections. I always had something to say. I was even kind of a know-it-all. But then I learned it was better to shut up."

"Yeah. But what did you want?"

"EVERYTHING! I wanted everything. I wanted to work at the UN, work as an interpreter, solve all world problems, help make world peace. Actually, it's funny that I wanted to work as an interpreter, because in truth I had absolutely no facility for language. But I did marry someone who does. . . . I wanted to design clothes. . . ."

"Let yourself feel now all that wanting energy that you had then. Just try it on."

She pulled herself up in her chair and began gesturing with her arms regally. But then she stopped and shook her head. "I don't know. It seems kind of . . . grandiose, you know? Just to want like that. It's hard to put that . . . crown back on. You know what I mean?"

"Oh, go ahead," I urged. "What if you did put the crown back on right now? What would you want?"

"If I could do anything?"

"Absolutely."

"Then I would tell my story to everyone I meet, not because they should want to know about me per se, but because it shouldn't be a secret. It's important to know you can live through things and get better and be strong."

"Good, what else . . ."

"Let's see. There's something about school and learning. I wish I could do it over. I didn't do my best at that. I just took what I had to and worked for grades. Now, I'd take whatever interests me, even if it's not practical. In fact, the more impractical, the better.

"I'd get a dog. I would. It's not very practical, but I would.

"I would pretend it was my birthday every week and have a party every week, just so I could invite different people over.

"I'd express my opinions. I know a lot about many subjects, and I have an interesting perspective on things.

"I would stop being so sensible all the time. I wouldn't give a damn about what the world thought about me. I wouldn't stick to things just because I signed up for them. I'd sign up for something today, then do something different tomorrow just because I felt like it. I'd be like a butterfly going from flower to flower.

"That's so different from what I learned growing up," she said to me, her eyes strikingly clear and alive, "which was that there's only one door, and you have to go through it, and then you have to make the best of it. I want to make room to change my mind, to explore and to play.

"I see now that the more I struggle to know what to do with the rest of my life, the further it eludes me. I want to play without knowing. Life's not about finding the answer behind one door! It's about . . . *how many doors can I open?*" With this, she threw her arms open wide, smiling from ear to ear.

What if the truth was *not* that women want too much, but that most women allow themselves to want too little? What if, instead of being hushed and taught to be careful about our wanting, we learned from a young age to take our wants seriously and go after them unabashedly? I invite you now to spend fifteen minutes wanting with the uninhibited exuberance of a child.

If you've done the exercise, you now have in front of you a list of your wants—ten, fifteen, twenty-five, maybe fifty or more! In my workshops, I often challenge women to write down a hundred wishes. After first looking at me like I'm crazy, most women become quite engrossed. You could slice the concentration in the room with a knife. It's a chal-

⪫ INNERCIZE 13 ⪪
Claiming Your Wants

Take a pen and a piece of paper (or turn to a page in your journal) and for the next fifteen minutes write down as many wants and wishes as you possibly can. They can be for material things, such as a car or a house by the ocean. They can be for something you'd like to do or accomplish, such as "I want to sing at Carnegie Hall" or "I want to lose thirty pounds." They can even be for things outside your control, such as "I wish for world peace" or "I want to see a cure for AIDS in my lifetime." It may help you to think about the different areas of your life, such as relationships, family, friendships, career, learning and achievement, your physical health, and spiritual development.

Whatever your wishes are, allow your imagination to run free. Don't judge whether they're practical or feasible or even physically possible.

Notice what happens to you as you do this exercise. Do you get excited? Or afraid? Does a part of you say, "Yeah, but"? Notice what outside voices arise within you. Perhaps a voice inside tells you this exercise is a "bad" thing to do. Do certain wishes make you feel guilty? You might even feel sad writing a few of your wishes. See if you can let yourself be with all of these things—especially the excitement.

lenge to come up with a hundred wishes, to push beyond what you always think about and yearn for. People usually first write down their material desires along with their most unfulfilled heartfelt desire. After that, people often begin to express subtler and more altruistic desires; they express prayers and wishes for others and the world at large. So, contrary to what you might expect, allowing yourself the fullness of your wants—admitting that you really *would* love to have a chauffeured limousine and a forty-room mansion in Beverly Hills or the south of France—doesn't turn you into a selfish monster. Instead it leads to a greater sense of oneness and generosity toward others. Because it's all part of the same energy, the same life force.

When I asked Michelle to name just ten things she wanted, she came up with this list:

"I want to be a weaver, be physically fit, be loved and valued, and have friends.

"I want to develop new interests and meet new people and become a photographer.

"I want to move to some place warm in a couple of years and have good relationships with my kid and grandkids. And develop a craft I could sell. I want to have status. I want to have *worth!*" she said. She made her hands into fists and shook them over her head.

When she lowered her arms, she looked a little dazed. "Wow," she said, "Where did all of that come from? I had no idea I wanted so much."

"You're a closet wanter," I told her.

"Yeah, I guess I am."

Once mobilized, her wanting took on a momentum of its own. "You know what?" she said as she came into the next week's session. "I thought of three more things I really, really want.

"I want to buy a bike and join a bike club.

"I want really *good* hand lotion, not that cheap stuff." She rubbed the imaginary emollient all over her hands.

She paused, her eyes glinting.

"And I *really, really* want a cheeseburger."

Obstacles to Wanting

If it was just a matter of waking up one morning and saying, "Of course! From now on I'm going to accept all of my wonderful wanting!" everyone would be doing it already.

Your wanting, like the raw wanting of a preschooler, is big and expansive. It can make you feel "bigger" than you're accustomed to feeling about yourself. At the same time, it can feel scary, vulnerable, even foolish. So naturally, outside voices flood in. Indeed, the bigger and more important the want, the louder the outside voices! You may have noticed this when you did the last innercize. If you started hearing in your mind, "You'll never get that," or "That will never happen," you can bet that you were getting very close to something very important to you. If you heard or felt, "How *dare* you want so much—who do you think you are?" then you *know* you've touched something close to your soul.

Why do outside voices get so strong when you begin to claim what you truly want? Because they desperately don't want to see you get hurt. If you already had what you wanted, or thought that you could obtain it without risking something you already have, you wouldn't have these self-attacking thoughts.

One thing that helps with these outside voices is to acknowledge them and acknowledge what they're trying to do. Try saying to them, "Hi. I know you just don't want me to get hurt and disappointed again. I know that you don't want anything bad to happen to me. I appreciate you worrying about me and trying to protect me." This will help your outside voices feel understood, and calm them down.

Another outside voice that many women hear is the one that says, "If you don't want it, you can't be disappointed."

Nobody loves feeling disappointed. Disappointment is a painful feeling. Of course, the more you open yourself to fully wanting something, the more painfully you'll feel the disappointment if you don't get it.

But the *fear* of disappointment comes from feeling that your "unhappy" feelings are unacceptable, that they won't get comforted and supported. Say you didn't grow up with someone in your life who would help you take a risk, someone you could lean on, show your disappointment to, and learn how to deal with it from. You may have learned to fear disappointment itself as an overwhelming feeling that leads to further pain, rejection and isolation. You may then have chosen to live a "contented" life, one that's good but where you don't take many risks.

Or, if you've had a number of disappointments in your life, you might start to build your life around *being* disappointed, in effect *becoming* the feeling of disappointment on a permanent basis by making the decision that you'll *always* be disappointed. In this way you protect yourself from both wanting and feeling.

Disappointment is in fact a kind of grief—a reaction to the loss of something you desired. If you honor and gently hold the disappointment inside you, and at the same time keep yourself open to the wanting behind the disappointment, you'll be able to weather your disappointments and keep going.

Another way to avoid the feeling of wanting is to concentrate only on what you *don't* want. "I don't want my boring job." "I don't want to commute." "I don't want to clean up after everybody all the time."

"Don't-wants" tend to be very loud. And they certainly are a form of wanting. But by themselves, they rarely *move* you.

That's because they only lead away from something, not toward something. Imagine a toddler learning to walk only in order to move away from unpleasant things—like a hot fireplace for example—but having nothing in her environment that she wanted to walk toward. How depressing! No wonder don't-wants don't fill us up.

The next time you think about a don't-want, let yourself pay attention to it. Take it seriously. For example, *why* don't you want your job? *How much* don't you want it? But don't stop there. Let the don't-want point you to what you want instead, and claim your want. "I don't want to stay in this boring job" may point to "I want an interesting job, in a new company, that pays me better."

Chances are, this feels a lot harder to say than "I don't want my job anymore." Don't-wants are familiar and safe and comfortable. You're already living with them. Wanting is a lot more challenging. It takes you out of what you're familiar with, into new territory.

The Foreclosure of Wanting

You may also believe it's wrong to want. I call the beliefs that tell us that wanting is wrong "foreclosures," because they foreclose on your wants before you've even felt them. I've found that foreclosure beliefs fall into one of three categories:

"What I want is impossible."

"Wanting is irresponsible."

"Wanting is unspiritual."

The first foreclosure, "What I want is impossible," brings to my mind Beverly, a woman who signed up for one of my workshops. She did the innercize on Claiming Your Wants, seemed to enjoy it, and even shared some of what she wrote with a small circle of other women in the workshop. But less than thirty minutes later she told me she "had" to leave.

"Why?" I asked her.

"Well, it was fun to write those things down, but I know that most of what I wrote is impossible. I can't afford it, and I never will." I could almost hear heavy steel doors in her mind drop to the floor with an enormous *clank!*

Any thorough list of wants probably includes a few impossible, or at least highly improbable, desires. As you learned in the last chapter, your inner self wants more than anything else to be listened to and validated. It doesn't require you to immediately drop everything and follow it. On a deeper level, when you allow yourself to want, you often unleash the disconcerting feelings that wanting brings. These can include regret and remorse or a painful sense of the distance between what you have and what you want. If Beverly had stayed, she could have dealt with "I can't afford it, and I never will" as *feelings inside of her*, not as a *fact*. If she had listened to those feelings, they could have led her to something more, something new.

At the same time, it's important to separate the good feeling of wanting from the painful feelings, and to separate the wanting from its actual manifestation. Nothing stomps on the tender shoot of wanting faster than immediately thinking about how or whether it can happen.

Just like feelings, treating wants as immutable facts prevents you from working with them. Let's say you've always had this desire to be an actress. But you didn't go in that direction in your life, and now at fifty, it seems highly unlikely to you that it will still happen. If that desire still lives strongly within you, that means there is something your inner self wants to express. Maybe it's your love of acting, or your love of movies, or your desire to be famous or glamorous or live life in a colorful and dramatic way. Whatever it is, the good feeling of the wanting can guide you toward fulfilling the most important aspects of your desire.

"I don't have enough money" is probably the most common reason people give for placing a lid on their wanting. With so many people deeply in debt, and so many feeling trapped in the wrong job or working way too many hours to keep their families provided for, I would never want to dismiss or make light of this.

At the same time, one of the worst things about money worries is the way they seem to tell you that you shouldn't want. They can feel like a 200-foot neon sign flashing GET REAL. WHO DO YOU THINK YOU ARE? This is very sad, because especially in the midst of daily struggles, it's important to remember the goodness of your dreams and the things you truly want. In fact, deeply listening to your wanting, and bringing wanting back into your life, is not truly dependent on money.

The truth is, nobody has a crystal ball. Within certain broad limits of physical reality, you simply don't know what's possible for you. No matter what your life or financial situation, when you dare to want, and when you have the courage to want without insisting on knowing how it will come to be, you allow the Universe to open doors for you.

The second foreclosure, "wanting is irresponsible," is an interesting one because it often affects strong and competent women who'd actually be very good at getting what they want, if they'd just allow themselves to feel it.

They don't, though, because they believe that such an open exploration of wanting is nothing more than irresponsible "dreaming" that encourages people to ignore real-life responsibilities and actions in favor of impossible, "pie-in-the-sky" visions.

If this describes you, I agree with you on this: Wants and wishes alone, without taking action in the world, and if used as an excuse for not taking care of absolute responsibilities such as the care and nurturing of children, do not lead to a fulfilled life.

But I invite you to consider the possibility that *not allowing* yourself the opportunity to want and wish for what's "impractical" is draining some of the color, warmth and fun from your life. It may also be keeping you from having more than you think is possible. Because, of all women, your very competence and practicality make you among the most likely to make your wants and wishes come true—once you allow yourself to feel them.

For example, I have a friend, a forty-three-year-old lobbyist on Capitol Hill, who is a super-pragmatist. She's not the kind of person who goes to personal growth workshops. But recently she shared with me something that happened to her. Though she had risen to the top of her game, she felt unhappy. One night, riding home on the train from New York to Washington, she had an epiphany. "I thought about how much I loved to dance as a child and how good I used to be at it, and how I had stopped. And I thought about my father, whom I love, who had done so much to make me believe in myself and become successful in my career, but who discouraged my dancing as soon as it became clear that it wouldn't 'lead to anything.' I realized I'd given up too much."

Now she dances again, just for the love of it, and it has restored her energy and brought pleasure back into her life.

I thought of the third and final foreclosure, "wanting is unspiritual," while conducting a workshop with a group of very wonderful, spiritually oriented women. Many of the women shared beautiful wishes for children and the planet. But they had trouble wishing much for themselves. In the discussion that followed, one woman asked, "Shouldn't we simplify life? I wonder if thinking about all the things I don't have, when I have so much, is the right focus, or if it just leads to feeling dissatisfied and discontented for no real purpose."

"It's true," I told her. "We have so much material wealth, and most of the people in the world have so little. But everything you want tells you something valuable about yourself. You can explore your desires without thinking that you should fulfill every one.

"Let's say you secretly want a Mustang convertible. Maybe that just says you want more fun and carefreeness in your life. The idea is to accept all that you are, and not label parts of yourself 'good' or 'bad.'

"Wanting isn't what causes problems," I continued, "but our relationship to it. The idea is to listen to your wants the way you listen to your feelings. Then you can move toward the wants that mean the most to you, and that are in accordance with your values.

"I also think that there's nothing wrong with a little dissatisfaction," I added. "In fact, it's good to be dissatisfied now and then. Gloria Steinem once said that gratitude is nice, but ingratitude is better. She meant that when you have high hopes and expectations, you notice what can be improved upon and have the drive to make it happen. Just don't sit on your dissatisfaction. Let it erupt in you. Figure out what you *want* and let the dissatisfaction push you toward making it happen."

The Ten-Degree Change

Maybe you do know perfectly well what you want. Maybe the problem, and the reason you've been avoiding wanting, is that the gap between what you want and what you have feels wider than the Grand Canyon.

Maybe you feel like you have nothing, or almost nothing, of what you want. Your life is a total disaster. You have neither a satisfying significant relationship, a great job, good friends, the right place to live, or a svelte body. Your inner self seems to be shouting, "Help! Everything's a mess! Do something and do it quick!!!" You have no idea where to start, and you feel completely overwhelmed. You want to forget about it all and reach for the chocolates.

The good news is that you do not have to solve all of your problems to begin to feel a lot better. You will realign with your inside simply by beginning to make what I call ten-degree changes. These actions can be as big as beginning a job campaign or calling a therapist, or as small as taking a walk, a day off, a bath, or writing in your journal. But the process of listening has taken place.

A number of years ago a client in her late twenties named Celia came to a session announcing that she had made a "terrible mistake" marrying Drew, her husband of three years. He was a "stick-in-the-mud," he wasn't sensual, he was boring her to death and if she stayed with him, it would ruin her life. "The only reason I married him was that I was miserable, and I needed someone to love me," she said. "Now that I have myself back, I have to leave him."

Before this session she had only spoken of him lovingly. She called him her "best friend." What changed was that she'd woken up some long submerged, and totally valid, wants. The trouble was that she saw only three options: leaving him, overhauling him, or settling for less than her truth.

But those weren't her only options. After determining that he wasn't completely closed to more sociability, we talked about some ten-degree changes. She could tell him she wanted more dates. They could go to plays, which she really enjoyed but which he felt were extravagant. As for being more sensual, she wanted him to take a course with her on massage for couples.

"But I asked him already and he said no."

"You did?" I asked.

Actually she had mentioned it to him once, knowing he wouldn't be enthusiastic, and he wasn't.

Unfortunately, this is something many women do to their wanting, not just with their husbands but in all aspects of their lives. They ask or try for what they want once or twice or maybe three times, and when they don't get it, they give up. They take the fact that they didn't get it to mean that it wasn't possible or it wasn't "right," it wasn't "meant to be."

Those of you reading this book who've spent more than, oh, a day or two with small children, tell me: Do small children ever ask for anything they *really* want just once? Do they give up after a single "no"? No way.

It goes back to women's sensitivity to others and their desire to maintain connection at almost any cost. Often, women won't even ask at all. They'll "intuit" whether a request might cause somebody discomfort, hold themselves back from asking, and then secretly be angry at the person they haven't asked for not being willing to give it to them!

In the end, although I'm sure he didn't become as sociable or sensual as she would have liked, Drew did respond and change to accommodate a more insistent and outgoing Celia. Their relationship became stronger.

Honoring and aligning with your wanting means finding the ten degree changes, finding what is possible right now. If that requires something from others, then that means asking for it, many times if necessary and in different ways, and not falling into the outside voice that says that a "no" means that you have done something wrong or that what you want is wrong.

No matter where you are in your life or how far you need to go, your

🥣 INNERCIZE 14 🥣
The Ten-degree Change

Take an area of your life where getting what you want seems "impossible." Now brainstorm ways that you can get a little bit of what you want. Just ten degrees, or even one degree, of it. If you're in a house with a fifties-style kitchen that you can't stand and can't afford to remodel, go to a store and pick out the tile that you'll one day retile it with, buy one tile, and put it next to the wall. Any little thing you can do to move toward the direction of your want will feel good. Repeat this innercize often.

daily happiness will be determined by whether you are acting toward the fulfillment of your inner self on that particular day, rather than by the product of what you've accomplished. Even if you don't feel anywhere near your dreams, you can feel as much if not more psychologically healthy than someone who already has what you desire. Your *direction*—toward or away from your inner self—matters more than your *location*.

When Wanting Feels Bad

There are times when wanting does not feel at all energizing or positive. Rather, it feels empty or even painful. You feel "hijacked" by your wanting and helpless before it. I call these sinkholes.

In sinkholes, all of your life energy gets sucked up by the feeling of wanting. In one form of it, you're obsessed with buying and possessing things, yet none of them fill you up. In the other, you're obsessed with one thing that you can't get, to the point where the rest of your life feels barren and colorless in comparison. So you "sink" into a feeling of pain and deprivation that feels almost unbearable.

What's happened in a sinkhole, as with other forms of suffering, is that your "I," your Larger Self, has disappeared. The want and need has seemingly become bigger than your self.

What makes sinkholes so painful is that they recapitulate some of the earliest and worst feelings you ever had. There really was a time in your life when you were utterly dependent on some bigger person to fill you up and take your pain away. Hopefully, you learned that you did have some control over that pain—that if you cried, someone would come soon to take care of you. As you grew, you learned more and more mature ways to take care of your wants, so that by the time you grew up you had a feeling that what you basically wanted and needed was within your grasp.

But in a sinkhole you lose that sense. An "impossible" want has taken over, and you lose the sense of having control even of your own feelings.

Sinkholes are not, however, a result of wanting too much. What they are, in fact, is a narrowing and tunneling of wanting. They often hide a fear of wanting for and believing in yourself.

One young woman named Dawn came to me depressed after the breakup of her first "serious" relationship. "I want to be back with Allen," she said. "That's all I've ever wanted." Her whole goal for therapy was to figure out a way to change herself to get him to come back, or to figure out how to change him so he would be more "mature" and able to control his temper.

When I asked her what else she wanted, what else gave her pleasure in her life, she couldn't think of a single thing. She didn't know that she had any wants, hopes or dreams for herself, and she didn't know that her life had possibilities, even though she was only twenty.

Sinkholes feel intensely real. In fact, they can feel more real than the rest of your life. They can be as painful and riveting as a throbbing tooth. So what can you do? Denying or angrily recriminating yourself for them are not good long-term solutions. You might convince yourself to stop wanting altogether, because wanting feels so painful.

The first step is to help your Larger Self get back in control, by listening with compassion to the part of you stuck in the sinkhole. Though it doesn't feel this way, there is a whole lot more to you than what's missing in your life. See if you can accept the pain—usually, it will pass in a few minutes, or at most a few hours—and be nurturing to it. Sinkholes are very tender places, usually related to unresolved needs from early childhood or lifelong difficulties. They deserve gentleness.

Second, take an inventory of your life. Remember, sinkholes represent an extreme tunneling of your wanting energy. When you're in a sinkhole, your mind tricks you into thinking that nothing will make you feel good except the one thing you can't seem to get. But the truth is, what works best is to get in touch with other true wants, wants that you can act on. So ask yourself, "What wants am I depriving myself of right now?"

It also helps to take a look at how well you're taking care of yourself. Sinkholes often get triggered when your resistance is down. That happens when you work too hard, eat too little, don't get enough rest or make time for people who make you feel good.

Sinkholes can also arise just as you're thinking about trying new things. They can be a last-ditch effort of your mind to keep you from moving forward. So ask yourself if there's something you've been wanting to do or some new direction you want to take. And then go do it!

You can also see if you can identify a childhood want that the sinkhole is hiding. This can help make them feel less overwhelming.

And finally, if at all possible, see if you can share what you're going through with someone who's a skillful listener. This should be someone who can be accepting and understanding of your feeling of deprivation, yet who knows that you are much too good to waste your life over it.

The hardest sinkholes are the ones where there really is a deeply held desire that for some reason doesn't get fulfilled. That's the situation Evelyn found herself in.

Evelyn was a tall and elegant woman in her mid-fifties who came to therapy extremely unhappy, she said, about the way her life had gone. "I never planned to live my whole life alone," she said. "I want to know what I'm doing wrong."

For more than twenty years she owned a bookstore-café in an artistic but small college town. She started it soon after her divorce from a brief, disastrous marriage that fortunately gave her a daughter, who was now through with college and pursuing her own life. The little independent bookstore was the center of literary culture in the town.

As her story unfolded, it turned out that most of the time she felt busy and happy. But when she had a moment of calm, the pain of being single "seared" her, and she felt like her life had been lost. She was also scared of growing old alone and never having experienced being deeply in love.

The first thing we settled was that she really wasn't "blocking" a relationship. She had done all the right things for years. The problem truly was that in a town as small as hers, she knew just about every available man, and none of them was right for her.

I thought our work then would be to help her get the courage to move. But it wasn't so simple. For the truth was, she loved the other aspects of her life. She had many friends, female and male. She loved her home, which she had decorated and redecorated for more than twenty years. She loved the way she knew the children on her street and had watched many of them grow up. "What am I supposed to do?" she asked. "Chuck it all and buy a new store somewhere else, and hope that some guy walks into that store one day?"

So we took a different route. First, she learned to stop blaming herself for the choices she had made in her life. Everyone has 20/20 hindsight, and *no one* can get through life without making what later looks like a "stupid" decision. She could never have predicted in the seventies that this town would not bring her a mate.

She took an inventory of her life and decided that she'd been telling herself for years that she was "too busy" to get involved in community theater, when in fact she was scared. So she took the plunge and joined the cast of a play.

Most of all, she learned to have a new relationship with that pained part of her being. She accepted what she called her "down days," which sometimes hit her pretty hard. She let herself be sad, and, for the first time in years, let friends of hers see it. Instead of feeling "foolish and pathetic," she discovered she felt relieved to cry and show others that she didn't always feel strong. What's more, she discovered that rather than being repulsed or overwhelmed by her sadness, as she feared, her best friends were "excellent," in her words, at giving love, comfort and support.

Three years after she left therapy, I got an amazing letter from Evelyn. A year earlier, she had finally decided to sell her business in order to buy another bookstore that had gone on the market in a much larger college town. She put $7,500 down as a deposit on the other store. Three weeks later, she went to the American Booksellers Association annual conference—"an event I normally despise"—and met a man. They started a correspondence.

"Mysteriously, my store wouldn't sell," her letter continued. "Three buyers fell through for the most peculiar reasons. But it didn't matter, because four months after we met, Geoffrey decided to move here to live with me.

"I don't miss that $7,500 for a minute," she wrote. "It's been eight months now, and I am so happy. I don't know why I had to wait so long to find true love in my life, but now that I've found it, I'm glad I never stopped wanting it."

To Thine Own Wanting Be True

Evelyn's example points to something I've seen often. Sometimes, wants have to be held and accepted for a very long time.

We've all seen books that suggest that you can always get what you want in a short amount of time. All you have to do is clear out your negative thoughts, get over all of your fears and inner blocks by realizing that they're just silly, and visualize in the right way, and it will miraculously happen.

I haven't seen this to be true for anyone I've ever met, including myself. It simply doesn't seem to be the way life works. Yet wanting is still a gift, even if a want takes years, or even decades, to be fulfilled.

Let the process of wanting guide you. When you first listen to your wants again, be *extremely* supportive to them, even if at first they appear grandiose or ridiculous. Trust the process of your own evolution. Of course, nothing can guarantee that your wants will come into being, but wanting allows what's most important and precious in you to stay alive, and keeps open the possibility of your wants being realized.

You need never give up on a deep want. Some will take a different form. Some may take a lifetime to come about. And some may never be fulfilled. But even then, keeping your heart open to your wants enriches you and everyone around you in all sorts of subtle ways. You may even end up passing down your wants to future generations. Your daughter or granddaughter may, possibly without even knowing it, achieve the dream you had once dreamed.

CHAPTER EIGHT

The Voice of the Larger Self: Accessing the Spiritual Guide Within

Deep within us all there is an amazing sanctuary of the soul, a holy place, a Divine Center, a speaking Voice, to which we may continuously return. Eternity is at our hearts, pressing upon our time-torn lives, warming us with intimations of an astounding destiny, calling us home to Itself.
— Thomas Kelly, *A Testament of Devotion*, 1941

For the past four chapters we've explored pathways that lead you to reclaim, more and more, your own self, your own needs, thoughts, and feelings, indeed your own body. This reclaiming is absolutely vital. And yet intuitively we all know that there is more to life, and to the self, than this. There is a place inside that knows that life is not a constant battle between the self and others. There is a place inside you where the distinction between your self and everything else breaks down, and where it becomes clear that your life isn't measured by how many of your goals you have reached.

Deep down at the center of your being, there is Something that holds you with infinite kindness, caring and respect. It doesn't measure, it doesn't keep score. It doesn't value one person's growth or accomplishments more than another's. It doesn't judge you for the ways you haven't lived up to what you knew was true, or for the times you held back when you could have moved forward. No matter what you've done, how far you've come or how far you think you have to go, it considers you and your life, the beauties and flaws, triumphs and failures, both precious and sacred.

Most of us have been taught that this type of wisdom and compassion, if it exists, is "out there" somewhere, that it doesn't speak to us from within. What I've been humbled to discover is that if we're open to it, it will make itself manifest directly within our own bodies.

The passage that opened this chapter was written by a Quaker writer and educator named Thomas Kelly more than six decades ago. Though I've always felt myself to be a spiritual person, until a few years ago, I would have believed that the words he wrote were mostly metaphorical, and probably a little embellished. An "amazing sanctuary of the soul" deep within us all? A Divine Center? A speaking Voice? Those images weren't meant to be taken literally, I thought. Or if they were, only special people—mystics, or people who spent their entire lives in prayer and devotion—could have that experience.

But I've learned differently. There is in fact a place inside you *that you can feel*, that can speak to you, no matter who you are. And not only can it speak to you, it can bring you to a sense of peace and rightness about yourself that seems to come from a wisdom and intelligence far beyond your normal consciousness.

Discovering the Voice of the Larger Self

Back in Chapter Two and later chapters, we talked about the Larger Self. The Larger Self, as you recall, is the awareness that pulls together all of the smaller "parts" of you, the various aspects of the temporal self. The Larger Self is the "you" behind all of your ephemeral thoughts and feelings, the "you" that contains all of your memories, and most amazingly of all, the "you" that can heal you, by moving you toward actions that lead to greater wholeness and fulfillment in your life, and by giving compassion to all the hurt places inside of you.

Yet for all of that, the Larger Self isn't something you can easily name or categorize. Categories don't fit it. Like the air, it doesn't begin or end anywhere. It's a kind of Void. For that reason, it never occurred to me that one could connect with it directly. For a very long time, I helped women get in touch with their inner voice by teaching them about the first four pathways, helping them to identify what they knew, sensed, felt and wanted, and helping them to trust their inner selves more. This brought them in touch with their Larger Selves in many ways.

But one day, not fully realizing what was happening, I led a client to contact her Larger Self directly. Something extraordinary happened: The Void *talked back.*

Abby was a very bright woman, an insurance executive in her mid-thirties, whose last relationship had ended badly, and who hadn't gone on a date in several years. She had decided, in a very rational way, that wanting a relationship and trying to find one wasn't worth the tremendous investment of time, emotion and energy it takes. Most relationships, after all, don't work out, and even if they do, she reasoned, they were likely to lead her to make compromises that she might later regret. She had just bought her own townhouse and was excited about decorating it and making it just the way she wanted. Her goal in therapy, she told me, was "to learn how to be alone better."

For the first few sessions, we dealt with the issues that were most pressing for her, which all pertained to her work. Relationships, past or present, definitely weren't on her mind. Yet I was aware that we hadn't touched on the issue of being alone. In order for her to do so, it seemed to me that it would help if she could learn how to sense into her body, to get a larger, more complete sense of what the issue meant for her.

In her fourth session, I guided her into the first stages of Focusing, sensing into her body. Again, work issues arose. After sensing into them for a few minutes and gaining more clarity about them, she began to talk about feeling herself at a crossroads. "I have such big questions," she said. "Am I supposed to stay in this job, in this career? The answers aren't clear."

I had been doing a lot of thinking at the time about the nature of the inner voice. Where did it come from? How did it direct us? Given the questions she was asking, I suggested that she go to her "inner knowing place" and ask it what it wanted her to know. It was a suggestion I had never thought to make before.

What happened surprised me. After about thirty seconds, she said, "It said that I'm here to love and be loved and I need to be rejoicing in myself."

She didn't say anything more. A quiet stillness that seemed both perfectly natural and slightly otherworldly seemed to have settled over her. After lingering in the stillness, I said to her, "See if you could ask that place if there is something it wants you to bring back into your life from there."

"It answered that I have a tremendous capacity to love.

"That brings sadness," she continued, very calmly. "I've told myself I can't have it, or won't find it, for so long."

A few minutes later she opened her eyes. "That was amazing," she said.

As she explained what had happened, it was clear that it *was* amazing. Not so much for the message it brought her—it's not surprising that a woman would realize she didn't want to close off the possibility of love—but for the feeling that filled her. She didn't feel sad or upset at all. She felt totally peaceful. More surprisingly, she also felt absolutely certain that the message was true. Her attitude toward potential relationships changed on the spot.

She made rapid progress in therapy—and she began dating again. Two years after completing therapy, she had gone through two relationships that did not become permanent, but she was not feeling anxious about it. She had made new friends, reconnected with her mother in a much deeper way and become a Big Sister.

I'd never seen anything quite like this happen in therapy before. But it was so beneficial to Abby, I wanted to see how some of my other clients would respond if I did something similar with them. I thought it likely that Abby's experience would be unique to her, or that it would be especially profound. It didn't turn out that way.

In almost every case, women would get messages, most of them very simple, and all of them extremely affirming, that were accompanied by strong spiritual feelings, especially a remarkable—and very palpable—sense of peace. As a therapist, I was accustomed to the entire range of human feelings occurring in my office. But this type of peace I had not seen before. The closest thing I have found to it, I've discovered, are descriptions I've read of the experience of *grace*. The sense of grace would linger for days, or even weeks.

Sylvia was a longtime client who came into a session very agitated, worried that she was spiraling into one of her cyclical depressions. After an inner voice attunement, this is what she reported:

I saw a big hand with golden light all around it. I put my hand in it, and it took me up. It wants me to know I wouldn't have to go down into a depression like last time. It wanted me to know I could put my hand in the hand anytime.

She came into her following session feeling excited and happy. "I had a terrific week," she said.

There's been a calmness for me all week. I saw the hand, as I saw it that day in your office, every single day. It's the most beautiful hand. It's white and unlined, it almost looks like a sculpture but it's very much alive. The hand appears whenever I'm anxious or troubled, and I actually place my hand in it. Maybe it's the hand of God.

The In-Dwelling Place

Of course, human beings have had transcendent experiences since the beginning of time. But what I was seeing was different from anything that I had seen, read about, or experienced myself. The difference was how much my clients felt this experience right inside their bodies. Indeed, it seemed to come from a very specific place.

Every religion has its version of the God Within. Judaism calls this the *Shekhinah*, which is thought of as a feminine aspect of God, and which is sometimes translated as "The In-Dwelling Place." When I guided people through this process, it actually seemed like there was a place in the body where the Larger Self seemed to dwell. At least, this was where the voice of the Larger Self seemed to "come from," because people intuitively tuned into that spot and reported that they felt the message emanating from there. It seemed to be a place somewhere right in the middle of the chest or slightly lower, and a few inches below the surface. One woman expressed it this way:

I go down inside and it seems kind of dark, and then it's almost as if there's a little compartment space that's reserved just for the inner voice. I think of it as like walking into a huge, empty cathedral, and coming to the tabernacle where they keep the host.

It's somewhere right in the center below my heart. But it's not physical. I don't visualize it there, it's more like a presence. It's housed in the body, but not really part of it. It's as if it's on a separate plane.

Another woman referred to finding "a diamond shape, like a small shield or plate, right under my solar plexus." A third called it "a warmth in my chest. That's where the bedrock is located. The chest and the diaphragm." However, every person is different and this is something to feel for yourself. *Please* don't worry about finding an exact position.

I have heard countless Larger Self messages by now, and what strikes me most, besides their incredible gentleness and warmth, is how they share themes that have been repeated in the sacred texts of all religions: You are not alone. You are loved, exactly as you are. You have a path and a purpose all your own for being on Earth, and you can start unfolding toward that purpose at any moment. You are larger and more protected than you think, and needn't defend yourself as much as you imagine. Love is the most important quality to manifest in all of your relationships. I'll talk about the implications of these messages, and how you can apply them in your life, later in this chapter.

The following innercize is adapted from what I have done countless times in my office as well as for myself to access the Voice of the Larger Self, the spiritual guide within. I call it the Inner Voice Attunement.

This innercize, which may take some practice, is well worth it. The following are a few tips to help make it work.

- To begin with, the voice of the Larger Self will be difficult if not impossible to hear if there are many outside voices or surface emotions that need a listener first. If they're not heard, then even if you were to get a message, it might be a very distorted version of what the Larger Self wants you to know. That's why the Voice of the Larger Self is the last of the five Pathways.

   It's as if your inner self is a room. To hear the voice of the Larger Self, you need to make the room mostly empty, not by denying or throwing out what's there, but by meeting, acknowledging and hearing the concerns and immediate feelings that are filling the space. Then, once you've made the room mostly empty, the walls and the foundation that have supported you all along begin to speak. That is what the voice of the Larger Self is like.

INNERCIZE 15

The Inner Voice Attunement

This takes about five to fifteen minutes, and is best done in a quiet, comfortable place where you can sit without being interrupted. You may find it helpful to record the exercise and play it back, or else have someone else speak it to you. Read it slowly and calmly, pausing for a few seconds at each ellipsis, and longer (at least thirty seconds, and longer if necessary) between each paragraph.

Let your body find a comfortable position, allow your eyes to close, and take a few deep breaths.

Letting go of any thoughts about the past or future, bring your awareness to your body, beginning with your feet. . . . Sense your feet connected to the floor, as if to the earth below you . . . slowly bring your awareness to your legs . . . let gravity and your breath bring your body into greater contact with the chair you're sitting on, sensing your back totally supported. . . . Bring your awareness to your shoulders, your neck, allowing your head and facial muscles to completely relax. Sense your arms, and your hands resting comfortably. . . . Just let your body be a body.

When you're ready, begin to invite your awareness to the whole inner area of your body . . . and give those inner places a warm, hearty "Good morning" (or afternoon, or evening). . . . Take a few moments to sense into those inner places.

Now gently ask yourself, "How am I inside?" Let your awareness rest lightly on those inner areas, and sense whatever comes to you. You might become aware of a subtle feeling or sensation, like "jumpy," or "tight," or "a pain in my chest." . . . You might become aware of an emotion, like sadness. Or you might become aware of an image. . . . Whatever comes, simply welcome and acknowledge it for at least a few breaths. Notice, without judgment, exactly how it feels in your body, without trying to change it or make it go away. Take time simply to be with it. If something distressing arises, treat it softly and compassionately, like you would a dear friend who's hurting, letting it know you understand just how it feels that way, without trying to fix it. [Pause here for a minute or two.]

When you feel clear and ready, go to the Inner Knowing Place, in the center of your body, the place that knows everything about you, that knows everywhere you've been and everywhere you're going . . . and gently and slowly ask that place, "What do you want me to know today?" Listen or sense what comes. If after a minute or so, nothing comes, ask the question again, and listen quietly to whatever arises.

Let whatever you received sink in. Then ask, "Is there anything it wants me to bring back to my life, from this deep place?" Listen again to what comes.

When it feels complete, thank the inner place for whatever message it brought you, knowing you can return to this place again.

Now slowly, return to this time and place.

- Feel free to ask the two "inner knowing questions" two or three times, and let the answers take time to emerge. You don't have to get an answer to both questions.

- Remember, too, that you are seeking to *sense* something in the middle of your body—something that may or may not translate immediately into words. For example, recently a woman who was facing what felt like unbearable work pressure did an inner voice practice. What came to her was a sensation in her chest of being "lifted up." Because of her life experience, this had tremendous meaning and healing power for her, but it was mostly a wordless sensation.

- If nothing comes, it could mean that you need to cultivate your ability to tune into your subtle senses more, or that you need to spend more time with what is disturbing you, listening to it and giving it compassion until you reach a level of equanimity. It could also be that you believe so strongly that your Larger Self will be critical of you that you can't let its simple, affirming message come through.

• Try to resist the temptation to attempt a long dialogue with the voice of the Larger Self, or ask it a barrage of questions. Instead, be as quietly receptive as you can be. Less really *is* more in this case.

• The Larger Self isn't the same as intuition. Rarely has anyone reported a message that was "psychic" in the sense of presaging a future event in any way. It seems more involved with personal healing than with events on the temporal plane. The voice of the Larger Self is not judgmental or authoritarian. If it makes you feel bad or directs you toward anger and judgments against yourself or other people, it simply is not the Voice of the Larger Self.

You met Penny, the thirty-six-year-old systems analyst who wanted "everything," in the last chapter. What I only alluded to there was that she had grown up with terrible abuse, both physical and sexual. She had made it through by cultivating an indomitable sense of herself, despite everything. Yet it had not been without cost. She felt disconnected from other people. The walls around her and her past were thick, and the dismantling we did, brick by brick, came at the price of tremendous pain.

About a year before the session described in Chapter Eight, she had just gone through a very difficult period of therapy, and she needed time to take a breather, to rest and integrate what she had been through. I offered to lead her through the inner voice attunement, almost as a treat, and she was game.

She was very deep within it when I asked her what it wanted her to know today.

The first thing that came was, "I'm okay *now.*" It sounded like she was getting the message that in the present, she was finally safe.

Then the atmosphere changed in the room. A minute went by, and tears started pouring down her face. "I'm getting that I've never . . . I've never been alone. That I'm, um, I'm being watched out for . . . and my dog . . ." And here she gasped. "My dog is leading the way!" She shook and quivered.

I can't describe to you the thickness in the air, the emotion in the room. Tears were rolling down my cheeks as well. I didn't say anything for a long time. Finally I asked, "What does it want you to bring back to your life, from this place?"

"It sounds so clichéd," she said, "but I'm not as alone as I thought I was. I haven't been alone and it's okay not to be alone."

When she opened her eyes, she told me more about what happened. "When I was a girl," she explained, "I had a German shepherd named Ranger. She's been dead for almost twenty years.

"But I saw her, clear as day, *right there*," she said, pointing to the right side of my chair.

The hair stood up on my arms. I was in awe.

"Ranger," she continued, "was the one unconditional love I have ever had in my life, the only person or animal in the world that I ever felt totally safe with. And I haven't thought about her in *years*.

"I also saw an image of a big zipper running all the way down the front of me. I unzipped it and stepped out of it. And it was all right."

A week later, she elaborated. "Ranger was standing very alert, almost as if she was protecting me, and I felt like she really *had* been in my family to help me. I also received information last week that was very blunt, but I couldn't put fully into words. It said that, even when I thought I was alone, all this time, I wasn't. But more than that, not only was I not alone, I've been mistaken to believe that the best way for me to live was to be alone with no one looking out for me."

"You are not alone" is one of the most common Larger Self messages, either as the whole or as part of the message. Another common Larger Self message has been "you can lean on me."

Most people have much shorter and less intense inner voice attunements than Penny's, which after all was part of very deep, reparative, long-term therapy. Yet they still have a strong impact on people.

Andrea was a lovely therapist in her fifties who came to a workshop I held. What she received was this:

As a therapist I often feel very deep feelings of compassion for my clients. But at times what I hear is overwhelming, it's too much. I was remembering that feeling of being overwhelmed when I suddenly felt like I was somewhere that I could rest. Tears come to my eyes as I speak of it . . . it told me that when the pain gets too much to hold it wants me to rest. It said *"I* will hold all of it, *I am* holding all of it." I can't forget the peaceful quietness that was there, the feeling of holding I had.

Connie's story

One of the first people to try the Inner Voice Attunement was Connie, a forty-five-year-old mother of four. Connie had married at nineteen and swiftly had three children, followed by a fourth child, a daughter, nine years later. Now her third child had left for college, and Connie felt utterly bereft. Nothing she told herself took away the pain she was feeling. She was crying often, yet getting no relief.

I spent the beginning part of a session just helping her to disidentify and get a little distance from her pain, so that she could be compassionate to it rather than have it engulf her.

"I'm feeling how terribly I miss all of them," she said. "I can't stop thinking about them. I loved having them around."

"Just put a friendly arm around those feelings. *How much* you miss them. *How much* you loved having them around."

She was quiet for a moment. "But there's such an ache, such an awful ache, now that Lindsay is gone, too. I'm so lonely. . . ."

It wasn't easy for Connie to give herself compassion, because so much of her identity was tied up with being a mother. It would be another day when we would work on helping her find another focus for her life. Today we needed to deal with the sadness. Connie had done this work before, so she knew that if she could "step back" from the grief and give it compassion, she'd ultimately feel better. As she continued, she was able to find the place within her where she could empathize with her grief and keep it company.

"This part of me's feeling so sad. It's saying it just hates having such a quiet house, a house without kids."

"Really let that part know you hear its sadness."

"Oh, I am. . . ." She sat in silence for a few minutes, tears rolling out of her eyes, holding an inner dialogue. "It's starting to feel a little better. Still sad, but better. Not so torn up."

There was still a sense of struggle in Connie's voice, though far less than earlier. I sensed that she had reached enough equanimity that she could ask the Voice of the Larger Self what it wanted her to know today.

The difference was profound. Her face in repose, she said, "It wants me to know that the kids grow up, but it's not over. It's a passage, not an endpoint. Their leaving is just an event, something that happens." With a wave of her hand, she dismissed what, fifteen minutes earlier, had totally devastated her. "What matters is that I grow and evolve," she proclaimed. "It wants me to know that I'm not alone."

The glowing calm stayed with her throughout the week. She could recall it and bring it back to her any time she wanted. But the stress of life seeped in again. The pain wasn't completely gone, and the issues with her husband, her children and her own not fully developed self still needed more addressing.

Two weeks later she came in frazzled. She was in the midst of one of those days we all know about—shopping, a dozen errands, chores, a to-do list nine feet long. She wanted another "attunement," and I led her through it.

After it was over, her face was radiant. "I was somewhere else," she reported. "I felt myself being uplifted and held in God's grace and presence. I saw myself going through everything I have to do today, but in this light, almost weightless way. A few times in my life, I've had the experience of feeling so much in God's grace, but before, it just sort of happened out of nowhere, and from the outside, like taking a pill. This time *it came from within*. I've always heard about the God within, but this was the first time I really felt it."

The next session, she told me, "I had the best day after that experience last week. I was going through all the same ordinary things that I would ordinarily do, but feeling totally different. What was great was that the love that came through me was for me, too, not just for other people. It seemed to me that people were extra generous to me that day. I felt like, instead of me always getting caught up in everyone else's magnetic fields, from now on *I* was going to be the magnet."

Through therapy, she started to make steps to have a life of her own. A few months later, she wanted to go on a trip to Italy, on her own, without her husband or kids, to look at Renaissance art and architecture, a longtime interest for her. It was her first "solo" trip, not involving family of any sort, since she was in high school.

Her husband was mostly okay with it (as long as she left casseroles for a week in the freezer), but her youngest girl, her twelve-year-old, was very upset. She didn't want either to stay home or at the homes of her older sisters. She even held her breath until she turned blue. "I don't know if I can go through with this," Connie said.

We did an inner voice attunement. She got a feeling of total support, with the words, "This trip is part of your journey, too." It also told her, "Don't stop. You get hurt more by your fear of getting hurt than by anything that actually happens."

So she and her daughter had a very long talk. Connie listened to her daughter's feelings but wouldn't back down. Finally her daughter said, "Can I do one of your 'meditations'?" Connie guided her through it. When it ended, her daughter opened her eyes, smiled and said that she got, "Everything will be all right."

Collecting Sacred Moments

There's such a denial of the sacred dimension of life in our culture. We're way too material- and bottom-line-oriented to give value to what can't be seen. Many of our foremothers believed in an unseen dimension of good and bad forces animating the world, spirits and angels and demons as well. Their sense of the sacred powers always around them, in their fields and their homes and their hearths, illuminated their lives. Mostly we've left those old beliefs behind, calling them "superstitions." But what have we put in their place—goals and traffic reports and to-do lists? If everyday life is not sacred, what, except the occasional vacation or big accomplishment, will make us happy?

While in previous chapters I have cautioned against going past your feelings to "better" ones, there are times when you can take the perspective of the Larger Self and see what is sacred in you, in your life, and in the people all around you.

Indeed it is when your life is at its most difficult, when the challenges facing you seem hardest to bear, that you can help to remember yourself by *collecting the sacred moments*, the luminous moments that shine through the ordinariness of life. They can help sustain you by helping you to remember that you are always *more* than the person who is struggling to make it through the day. At that moment, when you step back within yourself to notice and acknowledge a sense of sacredness, you step into your Larger Self. You awaken the "I" from its slumber.

Sacred moments usually aren't big and splashy and they don't have to be tied to any ritual, although they can be. Samantha was struggling with her mother's illness, three kids, a stressful job and a marriage that was going through a rocky patch. I asked her if she could think of a couple of sacred moments from the week.

"The first thing I think of," she said, "was waking up real early last Thursday. I was all alone, and I could be still, and drink my cup of coffee and look out the window at the trees. That was a sacred moment for me."

Could she think of any more? I asked.

She looked puzzled for a moment, then her face lit up. "Yes I can," she said. "It was Friday night, and usually Eric and I are dead tired and the kids are cranky and it's lousy. But this time, the kids were playing around and started jumping on him, and he just laughed and rolled on the floor with them and everyone had a good time." She looked thoughtful. "That was our sacred moment of the day."

Sacred moments don't have to be perfect. Another woman felt that the forty-five minutes she spent with her husband in a traffic jam was sacred time, because they used the time for a good talk instead of fighting or getting tense.

Sacred moments can show you what you value. If you notice and collect them, you can string them together. Strung together, they form an alternate version, a sacred retelling of the life you are living.

Appreciation is another aspect of the Larger Self. I've found that the conscious act of appreciation has tremendous benefits. In fact, appreciation *appreciates*. That is, whatever you appreciate gets larger and becomes more manifest in your life, giving you even more to appreciate. I was talking to a saleswoman at a store in one of my favorite places on Earth, Big Sur, California. The views of the cliffs overlooking the Pacific, with the mists overhanging the mountains, are some of the most magnificent I have ever seen. I asked her about her life and how she ended up working and living there—there are hardly any businesses, and only 1,400 residents. She said she always loved the beauty of the Pacific. She'd been living thirty miles north in Monterey and couldn't understand how anybody could ever be unhappy living near such beauty. "I'd walk out every day and just appreciate how beautiful the vistas were. I never took them for granted," she said. It didn't surprise me that with so much appreciation of the landscape, a job and then an apartment would open up for her in a place that was even more spectacularly beautiful.

There's a children's cheer that goes, "Two, four, six, eight, who do we appreciate?" Let me change that a bit and ask, *Who* or *what* do you appreciate? What you sincerely and openheartedly appreciate is likely to be drawn to you. Acknowledging, and even more so, expressing appreciation is a great way to increase your own good feeling. One thing I like to do when I travel is leave a thank you note and a large tip to the women who clean my hotel room. They're not paid well, they often have families to feed, and they have made my stay more pleasant. Appreciating what they've done for me is acknowledging that we are all connected and that I depend on them.

There are times when your awareness of what you *don't* like in your life is so strong, it's hard to focus on what you appreciate, and that is okay. Yet even in the darkest times of your life, it's important to take a few minutes each day to appreciate *something*: a flower, the sun, your kids playing happily for ten minutes. Finding what there is to appreciate is like watering a seed that will grow and improve your life. It helps you stay connected to your self. It helps you keep the bud of your spirit open, without shriveling into resignation. I suggest thinking about a few things in your life that you do appreciate, however small. If you make a conscious effort to appreciate them more, and express your appreciation more fully, in a short amount of time you'll notice those things increasing in your life.

Blessing Yourself

I am the child, yearning for love,
I am the mother, so full of dreams for you
I am the angel, guarding your way
I am the voice of truth within you saying,

Walk in the light of love
Dance through the darkest times
Reach out to those in need
Bless who you are.
  —"Bless Who You Are," song by Hanna Tiferet Siegel

The messages from the Voice of the Larger Self are messages of *blessing.*
The feeling of grace that comes from them is the result of feeling, quite
literally, blessed. How strange and wonderful! There is something within
us that says we are blessed just as we are! There's something that knows
just how much we've goofed up and says, "I love you and bless your life
anyway!" And it's within our grasp to *feel* this. The only problem is that
most of the time, we either aren't aware of it or don't believe it.

But despite our limited normal perspective, you can step into the
perspective of your Larger Self and offer the blessing to yourself, your
life and other people that your Larger Self is always giving.

Let's begin with blessing yourself. The first reaction that many
women have to this idea is, "I can't do that!" Some people seem to react
as if it's almost sacrilegious, as if only God is allowed to bless us. Yet
clearly we don't believe it's sacrilegious to *curse* ourselves and *damn* ourselves—people do it all the time. If, as I believe, the Larger Self is our
point of connection to the Divine, then it's fully possible to bless ourselves, to make the connection to the universal Source that loves us and
wishes us well.

The Larger Self perspective is the opposite of seeing what's wrong
with you. From the point of view of the Larger Self, there are no good
and bad parts of you. It blesses *all* of who you are, giving every single
aspect of you love and caring. Not idealizing you, knowing exactly what
your strengths, weaknesses and limitations are, the Larger Self acknowledges the challenges you've faced and all the ways that you are

trying to grow. By bringing yourself in touch with that place deep down inside you, you can see yourself in the same way and write a blessing for yourself.

In this way, you can also bless your life, by imagining yourself as someone who in some way is being watched out for. Look with compassion on the story of your life so far, and imagine that you are extending a Divine wish that good things will begin coming to you. What would happen from now on if, indeed, your life were truly blessed?

You can then do a very similar thing regarding another person. To bless someone you know is to be in touch with who they are "deep down," seeing the luminous person below the surface, and extending from your largest self love, kindness and well-wishes for their present and future.

Rena, the mother of two children, one with cerebral palsy, did the following innercize during a workshop, and came out of it smiling broadly. "All of a sudden I saw Glinda the good witch from *The Wizard of Oz*," she related. "She told me that in the middle of all of the struggle and suffering, my true nature was very joyful. And all I had to do was tap my shoes together." Two months later, she told me that

⋑ INNERCIZE 16 ⋐

Blessing

Take some time right now to breathe, close your eyes and imagine yourself in the place of your Larger Self. Now imagine looking at yourself through the eyes of your Larger Self. Write down a short letter, blessing all of who you are, acknowledging where you've come from and who you are deep down. Allow the most caring and important message inside you to emerge.

Now pick one or two other people, and in writing, bless them, seeing their goodness. Finally, look at your life and bless all of it, even the bad times, and imagine that the rest of your life has been blessed. What will it look like from now on?

the blessing was still with her. "I could be going through a day feeling like all I do is survive and endure, and then I'll remember to tap my heels together," she said. "It gives me a lift. It reminds me to look for the joy."

Dancing with Joy

At the very core of human existence there is a paradox. On one level, we have to work hard to grow or just to get through the day. The demands of physical reality are so many, and the effort to grow is challenging. On top of it all, many if not most of us have gone through some very, very difficult times. Many, if not most of us, still are.

On another level, we're lifted up on eagle's wings. We're whole and blessed beyond measure. Within us is the ability to connect with a source of strength and healing that we barely know is there, and that we almost never tap.

Of all the stories of the voice of the Larger Self I have witnessed, perhaps the most remarkable one of all was Patty's. Patty suffered a childhood of terrible emotional, physical and sexual abuse. Despite it, she married and raised two healthy and successful sons. But when she was around fifty she suffered a breakdown. For four years, she struggled daily with a wall of despair, hopelessness and self-denigration that would often overtake her.

The first time Patty tried the inner voice practice, she had been feeling so down that she didn't want to get out of bed. In that very first session her Larger Self said, "From this place inside, we can solve any problem."

Her next session she reported that she still felt better from the one before—something I hadn't heard her say in quite a while. When she went to the inner knowing place she saw the child she had been, *dancing with joy*.

Patty suffered from chronic insomnia, so she began to speak the innercize to herself silently in bed at night to help her fall asleep. She also did it when she was confronted with previously stressful situations, and she wrote the messages she received into her journal.

Her energy level, sense of well-being and ability to cope with daily stresses all rose markedly. About a month after we first began doing this, she said,

> I thought I had nothing left inside to heal what happened to me in my childhood. Then I found this place. It was this place, I realized, that must have given me the strength to be a mother all those years when I felt so empty all the time. This place is so strong and whole and peaceful, despite everything I'd been through, and it's so filled with love. It feels like it comes from God.

In another session, she said, "How do I express it—there's a safety being inside me, a safety, maybe, being me. It wants me to remember that wherever I am, there's a place I can go that's safe and nobody can get to me."

In a few months she was able to cut her sessions down from twice to once a week. She began to do a great deal better. She returned to volunteer work and started to think about becoming a lay counselor in her church. Meanwhile, her favorite aunt, Edie, died, and her first granddaughter was born. A year and a half later I guided her through an attunement again. As she came to the place, she said, "That's incredible, it's not dark like a monastery anymore. It's not dark. It's bright, with lots of tall windows, like a great, steepled church. It's almost making me dizzy."

When I asked her what it wanted her to know today, she said, "I see myself dancing with Edie. We're like two little kids. We're holding each others' arms, swinging around. It's just light and airy, not heavy at all. Not like death. A celebration. I'm getting the words, 'It's okay. Life is good now.' It's amazing how much has changed."

Then I asked her what it wanted her to bring back to her life from this place and she said, "I was worried that I wouldn't live long enough to see my granddaughter get married, or have children. I realized that no matter what, I don't need to be unhappy or worried about dying and missing anything. Every day is a blessing!"

PART THREE

LIVING FROM YOUR INNER VOICE

CHAPTER NINE

Holding On to Your Inner Voice: The Foundation of Relationship

"I realized something this week," said Simone, a twenty-nine-year-old grant writer. "The choices I've made with my husband since getting married have expanded his life, but constricted mine. What's making his life better has made my life worse."

On the surface, Simone and her husband had what looked like the very model of a modern egalitarian marriage. They both worked hard at their jobs. They both cooked and cleaned and did the dishes. She even earned more money than he did. He would never, I was sure, say that she was "supposed" to fill a certain role.

But Simone was desperately unhappy. Though the reason that led her to therapy was a terrible work situation, under the surface was a problem she didn't want to face: a nagging feeling that her life, and her marriage, were not her own.

She had met Phil in the second year of college. His calmness and steadiness made her feel safe, and his love for her made her feel loved. She also loved how deeply he was committed to environmental causes, a passion she shared.

When they got married, in the summer after college, he started a business developing and distributing environmentally friendly farm products. Little by little, without realizing she was doing so, she made *his* life and career the center around which her entire being revolved.

To begin with, she became a grant writer. She didn't really like it, but it offered good benefits and paid well enough to support them while his business got on its feet. Then they moved thirty miles from the city so he could be nearer his suppliers and customers. And then they bought a huge but dilapidated farmhouse on two acres of land, which gave him plenty of room to work on new products—and which he spent 90 percent of his weekend time improving or repairing.

Her income, of course, was paying the mortgage. But though she felt stymied in her job and unclear about her own career goals, she channeled all of her energy into supporting him and helping him develop his business. It seemed like the "natural" thing to do, which she was sure would pay off in the end—eventually.

"You know, I always learned that when you got married, you worked together, you became part of a team," she told me.

"Yes, that's true," I agreed. "But I have to wonder, is he part of *your* team?"

Slowly and haltingly, she started to become aware of the differences she was submerging to be a member of the "team." She had stopped seeing her friends because he was less social. They had stopped going on dates because it seemed he would always rather be "doing" something. And she realized that she had fallen into acting quieter and more restrained around him, because her louder, more rambunctious nature seemed to "bother" him.

But she was terrified of looking at any of these things too closely, because instead of seeing them as changeable aspects of a mutual relationship, she saw each difference as a question of having to choose between *her* happiness and *his*. She couldn't see leaving him, yet she couldn't see how anything could change. Her marriage was good enough, she told herself. Of course, he wasn't very communicative anymore. And yes, she had grown quieter and sadder in their six years together. But there wasn't anything *really* wrong. They got along well together. She was devoted to him. After six years of marriage, isn't that about all you can expect?

"I think he needed me," she said in a session one day. Later, she said of the weeks before her wedding, "I had the strangest feeling that time was moving forward against my will, and I couldn't do anything about it. I guess I believed in fate and things happening for a reason, and it seemed to me that if I had gone this far, I was supposed to keep going."

"It's as if you weren't there," I reflected. The hopeless tone in her voice concerned me. "As if you weren't the one who was choosing. I hear you talk a lot about what other people want—what Phil wants, what your boss wants, sometimes what your parents want. In this case, I hear you saying that Fate wanted it. Who is Fate?"

"God, maybe God wanted it for him."

"But what about what God wants for you?" I countered. "You're doing something very dangerous. You're resigning yourself to being unhappy."

I was trying to wake up Simone's inner self. She needed to resist the voices telling her she was "fated" to be less than who she really was, destined to promote her husband's happiness, and their future children's, at the *expense* of her own. And I hoped she would do it soon. She and Phil had started to talk about having children, which would make Simone's "fate" a lot more complicated and less malleable.

Popular culture sometimes gives the impression that American women are calling the shots with their partners and making and breaking relationships at the drop of a hat. But attachment is such a strong force in the vast majority of women's lives that countless women do what Simone did, subtly accommodating and adapting to their husbands and making them *bigger and more important than themselves.* Waiting for validation from their husbands, they don't hold on to what is true for them, nor ask for what they need directly. In a way, they ask their men to give them permission to be who they are.

There is a difference between wanting validation, which we all need and which few women get as much as they deserve, and waiting for a man's validation to trust your inner self. The old choice—the only choice women were given for thousands of years—was to give themselves up for connection. Unless she was very, very, very fortunate, she couldn't keep her full self once she was "taken"—a fitting word—nor was she free to reject connection to maintain herself.

But now women have a new choice. They can stay true to themselves *within* relationships. In fact, if you have a basically healthy relationship, you can have more of your self and more closeness in your intimate relationship than you may have thought possible, if you are willing to both honor yourself and to say your truth in a way that brings you closer together, not further apart.

The first step is to ask yourself the most important question of all about your relationship. While I am writing here mostly about heterosexual relationships, I have worked with many lesbians and lesbian couples and I have found this to be true about same-sex relationships as well.*

---

*With apologies to my lesbian clients and readers, I will use the pronouns *he, him* and *his* to refer to the other partner for the rest of this chapter.

The most important question of all, surprisingly, is not, "Do I love my partner?" It is, "Do I like the *me* that I am when I'm with him?"

Do I Like the Me that I Am When I'm with My Partner?

This is an enormously powerful question. It is especially important in the early stages of a relationship, in those days when you are first becoming attached and establishing the ways you relate to one another, the particular "dance" the two of you have. But it is always valid and useful.

This question is not the same as, "Does *he* make me feel loved?" or "Does *he* make me feel special?" or even "Does *he* make me feel good about myself?" This is about the qualities the relationship brings out in you. If you feel comfortable in your own skin, if you feel like you're being *more* of whatever qualities you most enjoy about yourself, then you know you're on to something good.

Conversely, if, when you're with someone, you like yourself *less*, then no matter how much you love him or he says he loves you, or how many ski trips to Aspen he takes you on, there is a huge problem in the relationship that must be addressed.

Listen to Marcela, a thirty-one-year-old political activist, talk about her two most recent relationships: the one with her husband of two years, Andre, and her previous one to Justin, an activist like herself, with whom she had a difficult and painful relationship.

> The me that I am when I'm with Andre is the me that I recognize from when I was a kid, from the days before I cared what boys thought, before I realized that other people might not like me if I was myself. With Andre I feel wonder and delight, a kind of "gee-whiz" feeling about life, just like I did when I was a girl. I feel more and show more than I used to, because I don't have to guard myself, I don't have to act tough around him. He saw the me that I knew I was deep down inside even when I was hiding it, and that's the me he loves. It makes him happy just to see me be myself.

What Andre loves about Marcela is the person she truly is. And because of that, Marcela's inner self is free to blossom. She is not busy trying to change herself to "please" Andre. She *is* what Andre loves. This is a woman's true birthright: to be loved, honored and respected for the particular qualities and gifts that she brings to this world. For this to happen, two people must be equals who want each other to be as large as they can be.

This wasn't the case with Justin, the man Marcela dated before Andre.

> I was crazy in love with Justin. We thought and felt so much alike. In fact, I was working in another field at the time, and he was doing exactly what I wanted to do with my life. But he had to see me as a protégé, and I went along. It wasn't a conscious act, but it was an act. I shrunk myself. I made myself second place.
>
> Because I did that, I stopped feeling confident in myself. My work suffered. It made me doubt all of my abilities because the relationship required me not to be as good as him. And because I doubted myself, even though I was getting all these signals that it wasn't right, I didn't trust myself. I avoided talking to my best friend about it, because I knew she'd say "Marcela, what's going *on* with you?" I'd even tell friends that I couldn't believe what a jerk he was being, and the next day talk myself out of feeling that way.

All the signs of problems were there with Justin. Marcela was avoiding talking to her best friend, she talked herself out of what she knew to be true, and most of all, she felt worse about herself. Love should never, ever make you like yourself less. That would indicate that somehow you are changing yourself against the wisdom of your inner voice in order to keep another person's love. And you may be doing that because deep down you sense that if you were to be honest and open, saying what you know, sense, feel and want, he would leave.

The only way to find this out is to follow your inner truth, honestly saying or showing what you are afraid will drive him away. If it doesn't, then you have learned something very valuable about yourself and your partner, and you've deepened your relationship. If it does, you've lost an illusion, a false relationship. It's false, because if the "love" you receive from someone is making your soul shine less brightly, then that *itself* indicates a deficiency in that person's love for you. Love, by *definition*, means loving the true you, wanting to see your strengths and your goodness and to see them flower.

Justin did leave, and for a while Marcela felt crushed. But eventually she left her job and proceeded to find work exactly at Justin's level. Being out of the relationship with Justin, she reestablished the most important relationship she had—the one she had with herself. That is so critical for women. You are the one whom you will have to wake up to every day of your life. You are the person you need the most.

The best thing you can do to find someone with whom you can be joyfully and freely yourself is to courageously follow what you know, sense, feel and want right from the start. What I tell my single clients is that I hope their true selves become so irrepressible that they discover very quickly whether the person they're with is the right one for them.

Giving Your Self Away

Both men and women have a drive toward attachment. It's not uncommon for a man to meet someone one day, and decide, with often even less rational forethought than women, that she is, or could be, "the one."

The difference is that, no matter how head-over-heels in love he is, it's very rare for a man to define himself *in terms* of the relationship. But many women, as soon as they get attached, begin to feel that there's no separation between themselves and the relationship they're in. It isn't just one important aspect of their lives. It's who they are.

That's what happened to Deena, the attractive, thirty-two-year-old fashion designer whom we first met in Chapter Four, who used her *knowing* with her boyfriend to avoid making the same mistakes she made losing herself to her ex-husband, Glen.

She recalled how her relationship with her husband began. "I was nineteen, and Glen lived in the college dorm next to mine," she said about the time she met him. "That's when it started, me forgetting myself.

"The first time we saw each other, we didn't even talk, but I could feel the fireworks between us," she remembered. "The next time I saw him, he asked me if I was going to see *The Shining*, which was playing that night. I told him I wasn't really into horror movies. He said, 'It's my favorite movie.' I ended up going with him, and sat in the back shaking."

After the movie they went back to his room and talked. At some point he mentioned that he liked girls who were comfortable in jeans and a sweatshirt. Deena, being a future fashion designer, never did like sweatshirts and jeans, but the next morning, she rummaged through her bottom drawer for a pair of old jeans and a sweatshirt and put them on.

Thinking about that morning, Deena smiled ruefully and shook her head. "I knew I wasn't being myself, but I didn't think of it as a bad thing then. I thought of it as changing for my man."

Before Deena met Glen, she still had some connection to her inner voice. "I was pretty full of myself in college. I was very outgoing. I enjoyed my classes. I wanted to be an artist." But when she met Glen, all the signals coming from her inner self became unimportant to her. She was powerfully drawn to Glen, and the strongest feeling she had ever known was telling her that having Glen fall in love with her and marry her would make her happier than she had ever been.

Somewhere inside of her there was also a voice saying, *Hey, I don't like jeans. That's not me.* But Glen's voice had already become so loud to her. Besides, there was also an excited, even thrilled voice inside her saying, "I'm changing for my man!" *If I'm already willing to change myself for him,* this voice said, *it must mean I love him, and he'll love me.*

I've been surprised to discover how many women, even young women who fully assume that women are equal to men and can do anything men can, still believe deep down that in order to get or keep a man's love, they have to go along with what he wants to do and pretend to like it. They still equate *relationship* with *changing for the other person.*

This is not to say that most men in the courtship stage don't try to make a good impression as well, or that they wouldn't spend a Saturday morning at an art museum with their girlfriends, if that was their interest—though it's not uncommon that a man never would, or she would never ask him to, even after they've gone six times together to watch his favorite college team's football games. But the difference is, once they were a couple, very rarely would a man pretend to love art. Sad to say, generally speaking, she would probably feel lucky and excessively grateful if he managed to act graciously interested for three hours.

There's a life-enhancing aspect to going along with what your partner enjoys. Women want to be changed by love, to be stretched and to discover new interests. The danger is they can inadvertently set a pattern that says *Your interests are more important than mine. What you do is more important than what I do. Where you go, I will follow.*

Very soon after meeting Glen, Deena stopped attuning to her inner signals and started attuning to only one thing: Glen's feelings and reactions. Her focus became figuring out what would make Glen happy and preserve his feelings for her so as to attain the loving attention from him that gave her so much pleasure. This is the essence of losing yourself in a relationship.

This caused a vicious cycle. The more she desensitized herself to her own basic urges, opinions and feelings to act a certain way for him, the more she was like a plant cut off from its roots, unable to draw nourishment through itself. This made her more dependent on his love and ap-

INNERCIZE 17

Returning to Yourself

When you find yourself going over and over in your mind, "What does he feel? What is he thinking?" you are indeed "out" on someone else. Your attention is outside of your body, no longer paying attention to what's true for you. When you notice yourself doing this, imagine literally pulling yourself back into your body and landing your awareness there. Ask yourself, "What's happening inside of me right now? What do I feel about him? What do I know? What do I sense? Am I sure I like *him*? Is he treating me in a way that feels good to me, or am I trying to get him to?" Notice the *feeling* in your body that made you go out of yourself, which is usually some variant of insecurity or not being "good enough." Acknowledge that feeling, let it be there, and give it a lot of compassion. Then take a slow, deep breath, and concentrate on staying within yourself, and accepting yourself as you are. This, by the way, applies not just to intimate relationships, but to any person or situation (a party full of strangers, for example) where you find yourself going "out" of yourself and on to someone else.

proval to feel good. And the more she was dependent on him to feel good, the less she was willing to risk losing Glen to reestablish her connection to herself. Over time, she lost touch with her own outgoing and straightforward nature, allowing Glen to always be the center of attention while she slipped into the shadows.

Disconnections are "Whole-some"

> *Even when I know I have a right to be angry, I forgive my husband before I should. I'm afraid of losing the connection, even when there shouldn't be a connection. I want to make a stand, and physically separate, like go to a separate room, but fear that we wouldn't come back together.*
> —Naomi, age thirty

Deena, in effect, was trying to create a *premature* "we-ness" with Glen by trying to become what Glen wanted. The sad thing about this we-ness is that Deena did not yet know Glen, so her attempt to be what he wanted was destined to get in the way of her truly learning to see *him*. That is the tragedy of submerging yourself for your partner. Like being identified with your own feelings, being identified with your partner leaves you no place to step back and see him for himself. In Deena's case, had she done so she might have realized that Glen was a moody, self-centered young man with far less sense of direction than she had, who tried to make himself feel bigger by tearing her down.

In relationships, the important thing, as in all other aspects of your life, is not to be self*ish*, but self-*oriented*. This, if you recall, doesn't mean orienting *to* yourself, but *from* yourself—making yourself the starting point. This doesn't mean you don't see or recognize other people's needs, or try to meet them. In fact, you may see them even more clearly. And if you're solidly coming from your own inner self, you can respond to other people very well without fear of getting permanently lost. When you live from your inner voice, you can *sense* when you want to extend beyond yourself, and still hold onto who you are.

Women often lose themselves in relationships in very subtle ways, scarcely aware that it's happening. It can happen when you've "fallen in love," and you're so euphoric that you think the two of you are *perfect* together—so perfect that anything that ruins this image of perfection is quietly "forgotten." This makes me think of Morgan, a twenty-four-year-old veteran of several great romances. "The first six months are always the best," she said. "It feels *so* wonderful. It's *so* sweet. It's *so* tender. You're just getting to know each other. You're getting to know how the other person is. You get butterflies just thinking about the other person." But when she explored what she actually shared about herself with her last boyfriend, she realized that it was in fact a highly edited version of who she was.

Then there's the problem of despairing whether you'll ever really find someone who resonates with you. You start thinking that maybe you're just too picky, or else there are "no good guys out there." "I've met eighteen guys in the past three months, and none of them were right," said Haley, a twenty-six-year-old meeting planner. "All of my friends are seriously involved with someone. I'm afraid I'm going to end up at thirty-five spending Saturday nights with my mother eating Häagen-Dazs and watching Lifetime TV."

Because of this, Haley said, "When I finally do get involved with a guy, I get all wrapped up in him. I close my eyes to what's not right and think, this is pretty good, maybe it'll get better." Women like Haley don't so much fall in love as fall *into* love—or fall into attachment. When they meet someone whom they're attracted to, who wants a relationship and who meets a certain bare minimum of the requirements for the kind of partner they want, they attach their desires for a relationship onto him and try to "make it work."

Let me say that I absolutely don't believe that experiencing the state of "falling in love" is necessary for two people to love each other. I've encountered many people in wonderful long-term relationships who never went through that stage with each other. But they definitely had more than just attraction and minimum requirements between them. They felt a deep sense of well-being with each other, and a feeling of bringing out the best in one another, that "liking the you you are" I speak of.

In fact, falling in love has the danger of feeling so great that you get fooled into thinking it's the ideal or the only "real" state of love, and so you try to keep it or get it back. Let it go. If your love withstands the test of time, it will never be gone completely. But it's the blossom of love, not the fruit. A woman who wants to live from her inner voice knows that only when that feeling of lovestruck oneness begins to fade can she start to learn whether this particular relationship is worthy of her devotion. The way to do this is to learn to tolerate small disconnections.

For many women this is easier said than done. But think of it as a set of emotional "muscles" you'd like to build to counteract the powerful tendency toward connection. This is the time to develop the practice of knowing who you are and what you want in the presence of this person whom you hope is becoming your lifelong partner. If the two of you have a disagreement, stay with what's true for you and don't agree with him until you're absolutely ready to. At the same time, don't expect or require him to see things the way you do or be perfectly attuned to you.

I strongly suggest that when differences emerge, you *not* try to keep the peace, *not* try to preserve harmony above all else. If you preserve harmony now, how will you ever learn where the two of you conflict, and what will happen when you do? You literally want to welcome the times when you know he feels one way and you feel another, so you can practice holding on to what you feel and want anyway, and reaching to connect with him over the gulf between you.

There is a powerful, unspoken cultural assumption that a woman *should* go along with the man, if it's important enough to him and she "really loves him," while a man is under no such obligation in return. For this reason, holding on to your own position may trigger outside voices saying that what you're doing is "wrong." Yet one of gutsiest and most important things you can do for your future is to establish your relationship on your own terms, one of them being that you expect him to compromise as much as you do. You're not the *designated* compromiser.

To Love You Is to Know You

As we saw in Chapter Four, learning to say, "What do I know to be true?" is especially important in intimate relationships. Aside from what you know to be true for you, there is another very important "knowing" involved in relationships: what you know to be true about your partner. I invite you then, to try the following innercize.

⋛ INNERCIZE 18 ⋚
What Do I Know to Be True about My Partner?

At a time when you're feeling neither extremely angry nor madly in love, take at least twenty minutes to write down everything you know to be true about your partner. Put aside, for the moment, what you *feel* about him and write all the facts you've collected, observed and inferred—everything from "I know that he was born in Minneapolis and has two brothers and a sister" to "I know that when things are not going well at his job, he gets very snappy and quiet around me." Let yourself be surprised by how much you know—in other words, let one "knowing" touch off other "knowings" that you didn't realize you knew.

After finishing this list, take a really good look at it. First, are there some simple, normal facts that you don't know about him, that you should know after however long you've been together? Are there things you've written that are obvious red flags, such as "I know his drinking is a problem" or "I know that he always has to be the center of attention"? When you take in the whole list, do you like and *admire* the person you've just described? Most importantly (and this will be more accurate if you do this innercize after the first thrill of love has worn off), do you *want* to know more about this person? Is he becoming more interesting to you, the more you know him, or less? Do you think you'll find him interesting five, ten, twenty-five years from now?

Knowing is a critically important self-protective pathway for women in love. Romantic love can feel absolutely euphoric, but unfortunately, it can also very well be blind. Just because you have given your heart to your partner does not mean that he has done so as well, no matter what he tells you, because it's not hard at all to say the right words, or to mean them in the moment but not *really* mean them.

Speaking of words, it's a shame that English doesn't have two totally separate words to distinguish between "love" that has nothing to do with reality and "love" that is reality-based. If it did, it would be much easier to enjoy each separately for what they are, and not get the two confused!

At some point you probably want a love that's reality-based. The only way you'll find out if you have that is to use your knowing. Optimally, your partner will simultaneously be doing this same type of investigation himself, but if he doesn't, *you have to.* "We love each other, it'll work out" is putting the relationship ahead of yourself.

True knowing is not just protective. It's at the heart of abiding love. Knowing gets below images to the person underneath. If you're like most women, you have an image of the kind of man you like, or are attracted to, but when you get to know the person, the image matters less and less. You can discover that the person you're with is much less right for you than you thought based on his image, or, conversely, that someone who didn't fit your image is the most wonderful human being you've ever known.

We all want to be known. But since men often don't act as if they care about being known, we can forget that in order to love them, we have to know them. If you don't know him, or don't act from what you know about him, then you're actually trading love for the trappings of love—for him acting in a way that makes you "feel" loved. More accurately, you're trying to re-create the kind of love you got, or should have gotten, when you were a child. Children, after all, love their parents with an unconditionality that is heartrending—but they don't *know* them.

The deepest knowing of all is knowing who he is, not pretending he's what you want him to be—but knowing who he can be as well.

There's a way in which we all can pretend to ourselves that our partners are what we want them to be, not who they really are. This can happen to us whether we've known our partners for three weeks or thirty years. It's human. But it doesn't work. In love, you can see who someone *can* be, and call it forth from him—but only if you know and love, or at least acknowledge in a nonjudgmental way, who he is right now.

Really loving someone involves having three separate visions—three different pairs of eyes. With one pair of eyes, you see him without any of his flaws, a lot better than he really is. These are the eyes with the rose-colored glasses. You need this pair of eyes, and you always will. Reality is too harsh to look at all the time. You've got to have a *little* positive illusion in life, or it's all too much!

With the second pair of eyes, you learn to see him and get to know him exactly as he is, with all of his weaknesses and imperfections. You get to know what he's like, beyond the ways he relates to you or fulfills you. You notice his "sparks," those places and moments when he feels happiest and most fully alive. You also acknowledge the ways in which he truly is not all that you wish he could be, and you acknowledge, with compassion, the part of you that wishes that he was.

And with your third pair of eyes—your Larger Self eyes—you see *his* Larger Self, you see the goodness, even the greatness that is within the flawed man before you. You see what his deepest yearnings are. You see the potential of who he can be for *him*self (not what you would like him to be, for *you*rself). Simply by seeing that, and *holding* that inside you, you draw it forth. With that knowledge of him, you can tell him when what he's doing is not in keeping with who he is deep down—not for your sake, but for his own. And of course, when he chooses to align himself with the greater nature of his being, that benefits both of you.

In love, all three of these visions, especially the second and third, co-exist at once. You enjoy the first, and you hold the second and third as true, even though on a logical level there are places where they contradict one another. This kind of knowing is one of the most wonderful gifts a true lover gives her or his beloved, and it's the effort of a lifetime. But if you don't make that effort for your partner, how can you expect him to make the effort to know you?

There is a beautiful scene near the end of a great little movie called *Green Card*. In it, a New York society gardener enters into a marriage of convenience with a French musician; she wants a beautiful apartment with a greenhouse that the landlord will only rent to a married couple, and he needs a green card to stay in the United States. Everything is fine until the INS, having become aware that phony paper marriages were occurring, sends them a letter stating that they will be interviewed separately about their partners. They have only a few days to learn the minute details of each other's lives in order to convince INS interrogators that their marriage is genuine. In the course of telling each other and quizzing one another about their life stories, they fall in love.

Near the end of the movie, as we watch the woman tell her female interviewer everything she knows about the musician, we can see in her face and hear in her voice all the admiration, understanding and love she's grown to feel for him. We, the audience, get the point—these two know and love one another more than some people who've been married twenty years.

Miss Clavel Turned On the Light . . .

And said, "Something is not right!"
—Ludwig Bemelmans, *Madeline*

We've talked about the heights of love—now let's return, reluctantly, to some of the difficulties. Even in good relationships where there is a genuine loving bond, flawed and imperfect human beings have a tendency to make a mess of things. And sometimes, unfortunately, sensitive and intelligent women can give their hearts to the wrong person, not seeing the dangers, and having once done so, lose the perspective they need to see their way out. Let's look at a few ways to avoid, or at least identify as quickly as possible, these hazards.

Sensing, like knowing, is a powerfully self-protective faculty. Your inner senses come from your instinctual self, the part of you that operates below all the words and deceptions of the mind. It's not distracted by thoughts like "I need him" or "he needs me" or "he's so good to me" or "we're so good together." It just senses what it senses, and if it senses danger or falseness, it registers it. In his book *The Gift of Fear*, Gavin de Becker, an international security expert, writes of this innate faculty, which he refers to as intuition:

> Trust that what causes alarm probably should, because when it comes to danger, intuition is always right in at least two important ways: (1) It is always in response to something, (2) It always has your best interest at heart . . . [B]ut our interpretation of intuition is

not always right. Clearly, not everything we predict will come to pass, but since intuition is always in response to something, rather than making a fast effort to explain it away or deny the possible hazard, we are wiser (and more true to nature) if we make an effort to identify the hazard, if it exists.

If you sense something wrong in your relationship, the first step would be to acknowledge to yourself that "something doesn't *feel* right." You needn't know yet what that "something" is, but you know it's *something*. At some point, when you're clear that this is no passing feeling, you will probably need to talk to your partner about it.

Rather than asking him or accusing him, calmly tell him what you sense, as in, "I sense that you're not telling me the whole truth" or even, "I sense you're having an affair." Then listen, very carefully, to his answers. Let your inner senses tell you whether he is telling you the truth now, or if he is still lying or concealing. Notice if he tries to sidetrack the conversation to avoid dealing with your question, and bring him back to it, until you feel fully satisfied and "right" inside. And finally, notice if your senses tell you whether there is any hope he will be truthful to you from now on.

To listen to that little sense of "off-kilter" inside is to step into the unknown. It can feel easier in the short run to accept things as they seem, to override what you sense and hope that time will take care of everything.

That's what Amanda did before she found herself in the ultimate soap-opera situation—her husband in bed, in her own house, with one of her best friends. "What gets me is that I sensed that something was going on, but I couldn't believe that they would do that to me," she said. Afterwards, she said, she "couldn't believe" that she let it happen.

Her choice of words is interesting. If you find yourself saying, "I can't believe" something, *notice* what you've just said. You didn't say you *don't* believe it, did you? You said you *can't* believe it. So maybe you can ask yourself, "*Why* can't I believe it?"

See if you can allow yourself to explore that question. What will happen, and what may you have to give up, if you let yourself believe what your inner self may already have decided is true?

The irony is that most women are extremely good at sensing. They can sense when their mother's feeling lonely. They can sense all the subtle and intricate social nuances involved in creating and hosting a successful dinner party. The reason they don't listen to their senses in relationships is usually because they know it will cause conflict, and they're afraid of loss. They may question whether they should bring up what they sense because they don't know it for certain. But you don't have to fall into the trap of waiting until after the fact to trust what you sense. Sensing can be an early warning device—kind of like a mammogram—a picture of something wrong long before it gets out of control.

Enid and her husband had just gone through a rocky patch in their marriage. She was aware that he had a woman friend at work with whom he ate lunch and talked, and she believed him completely when he said it was platonic. But when she met Vicky and talked to her one day at her husband's suggestion, she sensed something.

"That night I told him, 'I believe you that you're not having an affair, and I think it's good you can talk to someone, but you're going to Vicky with too many things about us that you then don't think you have to tell me about. You've got to stop. Otherwise we're going to get in trouble again.'"

Feelings, the next pathway, of course, are central to relationships, and for the most part you can trust them. Yet obviously, there are times when they can lead you completely astray. Unfortunately, the spell of love can feel so good that a few euphoric days can keep a bad relationship going for months. This is because the *feeling of love* is easily mistaken for the *feeling and reality of having a love relationship*. But the two are actually separate feelings. This is why the intensity of how good someone can make you feel, by itself, makes for such a poor barometer for whether you are in a good long-term relationship or not.

So here are some questions to ask yourself: "Does my partner make me feel wonderful one day and terrible the next? Does he make me feel wonderful if I act one way and awful if I act another?"

Or, perhaps most commonly, did he used to make you feel wonderful, but now he doesn't? As Fran, fifty-two and divorced, sadly put it about the man she had dated for the past six months, "He made me feel like I was eighteen years old again. Now he makes me feel like an old hag."

The temptation is to believe that something you did caused this to happen, and that you can now do something to bring the good times back. Unfortunately, that's rarely the case.

If you answer yes to any one of the above feeling questions, take it as an indication that you need to think seriously about disconnecting. A relationship that ceases to bring pleasure and good feeling, or that constantly bounces between pleasure and intense pain, is not a love relationship, because it's not a *loving* relationship, no matter how intense the pleasurable moments were or even still are.

Risking It All

Sometimes you simply have to risk the relationship to keep yourself. That is what Simone ended up doing. Simone had given up much of her own development, and even her own self, in her relationship with Phil. That began to change the day she learned about an opening for a part-time grants consultant, twenty-five hours a week. She saw it as a chance to get out from under her tyrannical boss and have some time to rethink her career. She knew that although it would be a stretch, they could afford the loss in her income now that Phil's business was well established. He, however, was adamantly against it.

That did it. Though she didn't apply for the job, a few days later they fought for four excruciating hours about everything. "You honestly don't think what I do with my life is as important as what you do," she told him at one point. It was an agonizing, inconclusive fight, and it had to happen. It exposed the illusion she had built her life around. "I thought I was doing the right thing," she said. "I thought that if I unconditionally supported him in his career, he would automatically support me. But that's not what happened."

A week later, she went apartment-hunting, found one, and told him she was leaving. "I'm unhappy," she told him. "I don't blame you. I'm just unhappy with the way my life is going. I need it to be different."

At first he accepted her decision. But before she could pack her belongings, he told her he didn't want her to go. "I still love you," he said. "I still want to be with you. I want to work it out."

She didn't move out. Little by little, they had the discussions they should have had all along, about her goals and what *she* wanted from life. "It's odd to realize how much I spoiled him," she reflected later. "I made all these decisions because I loved him, and then I ended up hating him. And he had absolutely no idea."

She also began, for the first time, to question his business purchases, not automatically agreeing with them out of gratitude that he consulted her at all. He was surprised and angry at first, but he listened. And they started going out and having fun again.

Over time, the changes held. "He's a totally different guy," she told me four months later. "He supports my career search completely. I don't give in to him the way I used to, yet we've both gotten better at listening to what the other has to say.

"But the craziest thing is, he doesn't think he's changed at all. He says I'm the one who changed."

I've seen this happen with other couples. I'm speaking here of normal men, not the ones who are abusive and pathologically controlling, but when a woman decides finally that she values herself so much that she is willing to question whether her relationship has a future, it's not uncommon for a man to suddenly "remember" that their relationship is worth making an effort to keep, and worth making concessions for. Until then it had been too easy for him to shrug off his partner's complaints.

Letting Go

There is no decision more critical to a woman's life than whom to commit her heart to. Nothing, except having a child, affects the course of her life more profoundly. Especially in your twenties, but at any time in your life, there are three questions to answer: "Who am I?" "What is my journey in life?" And "Who's going with me on my journey?" Hold out for the highest, best answers to these questions. If a relationship makes you feel bad about yourself, if it makes you settle for less than someone who honors you in every sense of the word, then it's time to consider using all the powers of your inner self to begin letting go.

Cara had one of those blazing romances that for no apparent reason turn into "trying-to-make-it-work" relationships. She'd been trying to make it work, she calculated, for eleven months before the evening she called it quits.

> I had just gotten this huge promotion and I wanted to celebrate with him. So we went out to dinner, but he just wasn't going to get excited about it with me. I knew he *could*, since he used to be more supportive of me, but that was no more. It hit me in a moment of crystal clarity that I didn't want to live the rest of my life working so hard to barely get little bits and pieces of what I need. After dinner, I said to him, "You know what, Stan? Let's just be friends."

One of the most common, and painful, kinds of relationship that is detrimental to your inner voice is one where your partner refuses to fully commit his heart, even after years of you being together. At a certain point, a relationship that is fully loving *must* be committed. For love to grow and flourish, the exit door has to close. Commitment is a decision and an intention. At some point a person has to decide that the one he loves is the one and only person for him. A relationship can't grow, nor can someone grow within a relationship, if he or she is holding onto the thought that somewhere out there, there may be someone better.

Being committed to a man who won't commit his heart to you is like smoking a pack or two of cigarettes a day. Each day it goes on, it's hurting your insides a little bit more. What keeps it going is the fact that *your* heart *has indeed committed*. Commitment aligns your feelings and thoughts, so naturally your thoughts tell you that nobody out there could be better for you. Your energy is going into changing his mind, not finding someone else. The longer the relationship goes on, the stronger you will think and feel that nobody else is out there for you.

There is a two-step process to dealing with men in a long-term relationship who won't commit. The first step is to help him talk about why he feels noncommittal, and to listen to those feelings nonjudgmentally. If he has feelings that he thinks you don't want to hear, and therefore he doesn't express them, naturally they will get stronger. The same thing would happen to you if he denied feelings of yours. If you listen, however, and attempt to understand how he feels, without judging, correcting or trying to argue his feelings away (no matter how much you may disagree with them), he may discover, to his own great surprise, that his feelings have changed.

This can only work if he is honestly willing to sense into what is getting in the way of making a commitment, and to talk about it, and if your relationship has enough trust that he feels free to say out loud what is really going on, messy and hurtful though it may sound at first. If you don't feel you can handle that role dispassionately, or if he doesn't think you can, then seek the help of a skilled therapist who can help him clarify what he feels.

But if he's not willing to get help to clarify his feelings, and he continues to make no effort to make a decision, the next step is: *good-bye*. Quite simply, as long as you see him, he doesn't *have* to make a decision. He doesn't have to confront himself. It could go on this way forever, or until he finds someone else. This decision, by the way, is not a decision about a ring or a ceremony. It's a decision of the heart. He can be married to you and still refuse to commit himself, and the problem, and its solution, are still the same.

Women can find themselves in relationships or marriages lasting years or even decades that are tremendously detrimental to them. As one client, a banker in her forties married to an alcoholic, asked me, "How did I get this way? I'm an independent professional woman. How did I let my life end up like this?"

"It happened little by little," I told her. "If someone approached you and said, 'sign your life over to me' in one big chunk, you'd never do it. But because it happened bit by bit, it was easy not to notice what was happening.

"You invested in him, and in your relationship with him," I added. "And the more you invested, the harder it became to walk away from that investment, and admit that it wasn't going to pay off."

The key to saying good-bye to a harmful relationship is to accept, even on faith, that there is something better that is meant for you in your life than to give your love in exchange for the attentions of someone who hurts you or takes too much from you or refuses to commit his heart to you. When such a relationship fails, it doesn't mean that *you* have failed, or even that you did anything wrong for staying in the relationship as long as you did. The power of your love was never in your partner. It is in you, in your ability to give and receive love, and it always has been. Breaking away from a harmful relationship is an act of enormous courage. It takes courage to believe in better possibilities for yourself after being invalidated for so long. When you do feel happy again—whether through a relationship or not—it will feel that much sweeter.

Back in Chapter Three, I spoke of Sally, who was married to a bank president who emotionally abused her. It took her nine months, but she decided there was no way she could ever feel happy or safe with him, and left him. Six months later, she reported:

> All I know is I feel better and better. I never felt like myself. I was always worrying if he was mad about something. Now I feel balanced. And I guess I've learned. I'm not even attracted anymore to those big, gregarious, I-know-you-want-me kind of guys. I go for the nice ones now.

At first, losing that connection will most likely feel like it leaves a terribly painful void in your life. But nature abhors a vacuum. If you are committed to feeling it, and working through it, and seeking the support you need to grow through it rather than give up on yourself, there is a very great likelihood that in the end you'll be happier and have more good feeling in your life than you did before, whether you have a new partner or not.

I believe that when a woman says "I deserve more" to a man, and by extension to the Universe, and *commits herself to her self*, the Universe wakes up and pays attention.

Sometimes the man does, too.

Virginia, a thirty-nine-year-old sales representative and a single mother of a twelve-year-old daughter, had been with Greg, who wouldn't commit, for three years before telling him good-bye.

> We broke up the day after Valentine's Day. In my mind, it was a permanent breakup. I started to date a few men. I didn't sit around hoping he would call.
>
> On Easter morning I received an e-mail from Greg saying he absolutely adored me and was totally miserable without me. I was

hesitant, but I talked with him over the phone and then I agreed to meet him. We got back together.

Our relationship has never been better. His entire attitude and behavior have changed. He appreciates what we have together now, and he's fully committed to me. I'm different, too, now that I feel secure in his love. No date's set yet, but we're planning to get married next spring.

CHAPTER TEN

Deepening the Connection:
Living from Your Inner Voice in Relationships

"I can't stand it anymore!"

Trudy, a thirty-six-year-old physical therapist with three children in grade school, returned to her profession when her youngest entered first grade. Before she returned, she and her husband, Scott—an engineer—had discussed the changes it would make in their home life, and he seemed to be agreeable. But now, more than a year later, he still wasn't doing anywhere near his fair share of taking care of the children on weekday evenings. Whether it was dinner, homework help, or bedtime, most evenings he would "zone out" in front of the TV and pretend it wasn't happening. Trudy had resigned herself to his lack of involvement when she was a full-time mom, but now that she had a full-time job again, it was intolerable.

She had discussed it calmly with him a few times; she had screamed her head off at him as well. She tried to just accept it, but the only way she could do that was to think of Scott as some kind of half-adult or emotional cripple. She tried to understand him, since his father had done very little to take care of Scott or his siblings, and once talked to Scott about it from that angle. Scott agreed that made a lot of sense. But nothing she did made his behavior change for more than a few days.

"I never thought he would act like this," she said. "And I never planned to spend my entire life without a career. I told Scott a long time ago that I would go back to work as soon as all the kids were in school. And we could manage it fine, if only Scott would pitch in!

"It's not like he doesn't know what to do. He's a good father—on the weekends! Sure, he's tired after a long day of work, but so am I! I am very close to the end of my rope. One of these days, really soon, I'm going to snap. But what am I going to do—throw him out and tell him not to come back? How do I get through to him?"

Validation and the Gender Gap

> *I just want him to acknowledge my accomplishments. I could break*
> *my arm constantly patting myself on the back!*
> —Sheila, forty-one

Even in good relationships, patterns often get set that make a woman feel trapped, unable to feel that she's being her true self. Usually, these impasses involve situations where a woman feels that she can't influence her husband's feelings or actions. Indeed, psychologist and marital researcher John Gottman found that one of the strongest predictors of future divorce is the degree to which a woman feels powerless to influence her husband.

Besides influencing them, women want to be *heard* by their husbands and have their feelings validated and understood by them. People fight about issues, such as children or money, but what really hurts and drives people apart aren't the issues themselves, it's the feeling of not being cared about. For most women, it's expressed as, "Why can't he hear me? Why doesn't he listen? Why doesn't he care how I feel?"

It almost seems like some kind of tragic design flaw in the master plan. Why are so many women imbued with this desire for emotional validation from their husbands when so many men are constitutionally deficient in their ability to give it?

Not all, but most women are accustomed to the idea that they can share what they feel, get some kind of response that shows the other person heard them and hear what the other person feels in return. This, after all, is what women began doing with their girlfriends starting in grade school. This, to most women, seems to be what relationship and intimacy are all about.

Most men do at least a little bit of this kind of sharing during the courtship stage. But then many of them seem to stop. Women are all ready, especially after marriage, to go deeper, to get closer, to share more, and are surprised to find that that's not what their husbands had in mind at all. He sees the relationship as a given. He's not aware of whether he feels "closer" to his wife or further away, and because of that, he has no body-sense of what can cause her to feel closer to or further away from him.

Picture that for a moment. Your husband, if he is like most men, started out having no internal reference point for sensing the closeness of your relationship or what does or doesn't foster it. Years of being with you has probably led him to know to some degree what works and what doesn't, but only because you've told him. The sensory mechanisms, the acute sense-ability that tells you the emotional status of your important relationships (most of which are with other women) is only a very low whisper in his mind, if it is there at all.

Nor does he naturally concentrate his energy on the state of your relationship. Chances are, soon after you and he became fully "coupled," he stopped thinking of you and your relationship as his main focus, and began to focus most of his mental and emotional energy on the issue of his work and career.

Neither sex has a monopoly on empathy. The active process of stepping out of our own needs and feelings to become aware of the perspective, needs and feelings of another *without negating our own* is one of the most complex emotional tasks there is. In the beginning, however, most men and women in love do look to extend themselves to understand their beloved and meet their needs.

In many marriages one or both partners can't do this for the other adequately enough to establish a functioning bond. They fail to make the leap into mutuality enough, so the marriage is likely either to break up or to be very unhappy unless they get some help and commit to growing together. But more often, people reach a certain functioning level of understanding and caring for each other, a way of being that works to some degree, and then go no further.

Internalizing the Split

What I find with women who are distressed in their relationships is this: At some point in their relationship, a woman wants from her husband a validation, an affirmation, a connection in some area of her life that says to her *I see you, I hear you, I understand how you feel, I value you for who you are,* but it doesn't come. This becomes a hurt, a visceral feeling of pain inside her. She tries again to reach out for this understanding, and it still isn't met. Many things then happen. That bruise sits there between them. She feels inauthentic. The same process that happened to her in childhood happens again: She feels that she has to invalidate a part of herself in order to have connection and be loved. At the same time she's angry, seeing her husband as deliberately invalidating her, and also giving him the power to invalidate her.

The part of you that feels negated wants only to express itself and to tell your partner honestly, exactly, how it feels. It hates being silenced. It won't be dominated or held down. It's as if within women today there is an avenging angel, a visceral *No!* to the kind of silencing that women were forced to accept for so long.

Yet there is also the part of you that yearns for connection. Some women listen only to the part that wants connection. Others listen almost exclusively to the part that feels negated; the only time they feel themselves at all in their relationships is when they're angry. More common is when the two parts are at war with each other. This can create in women what I call a hit-and-run pattern of communicating to their spouses. That is when most of the time you go along, acting nice and taking care of him and the relationship, ignoring what is bothering you, and then periodically you blow up, telling him how mad and hurt you feel, in a very unmoderated way.

This blow-up may feel very satisfying and liberating and can sometimes lead to changes. But more frequently it ends up having no impact at all. Your husband gets angry and then shrugs off your complaint, frequently by focusing on the suddenness and intensity of your fury as a reason to say that he doesn't have to listen to you, that you shouldn't attack him that way, even that you're just being "crazy" (or, worse yet, "hormonal"). Meanwhile, you wind up not only feeling invalidated all over again, but "bad," and "sorry" that you've done something to break the connection; so you drop the issue and resume the status quo. You don't get the change you want, and you don't get closer.

The ABCs of Marriage

People have emotional needs all across the lifespan. They come to marriage looking to get many of those needs fulfilled—needs for love, comfort, security and closeness—and at the same time, if they are psychologically mature enough, to transcend those needs in the act of loving and understanding their spouse, and later, if they choose to have them, their children. It's not reasonable or real to think you shouldn't need or expect things from your partner. Everyone has to figure out what they truly need from their partner and how to fulfill it.

Emotional needs are vulnerable because they bring up the deepest fears people have—fears of being rejected and abandoned, and fears of being swallowed and engulfed, of not being allowed to be independent or to be who we are. We all come to marriage filled with memories, conscious and unconscious, of what happened when we went to our parents for what we needed or wanted as children.

The intimacy of marriage is a hothouse for all of these feelings and fears of dependency in both partners. When your partner doesn't respond as you hoped—or sometimes if he *does* respond as you hoped—not only do these feelings get triggered, but all of the defenses you have against these feelings get triggered as well, because your defenses want to protect you from all of this. They tell you you shouldn't have to feel all of this fear or pain, anger or sadness.

If you can apply the ABCs of Acknowledging, Being With and Compassion to both your own and your partner's feelings, you have a very different basis for your marriage. Instead of saying *I shouldn't feel this way!* or *You shouldn't feel this way!* you're able to step back and acknowledge all of the hurt and angry feelings that are there. Then you can allow those feelings in yourself and your partner, spend some time being with them and keeping them company, and they become less of a problem.

There's something inside us all that makes us feel as if listening to someone else's need or opinion, if it conflicts with our own, negates what we need or feel. But in the same way that you can listen to a part of yourself without agreeing with it, you can listen to your partner, or indeed anyone, with compassion *without* giving up your own position. You gain both closeness and true power by acknowledging what someone else thinks and feels.

An attitude of compassion to yourself and your partner, and acceptance of human frailties and foibles, is crucial to a marriage that allows both your inner self and his to emerge. People frequently talk to their spouses and children in the same way they talk to themselves. When you begin to let go of trying to improve yourself, and instead listen to your inner self with compassion, you can start to extend this new attitude to your family. Listening to their needs and feelings, and helping your spouse and your children feel heard, takes the heat out of arguments and changes things for the better far more effectively than trying to make things "right." All by itself, this creates an atmosphere more conducive for everyone's inner voice to start growing, with far less stress and friction.

No one can make you feel hurt or angry more deeply than the one you love with all of your heart. Sometimes the hurt and anger comes from something he's done, unwittingly or not. Sometimes it comes from your own deepest wounds. Probably most of the time it's a combination of the two. If you spend time with your own feelings first, welcoming them and listening to them, you can discern how much of what you feel is directly related to what your spouse has done and how much has more to do with your own feelings and history. Then you can talk to your partner from a place of clarity and without blame.

Elaine, a substance abuse counselor, told me what happened when her husband of twelve years, Alex, called her with the news that he'd been offered a position heading the pediatric cardiology department in a hospital, which would entail moving to Connecticut. "I know it means leaving our home, so I told them I have to think about it," he told Elaine.

It was a career-capping move. There was no way I could tell him not to take it. But I was furious. White-hot with rage. I felt betrayed. Abandoned. I stomped around the neighborhood in ninety-degree heat and humidity like a madwoman. *Damn* his ambition! He didn't talk to me about it! He didn't tell me this could happen! How dare he yank the whole family up to Connecticut! I hate Connecticut! Hate, hate, hate, hate it!

But at the same time I thought, *this is way too much.* I knew his job was precarious and he had to move on. I knew that relocating was a possibility, we had even talked about it already with our kids. I didn't hate Connecticut. What was I feeling? Envious, some. He was more successful at his career than I'd ever be at mine. Jealous, yeah—he loved his work as much as he loved me, maybe more.

Fear. That was it. I was boring, dull, mediocre. One day he'd figure out he didn't need me and he'd leave me.

We toasted over a $125 bottle of champagne the next evening.

Contending with Conflict

Conflict, in marriage, can be a very intimate act. It shows both a caring for yourself and a desire for another human being to be connected with who you really are. When conflict brings you both fully in the same room with each other, with neither one of you giving up something vital to yourselves, the relationship gets stronger. When it doesn't, the relationship gets weaker.

This may sound totally counterintuitive, but one of the major reasons marital conflicts get out of control is because spouses are afraid of each other's feelings. It may be hard to believe, but men are actually scared to death of women's feelings. They're completely undone by them. "For many men, Hell seems to have no fury like a woman who is even slightly disgruntled," wrote psychiatrist Frank Pittman in his book *Man Enough: Fathers, Sons and the Search for Masculinity.* "While a woman's anger is as terrifying to a man as the wrath of an angry god, we don't hear what a woman says when she's angry; we only hear that she is angry and we strap ourselves in, turn off our receivers, and wait in terror for the storm to pass."

Men have different tactics for dealing with their overblown fear of women's criticism. One man might get defensive, angry and hurtful, especially if he knows it will make his wife give up. Another man, having learned that getting defensive doesn't stop *his* wife, but only gets her more riled up, will do something more subtle. He will say *whatever he has to* to convince her that she's been heard so that she will stop bothering him. And a third man might simply be silent.

Women, for their part, are often just as fearful of their husband's strong feelings. They may feel overpowered by the sheer force of their husband's size, voice, needs and desires. As one woman said of her husband, "He's such a big guy! I feel like he fills up the room. When he wants something badly enough, I feel like I get washed out to sea." She realized that when she had that feeling, she had to deliberately walk out of the room and spend a little time on her own to figure out what she felt, before she went back to talk to him about it.

Women are especially afraid of men's anger and aggressive impulses. There also may be one part of you that wishes to see his vulnerable side, yet another part that is afraid of seeing him feel confused, lost or unhappy, without his usual mask of competence and control.

So what can you do? If either or both of your Attackers and Defenders get in control, very little can be learned. The greatest power you have in a conflict is to stay aware of yourself. Where are *you* in this conflict? Are you in your body? Are you saying what you feel?

Most of all, are you moving toward him or further away with your feelings? This is something you sense in your body. You can be shouting at him and still be moving toward him. When you're moving toward your partner, you feel open, honest, and full of heart. You're keeping in mind that you love him and want to be close to him, and want to resolve the conflict so that you can be closer again. When you're moving further away you feel tight, lonely and combative, you're thinking mostly about what's wrong with him, and you may feel hijacked by your pride. Usually, moving toward your partner with your feelings in an argument feels better, more relaxed and congruent, than distancing yourself, but you may not realize that until you move past your own fears of getting hurt and try it.

What if you've been trying to talk to him and move closer to him, and he deliberately says something to push you away and shut you up? *Don't let him call the shots.* Say, "What you just said makes me want to pull away and give up, but I don't want to do that anymore." By naming his move, it loses its power. You can stay open and keep moving toward what you want.

Yet moving toward also means being aware of the effect your words and feelings are having on your partner. If what you're saying or how you're saying it is making you feel closer to him but is making him feel further away from you, then that needs to be addressed. If your own emotional level is triggering your spouse to where he is not hearing you, then see if you can *calm down, but not back down.* That is, lower the volume of your emotional intensity but don't let go of your stance.

The key to all of this is to think of the two of you as being on the same side. If you consistently feel that you're not on the same side anymore, that he's no longer your friend and you can't talk about issues that are crucial to you, then you may want to consider getting professional help to connect honestly with each other again.

On a day-to-day level, I've noticed that just as men overreact to women's anger, many women tend to overperceive men's defensive reactions and interpret them as more hostile than they really are. When men feel threatened, they get disagreeable. They get "grumpy." I'm not talking here about abusive behavior meant to bully or batter another, emotionally or physically. I'm talking about what Buddhists refer to as "unskilled reactive behavior."

Nobody likes getting snapped at or barked at. It hurts and can even be a little scary. And grumpiness is unpleasant and off-putting. But if you don't get derailed by this, if you don't pull back from it or act like you're scared or appalled by it, it can be a great opportunity to connect on a deeper level with your partner. It helps to keep in mind that most likely there's something he's afraid of or needs, but is not consciously aware of, or has difficulty asking for.

Courtney, a thirty-three-year-old mother of a four-year-old boy, discovered this with her husband Sean. "He had been moody and a little rough with Brandon for a few days," she reported. "He had his 'force-field' around him, you know? 'Stay away!' "

She asked him if it was about her, and he told her no, which isn't surprising. If men are upset, it's more likely to be about their work than their relationship, which most women can't help but find a little disappointing. In the past, she had let him deal with his work problems alone, but this time she didn't.

"It's nothing I can't handle. We don't have to talk about it."

"Yes, you do have to talk about it. I'm affected by how upset you are. How do I know what's upsetting you if you don't tell me?"

"I don't want to burden you with my work problems."

"You moping and walking around in a huff all evening burdens me. Why don't you tell me what the problems are? Maybe if you bounce them off me, I can help."

In fact, Courtney, who had left a middle-management position to stay home with their son, had a lot of insight into the political problems Sean was dealing with at work. This opened up a new dimension in their relationship, where she helped him be more effective in his career, and he valued her advice and political mentorship.

What Do Women Want?

That was Freud's famous question. Is it really that hard to answer? I don't think so.

What do *you* want? Allow me to take a guess at a few things. First and foremost, you want to be close to your partner. You want to connect with him, and to have him connect with you. After that, you want your partner to be aware of you as a person, to take your thoughts and ideas as seriously as he takes his own, to treat your feelings as if they matter, and to treat your relationship as one of the highest priorities in his life. You want him to be equal partners with you in the difficult business of life, and to join with you to confront the challenges as they present themselves. You want him to be an involved and caring father who is empathic to his children.

You want him to be tender. You want him to be attuned to you when you make love, and honor your needs and desires even when they conflict with his own. You probably want him to remember special occasions and, every once in a while, to treat you in a special way, with a little romance, and to compliment you on how you look when you get all dressed up for him. You also probably want a good deal of touch that is not intended to be a prelude to sex, and you want him to say "I love you" with some regularity and without being prompted.

Nothing on this list, of course, is unreasonable to expect from any person of sound mind and body who claims to be the love of your life. Which is not to say that very many men are totally consistent about fulfilling every item on this list. But the effort a man would expend to become better at fulfilling this list would improve him as a lover, a man and a human being.

Aside from this list, you have your own specific wants and needs in this relationship, many of which may be variations on one of the above, that either he does or doesn't meet. When he consistently doesn't meet them, you feel a "disconnect" with him. You feel dissatisfied.

And yet, if you're like many women, wanting for yourself doesn't come easy, particularly if you perceive it to be in conflict with what someone else needs. In your gut, you feel that wants are supposed to be mutual; even the act of wanting more than he's willing or able to give feels like a breach in the relationship. So your first reaction to being dissatisfied is to take one of two courses of action: Either to act like it's fine, denying or minimizing your feelings of hurt or dissatisfaction to him and even more to yourself; or to get angry and accuse him of not *wanting* to give you what you want or need, while as much as possible not saying that you want or need it. Instead of saying, "I want to go out with you more often," you say, "You never go out with me anymore!" or "If you loved me, you would take me out on a date once in a while!"

Sometimes the issue of a denied want is not as deep as it seems. There are times when a man doesn't respond to his wife's request because he doesn't take it in that it matters to her.

This may sound unbelievable to you, especially when you're pretty sure you've asked him fifteen times. It's understandable if you believe that he's just being lazy, selfish and inconsiderate. That may even be true.

But men don't pay attention to requests the way women do, nor do they have antennae out to gauge other people's needs and respond to them. Men are not necessarily more selfish than women, but most of them truly are more self-centered. By temperament, training, or both, they simply are. So if in his own body it doesn't feel important to him, he may conclude that it can't really be that important to you. He's not conscious that he's thinking this, however, so he doesn't tell you. Besides, women often say so many things to men that men don't keep it straight. They don't know what's important and what isn't.

This is when you basically have to pull out the proverbial two-by-four. "*This* request is important to me, Bill. It really, really, really is. Do you believe me? Because I don't want you to tell me later that you didn't know." You might then tell him why it's important, and it's best if you can relate it to something analogous for him. But keep your message very focused on how *this is important*. Long-windedness will work against you. Optimally you can get the lightbulb to go off in his head, but if you can just get him to agree that he knows it's important to you, that works too.

However, there are more complicated issues that don't get resolved by the two-by-four method. This leads to the question of *why* you may find yourself angrily and bitterly saying things like, "You never take me out anymore," instead of saying what you want.

The reason is that feeling and expressing your desire directly to your spouse feels unsafe to you. It could be because it wasn't easy for you to get your emotional needs met as a child. Or, very likely, it's because you've repeatedly tried to express this need before to your partner and it has fallen on deaf ears. Of course, it could be a combination of both. But you've come to the point where it feels to you as if any serious attempt to get this desire met would only lead to a devastating "take-it-or-leave-it" showdown.

So you accuse and complain and get angry, not to get what you want anymore, but as a way of showing your partner how upset you are. As one of my clients put it, "I think the only time I feel safe to want from him is when I tell myself ahead of time, and I tell my husband, that I don't expect to get it."

But what happens when you use this approach? If you're lucky, and the two of you have a relationship built on trust and empathy, your partner can look past your accusations to address the feelings, wants and needs beneath. "I'm sorry we haven't gone on any dates lately," he might say. "Why don't we do something really special this Saturday night and go to a show? I'll call the sitter."

That, of course, is what you are really seeking. Your goal, in your heart of hearts, isn't to complain, or to fight or push him away. You just want him to acknowledge and accept your feeling that something is amiss, not as good as it could be, and to do something about it. In other words, you want validation for how you feel, and once you have that, you want to get close again.

Indeed, most likely if all he did was acknowledge and empathize with how you felt, you'd feel better. That's much more important to you than the date itself.

Unfortunately, in most relationships, what I just described—the fulfillment of your desire—isn't going to happen this way. Because you've probably just expressed in the strongest possible way how he's not meeting your needs. You've also implicitly accused him of doing it on purpose because he doesn't really care for you or about you, and you practically told him that you don't expect he will come through this time, either.

The Power of Positive Wanting

Ask for what you want. Let us be clear on this one: Subtle hints do not work! Strong hints do not work! Obvious hints do not work! Just say it!
—From an e-mail in circulation of men's advice to women

Accusations are very powerful. If you say them with a lot of strong emotion, they become even more powerful. Presented with a hopeless picture of how much he doesn't meet your needs, your partner—who is already, for some reason, not coming through for you—will give up even more, not out of anger or spite, but out of hopelessly accepting the judgments you have apparently made about his nature. *I never give her any presents? Okay, I never give her presents. I'm a selfish, inconsiderate and thoughtless person? I guess that's what I am.*

So how do you ask for what you want effectively, without sounding like a harpy? I call this the *power of positive wanting.* It's a matter of saying what you want in a way that makes it more likely that you'll get it by increasing the likelihood that he would want to give it to you.

Dr. Helene's Six Steps for Powerfully Positive Wanting

1. Tell him how what he did made you feel. However, don't say, "You hurt me!" or "I'm so hurt!" or "I'm so disappointed!" and start crying. That will only lead to a fight. Say *I'm so hurt* or *angry* or *disappointed that . . .* you were an hour late, you didn't do something special for my birthday, etc.

2. Say what you want. If you have to say what you don't want, go ahead, but be sure to follow it up with exactly what you *do* want. Figure this out and put it into words beforehand, so you can say it with conviction.

3. Express how what he did affected your connection to him. (e.g. "It made me think a lot less of you.")

4. Tell him that you don't want to feel that way.

5. Say how you *do* want to feel.

6. Convey how you *will* feel if he comes through next time.

Positive wanting works because you stay focused mostly on what you want, and even more importantly, on the *feeling* that you want with him—to feel closer. Everything you want that's sincerely from your inner self—even something seemingly frivolous like a romantic date—furthers your connection to him and your life together. So hold that intention inside you as the purpose behind what you say. You're not making this intention up; it's there already. You're just making it more explicit.

It doesn't work, however, if you are just saying the words. Strongly, even passionately invoke the feelings you're saying and express them. Just remember to talk *to* him, not *at* him, and be sure to invoke the positive feelings as strongly as the negative ones. Let him talk, listen to him, but don't let him sidetrack you with excuses or irrelevant arguments. The secret of "powerfully positive wanting" is to seek to connect with your partner—to feel yourself moving toward him, not away from him—as you say what you want and need.

Everything you want that's sincerely from your inner self—even something seemingly frivolous like a romantic date—furthers your connection to him and your life together. So hold that intention inside you as the purpose behind what you say. You're not making this intention up; it's there already. You're just making it more explicit.

Nothing can guarantee change. You can't *change* anybody. You can only motivate someone to want to make a change you'd like to see. Think about what it would take to make *you* wish to make a change you don't already want to make, and then apply that to your partner.

Consciously held positive intentions are the opposite of accusations. They create, over time, through subtle influencing, the kind of relationship, and indeed the kind of life you want. The intention of wanting closeness exerts a magnetic power. Of course your spouse could have problems, such as alcoholism, that you don't have the capacity or the responsibility to fix. But healthy men in healthy relationships naturally want their wives or girlfriends to feel close to them and feel good about them. When you tell them that it's possible and how they can make it happen, they respond—not always, but more often than not.

There is one more step. *Speak to his heart spot.* You want to speak to the part of him that you know is there that wants what you want, that wants to live from his best self, and that you know can come through the way you're asking him to. Telling him that you love him, and that this is getting in the way, can make a very powerful impact on him. And since he may not be coming through because he secretly feels incapable or incompetent, it may help him if you tell him why you believe he can.

"It's Got to Change"

I asked Mandy how her relationship was going, aside from the issue of the children.

"Pretty good," she said. "It's not perfect, but we get along pretty well. That's what's so awful about this. It's making me feel like I hate him, and I don't like that. I can't understand why he won't change or even make an effort when he knows how I feel."

I helped her to figure out exactly what she wanted (to supervise the kids cleaning the table and loading the dishwasher, to oversee their nine-year-old's homework, and to help get them off to bed most evenings). I then coached her to tell him what this was doing to her, how it was making her feel about him and how much she hated feeling that way, and to encourage him to be different.

"You can get as passionate as you want," I told her. "Just remember to move toward him with all of your feeling, and say the good things every bit as strongly as the bad."

She gathered up her courage and did it that night.

"Scott," she said. "You've got to listen to me. I can't live like this much longer. I'm too exhausted working all day long to do everything with the kids every night. It's got to change."

He protested that he had been changing, but she answered, "No, you really haven't. It's not enough. I'm killing myself. And when you don't help me, I end up resenting you. I even start to hate you. I start to think there's something wrong with you, like you're some kind of cripple or something.

"I *hate* feeling that way about you!" It was very important that she tell him this right then; otherwise he probably would have begun yelling at her. Sharing the negative feelings tells him how serious the matter is, and it's also staying true to yourself. But sharing the positive feelings, the deeper feelings you have in your heart, disarms his Attackers and Defenders, and makes it possible for him to hear you and change.

"I love you! I don't want to become one of those bitter women I see around here who stew about their husbands all the time. I love you and I want to be close to you, and I *can't* if you don't help me more with the kids!" Love, and the anger at being made to feel bitter and angry toward him, flowed through her equally. She was very passionately engaged, and she could see he was too.

She stopped and took a breath. "Do you understand what I'm saying?" He nodded. "Yeah."

She told him specifically what she needed. They went back and forth, pretty calmly, about some of the details. Then she finished with,

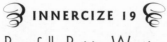

ᕽ INNERCIZE 19 ᕽ
Powerfully Positive Wanting

Take an issue where you'd like to influence a change, and write this down on paper.

The issue:

This issue is affecting me in this way in my life:

What I want, as specifically as I can make it, is this:

This issue is affecting my relationship, or my feeling about my partner, in this way:

This is the way I want to feel:

This is how I will feel about him if he makes the change I'm asking for:

This is why I believe he can do this:

"I will feel so much better about you if you do this. You can't even imagine. And I know you can do it. You are such a great dad. You're nothing like your father."

That affected him. "You really mean that?" he said.

"Yeah, I really do. You're a wonderful dad. You love them so much. You just gotta get in there and do it with me."

This worked. He changed and became fully involved with the kids in the evenings. Though she had to share with me some angry feelings (why didn't he do this before, etc.), she thanked and appreciated him for changing in the weeks ahead. And she meant it.

A long time later I asked him what made it work. "I guess I finally understood how much it was upsetting her. You might find this funny, but it just never sunk in before. And then when she said I was a great father, that I wasn't like my dad. That really got to me. I thought, okay, I'm going to do it."

Sex and the Inner Voice

> *When it comes to sex, my normal clock would run to about every nine days, and he's knocking on the door every three. I ask him, why don't you wait sometimes to when I'm really wanting it, and he says, "I can't risk that! It might fall off first!"*
> —Renata, thirty-two

For most women, sex is just one part of experiencing pleasure and expressing intimacy in marriage. Hugs, kisses, endearments, and a man showing his connection to her are frequently more important than sex itself. Most women find a man's willingness to extend himself to her very sexy, whether it's fixing something of hers that's broken or even, for many women, taking over with the children for a while. As one woman who considers herself "very sexual" told me, "emotional intimacy is still what's most important to me. Sex is just the icing on the cake."

Unfortunately, most men, at least until somewhere in their forties, tend to look at sex as the cake itself, and all other expressions of intimacy as the icing.

Of course there are many women whose feeling about sex for its own sake is every bit as robust as a man's. "I can't get enough of it!" said

Camille, a fifty-four-year-old consultant. "Through my whole marriage and my other relationships, sex has never been a problem for me.

"But it took me all the way until into my forties before I realized that I loved it," she continued. "That's the truth. Nice girls didn't feel that way, you know, when I was growing up. I honestly thought the reason I was enjoying sex so much with my ex-husband was that we were in love. Then when I was single again, it caused me some problems. Men misinterpret women who have a lot of sexual desire. But now that I'm with my partner, Mike, I'm totally free to follow my appetites. It's very refreshing."

But for many women, sex has a built-in ambivalence to it. As much as they may like or enjoy it, there still remains the ever-present possibility that it *could* feel like being invaded. What's more, in the background there's the knowledge, usually unspoken, that when your husband is making love to you, it's a little impersonal. There can be a sense of him needing to satisfy his sexual drive as much or more than expressing his love for you. This is different from the way most women experience their own feeling of making love to their husbands, which is much more personal.

That's why those other expressions of love are so important first. They require him to express *his* love for *her*, without a huge immediate payoff.

When two people first meet and are excitedly discovering the closeness they feel toward one another, both partners are passionately involved in experiencing this very intense way of feeling close. It's not that women stop feeling as much desire as that the ambivalence begins to become a factor, particularly when a man begins to take the relationship for granted, as men, to some degree, almost inevitably do.

Most men don't realize that the most important erogenous zone for a woman is her mind, and the most effective way in the world to arouse her is to make her feel, over a day or at least an evening, that she is the one woman in the world he wants to make love to. Chances are he once did this when they were dating each other and he was concentrating his attention on winning her love. Now it isn't so easy or natural for him to do.

Most of what people have learned about having better sex focuses on more effective foreplay and arousal. This assumes that a man and a woman are coming to sex from equal places, as if in the end there isn't a difference between the way she experiences sex and he does, or indeed between the way they each experience their marriage.

Many women have told me that foreplay isn't the solution it's made out to be, especially since their husbands so clearly have the goal of sex in mind when they do it that there's no sense of the moment. This is one of those little secrets women keep from their husbands, because the men are often so proud of themselves for their sensitivity in engaging in foreplay at all! As Faye, a fifty-two-year-old client of mine, said of her husband, "He doesn't see the big picture. I think he tries to figure me out like a manual—if it worked once, it will work again. I tell him, loosen up! Be in the moment! It's not a paint-by-numbers kind of thing!" But unfortunately, because of the way they're designed, that's exactly what sex for most men is.

Men's linearness, goal orientation and simple *loudness* about sex can make even a sexually positive woman begin to lose her sense of her own feeling. I wonder if women feel more sexual desire in their forties and fifties, as they often do, not just for hormonal reasons but because their husbands get less noisy about it, sometimes to the point where the women want sex more than their partners do.

Renata, the mother of a three-year-old girl, was married to Raymond, who thought of himself as a very good lover. And indeed, once she was aroused, Renata enjoyed sex with him a lot, and usually had orgasms. But it meant so much to him to have sex that over time it started to burden her.

"I wish it wasn't so tangled up in whether he feels good about himself or not," she said.

Indeed, when she caught a bad case of the flu and she couldn't make herself have sex for more than a week, he became depressed about his life. Though she was coughing and knocked out by cold medicine, she spent an hour one evening reassuring him. The next time she came to my office, she was furious. "What, I don't open my legs for a week and he goes down the tubes? Are all men like this?"

I asked her how he handled it when their daughter was born.

"That was different to him. He was all into how much it would hurt me. I think he thought he was being very manly and heroic controlling himself for three weeks. And he was very proud of being a father. But after that, we were doing it once a week, no matter how tired I was. Truth is, I didn't mind it too much. He was gentle and sweet about it, and it relaxed me."

But she was starting to mind it, especially since she was now home with little Annmarie all day and he, because of work stress, was acting more remote. He approached her every other day, and she rejected him most of the time.

"I want to do it, I really do. I don't know why I don't. He's sweeter, more open if he has sex. It lasts a couple of days. And I feel closer to him. 'Renata,' I tell myself, 'all you have to do is have sex with that guy every three days and you'd have a sweet, mushy man!' " She laughed. "But it's true! I can almost hear my mother, who I never told this to, saying, 'You've got to give men what they want, or they'll go somewhere else for it.' My girlfriends, too."

I asked her to listen to the part of her that didn't want to have sex, since it was obviously in control.

"Oh, it's very clear. It says, 'You haven't earned the right to have me like that tonight. It's such a kept, precious thing and you haven't earned it.' "

So we talked about the feeling of yielding, and being wanted for sex, and how she needed to help him understand how it felt different to her than to him. A few days later, she talked to him about it. "It's different for me than for you. When we make love, I have to take you inside me. It's not just about whether it feels good."

He was offended. "You make me sound like a rapist. Don't we always do it the way you want? First I turn up the lights. Then I turn *down* the lights. Then I open the window. Then I *shut* the window." They both laughed at his description of his efforts to do what she tells him so she can get in the mood. "I never do it a moment before you want me to."

"That's true," she conceded.

"We're married. We've done it a thousand times. I'm not some bad guy off the street, I'm your friend. Sex is for pleasure, for fun."

"Sure, you're my friend. But every time we do it, try to believe me, it's still the same for me, to open myself to you. And it's become so important, it doesn't feel like so much fun anymore."

Over time, he understood more about how it was for her. Eventually, because his pressure was making it impossible for her to know her own feelings, they made a deal: For a month he was to let *her* figure out when she wanted and how she wanted sex. He agreed to this with great trepidation, worried that she would never want him or worse, that she would become "bossy and mannish."

"See," she pointed out to him. "Deep down, you think sex is supposed to be something a man does and a woman agrees to."

In that month, she got back her desire for sex with him, and he, by necessity, learned more about how to get her to feel opened up and wanting of him before they got in bed. Both their sex life and their relationship became more equal.

Your sex life is a work in progress. It doesn't stay the same. Sometimes it's better than at other times. Sometimes it's more important to you than at other times. For some couples the sexual connection is tremendous, but for most couples it's like the rest of their relationship—sometimes special, sometimes terrible, mostly in between. In our culture, there's this constant background message, promoted by television and advertising, that the world is filled with people who are having much better sex than you are—and because of that, they're *glowing*. It's just a myth. Sex is a form of expression, but what's paramount is the emotional connection between you.

There are life-cycle issues. Motherhood, for one thing, gets in the way for many women. "I do feel more inhibited," said Celeste. "I used to be more spontaneous, more brazen. I liked being *dazzling*. It's hard to put away my mother self." Between children and the encroachment of work into people's home lives, people increasingly are having trouble relaxing enough to have sex in their own bedrooms. Some couples find it helps to arrange for a night out in a hotel. I've also heard a very good suggestion to send the children somewhere for the weekend, ignore the computers and the phones except for a prearranged "emergency" signal regarding the kids, forget all errands and chores and treat your home as if it were a weekend retreat.

Sex is something most of us have a lot of "static" about. It's like "soup": all these thoughts and feelings that we're not even conscious of, but that make sex a lot more complicated than we wish it were. Many of us have collected many negative attitudes about sex that we're barely aware of, a low rumble of outside voices. Because of that, I often suggest to clients the innercize below.

Another way to become more present in the middle of sex is to concentrate on your inner bodily senses. What does your body want, in the moment, if you get your mind out of the way? Penny, thirty-six, found that she could reclaim her sexuality, even after severe childhood sexual abuse. I vividly recall the time when she told me hopelessly that she had never wanted or enjoyed sex with her husband, and she was absolutely sure she never would. Her courage in facing her history was extraordinary, and it was followed by her equal courage in working on distinguishing the past from the present.

After going through many different stages, some in which she rejected sex outright, she was able to start freshly.

I now tune into myself when I have sex. I quietly pay attention. I ask my body, Does this feel right? If I get a no, I say stop, if I get a yes, I go with it. Then I ask again, does it feel right to keep going forward?

It's so wonderful, I'm enjoying myself so much. I used to want my husband out of my space, it was so visceral. Now I want him in my space.

Something that helped her tremendously was "skin-time." "For a couple of weeks, all I did was lie against him, body to body, skin to skin, and get into the rhythm of breathing together, and being aware, being

⧙ INNERCIZE 20 ⧙
Sex Soup

Sit down with a pen and a piece of paper, and for fifteen minutes, write down everything that goes through your mind when you think about sex—whether sex with your partner, or sex in general. When you start to run out of that, notice the felt senses that are associated with sex, and write those down as well.

present to myself," she said. "Nothing else. And then I began to feel an opening up. Now we still do it. We just breathe together. In a few minutes I feel myself relax and start to open to what my body wants."

Below is a useful innercize for any woman to do to sense into her own body's sexuality.

If you're seeking to improve your sexual relationship, go for ten-degree changes. Remember to keep an attitude of compassion for both yourself and your spouse regarding sex—and a good sense of humor. It's not easy for two people to be in the same place at the same time regarding sex, and the lifelong attempt to get in synch with one another is a triumph of faith and goodwill over logic. Considering the differences, it's a miracle men and women manage to have as good a time as they do.

Appreciation and Blessing

Of all the techniques for improving a relationship, appreciation may be the most effective. Remember: Whatever you appreciate, appreciates. It

⋺ INNERCIZE 21 ⋲
Skin Time

At a time when your husband is not feeling goal-oriented toward sex, ask him to try "skin time." Just have him hold you and be against you, skin to skin, and ask him not to do anything, but just breathe with you and feel you for a few minutes. Then, while breathing with him, let yourself sink into your body, sense what your body is feeling, and what it wants to do. Notice what happens, if you can stay with the closeness or if you start thinking about other things. Notice how it feels to you to be up against him—do you feel good, do you want more, do you want to pull away? Ask your husband, for this time, to let your body lead the way. End the innercize whenever you want, or take it wherever your body wants it to go.

gets stronger, becomes more a part of your reality. This is especially true in intimate relationships and with children. When you tell your partner that you appreciate something he's done, especially something that he doesn't do often or may not have realized you liked, something will go *Hey, that worked!* inside him. And do it more.

Even though your spouse may not see it, appreciating builds a storehouse of good feeling that helps when you want to tell him something that's bothering you. At the very least, he can't tell you that *you only tell me what you don't like. I'm not good enough for you.* Actually, he could, but you can quickly point out how it isn't true.

When you start to express to your partner what you appreciate about him, in most cases it won't be long before he starts saying more of what he appreciates about you. This begins an upward spiral in your relationship, making you both shine more.

What if you feel that the things you used to appreciate about him haven't been in evidence for years, and you wish he would do them again? Then you can still appreciate, by appreciating the things he used to do and telling him how much you'd love it if he did them once more. *"I used to love it when we took walks in the woods together. It would make me feel so good if we started doing that again."* *"I loved it when we took that week in the mountains and you relaxed and forgot about work and felt so happy. You looked so great to me. Let's do that again."* When you appreciate in this way, hold your positive intention very lightly and gently, concentrating on the joy you remember, not on the present-day lack. Sing out to him what you want.

Even though it may be hard if you've been feeling on the outs with someone you're close to, I highly recommend looking for some way to appreciate him at least once and preferably several times a day. Appreciating is like watering seeds. It doesn't usually take long to see what you've appreciated begin to sprout from the ground.

Blessing is a very special kind of appreciation—a deeper one, one that acknowledges not just one small behavior, but the core of a person. It also connotes a stronger expression of the profound goodness of the person or action being blessed, an expression that carries over time, even a lifetime. There's even the sense that the blesser is assuming the power to channel Divine energy to the one being blessed.

Blessing seems to be something people did more often in the past.

Children would hope for their parents' blessing. Now the only time someone might be personally blessed is when they hear "God bless you" after they sneeze. But it's a custom that deserves to come back in style.

You bless your spouse by identifying something close to his heart, something he values in himself or some way that he gives, and conveying to him just how *good* you feel it—and therefore he—is. After all, "And it was good," according to the Old Testament, is how God judged all creation. When you bless your partner, or your children, you profoundly impact them.

Appreciation and blessing had come up in a session with Gerri, because her husband, Bo, had been going through a very stressful period at work. "He doesn't let me in that much," she told me. "He gets very testy. We've fought more. He knows he can talk about his problems at work with me, but I think he really feels that talking about it won't make it any better, and I don't think I can change his mind." I suggested that appreciating and blessing him might help.

"I took to heart what you said about blessing," she told me the next week. "Monday morning, just before we both left for work, I said to him, 'Bo, I know we've had our fights lately, but I want to tell you that I see you go off to work every day, even though it's been hell lately, but you do it and you do it and you don't complain. And everything we

⊰ INNERCIZE 22 ⊱

Appreciating

Name three specific things you'd like more of in your relationship. Are these things your partner does, even a little bit? Is it something he used to do? Now concentrate on noticing when he does them, and appreciating him for it. If it's something he used to do, invoke as vividly as you can what he used to do that you liked so much, and appreciate it with as much gusto as you can muster. When he starts to do again what he used to do, even a little bit, notice and appreciate it. Do this consistently over time.

have, we couldn't have if it wasn't for you. I think you're a very brave man.'

"Well, he looked kinda shocked, and then he looked away. He did it so suddenly I got alarmed. 'Bo,' I said, 'What's wrong?' *'Nothing!'* he goes. 'I mean, nothing. Really. That was great. Thanks.' And he pecked me on the cheek and ran out the door. Wouldn't let me look at him.

"So I'm driving all the way to work wearing this big grin on my face, you know? Thinking, 'Men!' And when I get there, I turn on my computer and see this e-mail he sent to me. I had to show it to you."

She gave me the paper. It read:

Gerri,

I never felt good enough for my mom, and I never felt good enough for my dad. Today you made me feel good enough. Thanks, babe. Love, Bo.

In the end, it all comes full circle. The two of you ask yourselves and each other, "Do we like the 'we' we are when we're together?" And you get a "yes." In a good marriage, this "we" is a healthy living entity that grows, changes and matures. It grows from the way two people let down their guard and act upon each other like the forces of wind and water against the surface of the earth. It grows not only from the ways you fulfill each other, but from the ways you fail each other and how much truth and love, for yourself and your partner, you bring to dealing with those failures. As one woman said, "If he was exactly what I needed, what would I learn from that? I'm not here to sleep, I'm here to grow."

In a good marriage, even your battle scars make you proud; they testify to the seriousness of what you've accomplished. You know in your bones that what you've gained is far greater than what you've lost.

CHAPTER ELEVEN

Manifesting an Authentic Life

Hold fast to dreams
for if dreams die
Life is a broken-winged bird
That cannot fly
—Langston Hughes, "Hold Fast to Dreams"

"I don't know," Jana said when I asked her what she wanted. "I don't know what I want to do with my life anymore."

Jana, a thirty-year-old financial analyst, talked about how she had "fallen into" her career. "I remember in college being told, 'the world is your oyster.' What a laugh! One minute you're in college, surrounded by other students and this beautiful, intellectual, idyllic environment, and the next minute school spits you out and you're on your own. There you are—you're in the real world. Start! Go!"

After four months of looking, supporting herself with waitressing jobs, she landed a job with her present company, a huge, multinational construction and engineering firm. Through hard work she'd been promoted three times. But she felt constantly pressured to work even harder, spending many evenings and weekends at her job. What really bothered her, however, was that her work did nothing for her spirit.

She was so responsible, so determined—and felt so trapped. "When I was young, I was sure my life was going to be great. Now I wake up every morning thinking, this is it? This is my wonderful life?"

The Problem of Reality

I can handle reality in small doses, but as a lifestyle, it's much too confining.
—Lily Tomlin

Is it possible to live a life that truly reflects your inner self? When you sit down to pay your bills, and think about your job and all of the demands made on your time, it may seem impossible to live a life more in harmony with yourself. You may even feel that being realistic and adult means giving up on all of your childhood hopes for a wonderful, extraordinary life.

But reality, I've observed, is not as rock-solid as it appears. It is far more plastic and flexible. Your future is not bound by your past.

This is not to say that making changes is easy! There may be a few charmed people in the world, but from what I've seen so far, everyone's life is full of difficult and hard-to-change circumstances. But if you think back to where you were five or ten years ago, could you have predicted exactly what your life looks like now? Ten years ago, you probably faced a different set of "insurmountable" obstacles than you do today.

There is more interplay, then, between us and the world than we often recognize. "Reality" is not an unbendable set of rules and circumstances that we must mold ourselves to fit. It's just one more thing we have a *relationship* with, just as we have a relationship with different parts of ourselves and different people in our lives. It's possible, therefore, to improve our relationship with reality to make it one that includes our inner selves more.

In some mysterious way, reality responds to our thoughts, desires and strong intentions. It even responds to our imaginations. Often I've seen people's lives begin to change the moment they imagined that the changes they wanted were possible.

You don't have to be *bigger* or *braver* or *smarter* or *more organized* than you are to begin pursuing your inner visions—and you don't have to clean out your closets first! The most powerful thing you can do first is to start holding the intention—despite any and all evidence—that your inner truth can be made manifest in the world. You can begin challenging the outside voices that tell you that something you want to manifest is impossible because "that's just the way things are." You don't have to say these voices are wrong; you just have to allow that they may not necessarily be *right*. All you have to do is open the door of possibility just that little crack, and all sorts of new possibilities start slipping in.

Practically all of us would like to have more freedom, money, time or opportunity to pursue a life more true to our inner selves. Yet all of my work with women has shown me that it isn't those who *have* the most who come to live most fully from their inner voices. It is those who allow themselves to *want* the most.

VIA—Vision, Intention, Action

My goals for the future are to clean up the earth, bring world peace, and be president.
—Rachel, eight

"I forged my life when I was young," Jana continued. "I got a degree, then I got a career, then I got a boyfriend and a townhouse and a car. Isn't that what you're supposed to do?"

This is the masculine model of life. It labels as "failure" the pattern that most women's inner selves lead them toward. Most women aren't following a single trajectory. They're balancing several different paths, creating and re-creating their lives over and over again. While most men are quick to define themselves solely according to their careers, even very career-oriented women generally see work as only one part of what they do. Of course, for women with children, motherhood is a "career" in and of itself, one that almost invariably shapes whatever other career they have. And as long as the masculine model pays only lip service to the value of motherhood and child-rearing, women will pay an unfair price for being mothers, as Ann Crittenden points out in her book *The Price of Motherhood: Why the Most Important Job in the World Is Still the Least Valued.* Aside from being mothers, women are likely to consider their relationships with their partners, friends and other family members as equally important sources of self-esteem and self-definition.

Women also hunger for creativity and self-expression, either through their work or outside of it. They want to bring something into the world that is imbued with their personal mark, whether it is the design and decoration of their surroundings, a painting, a knitted sweater, a garden, a story or poem, a piece of music, a performance, a loving home, a scientific contribution, or a cause they believe in. They may also want to pursue a discipline or stretch their physical abilities, by taking yoga, perhaps, or running a marathon. These are all expressions of the inner self. Once, when Meryl Streep was asked why she acted, she answered "to lift up, to lift up, to lift up."

I asked Jana, "If you could do something different, what would it be?"

"I would sell everything, go to Europe, do odd jobs, paint people's houses, waitress, and live every day just for that day. Everything I own would be on my back. But would I really do it? No."

Sometimes you can feel that the life you truly want is diametrically opposed to the life you're living. This can make you want to dismiss your inner voice as totally impractical and unrealistic. Chances are, however, you don't really want to leave your entire life behind. But you do need to give voice to the part of you that says, "This isn't what I bargained for—or if it is, I didn't know what I was doing!"

Depending on your life, acknowledging that a big part of you feels this way can bring up a lot of sadness—and be a bit frightening. It is tempting to try to rise above how you feel, or, when that doesn't work, to complain hopelessly about your situation. But see if, instead, you can take this aspect of yourself seriously, and listen to it *thoroughly*, with compassion and respect. You may need to listen to it many times, but if you allow yourself to fully hear this side of you, the creativity and energy trapped within it will come to your aid, and you'll begin to get ideas about how to move forward while keeping what's important to you.

When Jana directed her attention to listen to what her inner self was telling her, "it said that I'm getting buried alive. I'm living like an indentured servant. I've got to stop being so good all the time, and change course. But to what? I don't know."

Maxine, a forty-nine-year-old lawyer with a son in college and a daughter in middle school, exuded energy and purpose. But she, too, felt like life had painted her into a corner. "I *loved* the law," she said. "But it's changed in the last twenty years. Everything's faster, more cutthroat. And my firm"—an old, established law firm with dozens of attorneys—"has changed, too. There used to be things you knew you could get away with but ethically wouldn't do. That's all gone now. It sickens me."

The work demands had grown as well. "It's even more all-consuming than it used to be," she continued. "My kids are almost grown, yet I've got less time than ever. Every professional woman I know feels the same way I do, and it doesn't make any sense. What's it all for?"

Maxine had a dream of writing a play about a nineteenth-century legal case, involving a very colorful and courageous woman, that extended women's rights. "The moment I read about this case, I knew I had to write about it. I'm *meant* to tell this story." But she didn't see a way out.

"You can't work for a big law firm half-time—you know, forty hours a week," she said ruefully. "And going out on my own, I could probably handle financially, but I'd hate it. I need people too much." She tried to work on her play with what little free time and energy she had. She was used to trying to do it all—she'd been doing so for twenty years—but it was wearing her down.

Though she didn't yet see how she could follow it, Maxine had the first part of bringing something new into beginning—she had a vision. What I've found is that there are three components to manifesting something of your inner self in the world: Vision, Intention and Action, or "VIA" for short. Generally, you begin with Vision, then add Intention and increasing amounts of Action, while continually revising and developing the first two. When all three are working in harmony, you are on the way to consciously creating from your inner voice.

Taking an Eagle's Eye View of Your Life

When times are tough, it's easy to see only the chances missed and the dreams lost. But in fact, you have always been actively creating aspects of your life, frequently despite outside circumstances. I invite you to claim and admire what you have created in your life so far. Within that creation, notice the threads that show up again and again. These are aspects of yourself that find a way to be expressed, no matter what, the way a blade of grass pushes through a crack in the pavement. What do you notice wants to live, even if its form keeps changing?

Felicia, a dance teacher in her fifties, came to a session feeling at loose ends in her life. In the course of the hour I asked her how she had started her successful dance school.

"It was sheer stupidity," she laughed. "I thought it would be easy. Get a space, put up a ballet bar, and get some students. I had just left my alcoholic husband, I had a one-year-old infant son to support and I needed to make a living. I left New York, came back home, borrowed a thousand dollars, and started the school."

"I realize now that I could have made it in New York as a dancer," she reflected. "But I felt so unprepared inside. I had no family support. I tell the parents of my students now that no one should have to do it alone. You need someone in the background who says you can do it. I've tried to be that person for some of them. At twenty-one, I was already divorced and had a kid, and I thought I was washed up. Now I look at former students of mine who are that age and see how hard I was on myself.

"A lot of my students have gotten accepted into dance companies," she continued. "I'm very proud of that. I feel like I have more of a future now than I did when I was young. Isn't that strange? And I'm at the age where I don't care what anyone thinks anymore."

We began to talk about what she would like to do with her future, the thirty years or more she probably had ahead of her. Her dream still was to be on stage dancing. She planned to audition for a national dance company of women dancers fifty and older. She also realized that she had been holding back from applying for a master's program in dance, out of fear of being rejected, and decided to apply.

In his book *Seven Arrows*, Native American writer Wolf Storm tells the story of Jumping Mouse, who goes on a quest to find the sacred mountains. In the course of his journey he becomes blind, but then is transformed into an eagle.

Think of a field mouse scurrying in the tall grasses. It can only see a tiny distance in front of it and watch the sky fearfully for birds of prey. Jumping Mouse had to lose his sight and learn to feel his way through the unknown before he could gain an eagle's view.

Most of the time we live our lives like Jumping Mouse, focused on and trusting only what we can see immediately in front of us, and it makes us fearful. But when you look at your life with an eagle's view, you look with the perspective of your Larger Self. You notice the overarching themes of your life, what has been important, enduring and continually unfolding, and you recognize your turning points, both the times you turned toward your inner self, and the times you turned away. And you begin to feel your way toward a sacred goal, in the midst of daily life.

"I've been told, you're so smart, you could be doing so much more with your life," said Selena, a stay at home mother of a five-year-old and a two-year-old.

> And there definitely are days when I feel like I'm going to go crazy with the kids and I'd much rather be out of the house. I'll have a really bad day and forget the four good days in a row.
>
> Those times I remind myself that this is what I wanted, and I chose it. I know I wouldn't be happier if I was working. That day will come when the kids are in school. Meanwhile, I love being there for my kids. I've made a conscious choice to enjoy this time in my life. For now I do yoga, I cook, I have friends over for dinner, I read books with my book club and I garden. Who's to say that's not following my bliss? It doesn't have to be monumental. It's the little things that make up who you are.

Holding the perspective of an eagle's view helps when you're trudging through your days and losing the sense of where you're going. It also helps you stand back and ask the question, "What needs to be planted or fertilized in my life right now so that I can live more fully from my inner self in the future?"

From Wanting to Creating

There's a wonderful scene near the end of the movie *Yentl*. In the movie, Yentl is a young woman living in Eastern Europe at the turn of the twentieth century who pretends to be a boy in order to be given the opportunity to study. But in the course of studying she falls deeply in love with her fellow student Avigdor, a handsome young man with conventional ideas. After she reveals her true identity to him, he realizes he loves her, too. But his love comes with the price of limiting her dreams and desires. Avigdor says to Yentl, "We'll get married, make a home, and have children. . . . What more do you want?"

She grins, shrugs her shoulders and says, "More."

Your visions start from wanting something more, something different. They start in those quiet moments at night, or that semi-dream time between sleeping and waking, or waiting at a traffic light as you notice a stunning sunset, when you feel a quiet surge within saying, "Something's missing in my life. There is more I want to be fulfilled." The seed of your vision is in that deep desire that keeps knocking at the door of your consciousness. It begins to grow when you pay attention to, rather than dismiss, these messengers from your inner self.

I had given Jana the assignment to write down a hundred wants and wishes.

"I can't believe how powerful it was for me to name the things I wanted," she said in her next session. "I feel like I'm starting from scratch again, remembering what makes me happy, what gets me excited. The list helped me do that."

We talked for a while, and I asked her if there were any wants in particular that stood out, that gave her a lot of "juice."

"I think what stands out the most," she said, "was how many of them have to do with expressing my creativity."

"What does your creative side want?" I asked.

"Well!" she said, her voice picking up. "I enjoy decorating. It's a challenge. I like to find things at antique stores, things you don't see every day, and use them in a completely new way.

"And there's one thing I do like about my job. I get to look at drawings and blueprints of these huge construction projects in the planning stage around the world. I get excited by them, even though I think most of them are just awful. They're total environmental disasters. But the idea of helping to build them excites me, despite myself sometimes.

"And I love to garden. I always have. I'm really serious about it. I read every gardening article I come across." She was talking very fast now. "I'm always giving friends and neighbors consultations about what they should plant and where. This past summer, when I got really really busy at work, I missed my little garden more than my boyfriend!

"But I don't think I can do anything with that," she said. "I don't think it's my real work."

"Don't dismiss it so quickly," I advised. "You don't need to have it all figured out." Instead, I suggested that she write down the essence of

Embodying Wanting

Look at the list of wants you wrote in the Claiming Your Wants innercize on page 158. If you haven't done that exercise or wish to do it again, take at least fifteen minutes to write down as many wants and wishes as you possibly can.

From this list, pick up to five wants that give you the most "juice." Write them down and place them somewhere where you will see them every day.

Take five minutes each day to read them over and allow the feeling of wanting those things to fill your body. For the time you are doing the innercize, stay focused as much as possible on the feeling of wanting, not on the obstacles to obtaining the want.

Now throughout the day, notice any small impulses you have in the direction of what you want. Then either follow through on those impulses, or simply make note of them, by writing them down or recording them.

what she wanted on a sheet of paper, and every day, just look at it, read it, and bring back the feeling of the want into her body. Then she was simply to follow any little impulses that occurred to her in the direction of her two desires.

Finding Your Inner Vision

> *A moment came when the kaleidoscope turned in just the right way, a way that fit me and nobody else, and I ran with it. I knew this was the way I could leave my imprint.*
> —Maxine, forty-nine

You may feel that you need to have the whole picture and know exactly what you want before you can follow a vision. But while some visions are immediately clear and complete, others get clearer and more fine-tuned over weeks, or months, or years, or sometimes decades. Trying to force clarity on your visions with your intellect stifles the process. Inner visions are *meant* to evolve. When you follow the uncertainty to wherever it leads, your visions become clearer.

For many women, the vision they most wish to find is of a vocation or avocation that fulfills them. The most important question to ask about this kind of vision is, "When I do this or imagine myself doing this, do I like and admire myself? Does it make me feel glad to be who I am?"

This was critical for Nikki, a mother of two who left her job nine years earlier when her daughter was born, and was planning to return to work again in a year when her son entered first grade. "I want to do something I care about," she said, "but I never figured out what I really wanted to do."

I asked her what she imagined doing when she was young.

"When I was a kid, I wanted to be a fashion designer. Then I wanted to go to Hollywood and become a makeup artist. But I was told that was wrong. Everyone discouraged me. Because I was really good at school, I made good grades. They thought I should do something important.

"Then I decided I would be a teacher. But the teaching market was terrible. So then I went to pre-law and political science so I could become a lawyer and represent down-and-out people. In the third year of college I realized I wasn't thick-skinned enough to do that. So I took accounting and my mother said *why* would you want to be an accountant. But the funny thing was, I liked being an accountant. I had a great boss and I made the best money."

Nikki had been eminently practical, and each of the careers she chose expressed valid aspects of herself. Her real love, however, was art, especially oil painting. For most of her life, she'd been what she called a "shadow artist," sketching whenever she could. But she had learned that art was "impractical" and "not important enough," since she was smart enough to do other things.

"But I probably can't earn a steady income from my paintings. At least not in a year."

"You don't know where it's going to lead yet," I replied. "What is a step that you feel that you *could* take, and that you'd *like* to take, toward your painting?"

This is a very valuable question to ask yourself. Frequently people separate the two halves of this question. Their vision seems so far off that no do-able step seems worthwhile to them, and no meaningful step feels like any fun. Yet only by doing what you both *can* and *want to* do are you likely to get started.

She thought about it. "I want to paint one day this week," she said. "Not all day, but a good part of it. And I want to sign up for an art course I know about, even though I'll have to miss several classes."

When she returned the following week, she was glowing.

"My whole day—no, my whole week—fell into place because of my painting. It put everything into perspective." Seeing how it made her feel, Nikki committed to painting one day a week.

Your true vison is your Larger Self seeking its expression in the physical world. As such, it grows directly out of your unique history, experience, gifts and traits. It doesn't depend on becoming some kind of special person, unless that special person is *yourself*.

Rebecca Maddox, the president of a company that has provided millions of dollars of financing to women business owners, wrote in her book *Inc. Your Dreams* that "an individual's success is usually born and maintained out of not more than a few unique, often very simple and unheralded abilities." She goes on to say that a successful individual is "someone who sees her uniqueness, who perceives even some very small differences that set her apart from others, and uses them to launch her life."

Most of all, it makes you feel good about being you. Think of the times when you feel best about who you are, when your particular constellation of values, personality traits and abilities all click together and you feel totally in your element. That's the seed of your inner vision. That's when you are truly being an instrument of Creation, in its never-ending process of expanding, discovering and expressing Itself. You yourself are a one-of-a-kind creation, never to be repeated, so what you have most to offer is equally unique to you.

Connie's vision—what she'd loved all of her life, but never felt she could pursue—was "hidden in plain sight." When the forty-five-year-old mother of four followed her inner voice to Italy, the first trip she had ever taken to pursue her own interests, she reignited her love of photography. Indeed, the trip was as much a rediscovery of photography as it was of herself.

One of her very earliest memories involved photography. "I remember sitting and studying the photographs in the *National Geographic* magazines at my house," she said. "I couldn't have been more than two or three years old at the time. I remember trying to look behind the pictures, behind the magazine, as if there *had* to be more dimensions to the picture. I wanted *so much* to see more."

Yet her parents saw picture-taking as frivolous. As an adult, months and even years would go by when Connie barely picked up a camera. Even then, a picture she took one year of a boat anchored to a dock won first prize in a photo contest. Yet she still dismissed her photography as a luxury she shouldn't "indulge" in.

"I *am* a photographer!" she exulted when she came back from Italy. "All my life I've been doing, doing, doing for others. But when I'm behind the camera, I feel like I'm being really me." Before, she could never follow through on her impulses to photograph professionally, but now she began doing small jobs and volunteering her talents, sowing the seeds for her photography career.

Once you have a vision, whether it's clear or barely formed, or

ॐ INNERCIZE 24 ॐ
What Do You Want Permission to Become?

Poet Natalie Goldberg, in her book *Wild Mind*, tells of a conversation she had with another poet where he asked her, "Who gave you permission to be a poet?" Poetry is such a devalued calling in America today that he knew that some important person in her life must have validated her right to pursue it. But women generally get so little "permission" or validation to pursue their visions, whatever they are, that one way to find one is to ask yourself, "What is it I want permission to become?"

whether it feels within your reach or nearly impossible, the next step is to begin to imagine that you can make it happen. This is the first step in forming intention.

"Sending Out the Monkeys" is an innercize for taking this step. It does so by giving your vision wings. It's one of my favorite innercizes to lead in workshops, not only because of how it makes people feel, but be-

⋛ INNERCIZE 25 ⋚
Sending Out the Monkeys

From the five wants you identified in Innercize 23 on page 253 choose one, two or at most three that have the most "juice" for you.

Make yourself comfortable and bring your awareness into your body, sensing this moment in time and space, and giving your inner self a very warm welcome. Now, bring the sense of your desire into your body, not the problems or obstacles involved, but just the good feeling it has for you, the excitement, and how it's an expression of something you want in your life. Take some time, giving it permission to get as big inside of you as it would like.

Now you're going to begin to send this out. Choose a method of locomotion for sending it into the world. You might imagine it as seeds bursting forth, or a shooting star, or whatever works for you. My personal favorite image is of the flying monkeys from *The Wizard of Oz*, when the witch calls out to the monkeys, shouting, "Fly! Fly! Fly!" Only these are flying monkeys that do *good* things. Imagine your desire as an alive, moving being, radiating from inside your body outward, traveling through the Universe to work its magic, reaching the right people, interacting with other people's living desires, combining and combusting and finding exactly who you need to meet to help you bring your wish into reality.

Share what happened with someone you trust—or just enjoy the feeling by yourself.

cause I get to hear some exciting stories later of seemingly magical events that were first imagined doing this innercize.

Intention

> *An aim in life is the only fortune worth finding; and it is not to be found in foreign lands, but in the heart itself.*
> —Robert Louis Stevenson

"That was almost a religious experience," said Maxine to a roomful of twenty women and men during a weekend workshop. "I saw shapes and colors. I saw this giant red flower opening, and golden pollen shooting out and spreading all over the world."

I had never heard her sound so, well, colorful. Her husband, who was attending the workshop with her, looked at her quizzically, as if to say, *Do I know this woman?*

"I'm going to write my play and see it performed. And I'm going to practice law ethically and sanely. And I'm going to have a life. I'm through with thinking I have to choose either-or. I don't know how, but I'm going to do it."

Intention puts *you* behind your vision. It's choosing to focus more on your vision than on your sense of the obstacles in your way.

Intention is amazingly powerful. When you set your intention and decide, "I'm going to do it, I don't care how, it's going to happen," incredible things can occur. And you are changed by the experience, as when Adele, who has a chronic medical condition, decided against the advice of her obstetrician and all of her family and friends to get pregnant again.

I lost my first baby and almost lost my life when I was seven months pregnant. When I realized that I still wanted to bear a child, my desire to have a child overrode the fear of what could be. I would never know if I could if I didn't try. My husband supported me once he understood how I felt. We had to block out the comments of all the people who tried to dissuade us.

It took several years of work. We had to save money first, since I wouldn't be able to work during my pregnancy. We had to research my health problems and medication interactions. Then we faced another wall of fear about the possible impact of my latest medication on the fetus, so we consulted experts and researched the literature again until we were satisfied that it was probably safe.

Then we took the plunge. I'd already faced death and been through my worst fears, so I wasn't afraid anymore. I was more worried for my husband and child than for me. There's a line from *Steel Magnolias*, "I'd rather have a few minutes of something great than a lifetime of nothing special." That's how I felt.

It came down to this: Was I ready to love so much that I was willing to take the chances? It actually surprised me how much I wanted it. I didn't even know why, whether it was because I wanted the baby or I wanted to show I could do it, but in the end, it didn't matter, I knew that I wanted to.

By carefully monitoring her condition every step of the way, Adele carried her pregnancy to term. With medication, her symptoms are still in remission, and she is taking care of her daughter, now a healthy, happy four-year-old.

When you hold and pursue a vision strongly and steadfastly and refuse to accept that it's impossible, it seems as if the Universe itself bends toward helping make your vision manifest itself. Not by intention alone, and not always in the way you imagined it. But out of the blue, doors open, obstacles disappear and what moments before seemed impossible suddenly becomes possible. Not easy, but possible. Yet that's so much better than impossible that it's enough.

Intention is a balancing act—actively going after a dream, yet allowing for help to come in unpredictable ways. To manifest your dreams, you need to be both active and receptive. If you don't allow for that—if, for example, you think that you can't apply to graduate school until you've paid off all of your debts, which will take five more years of working at a job you hate—you block the energy and creativity of the Cosmos. There is a saying, "You decide *what* your dream is, and let the Universe figure out *how*." This doesn't mean being passive. It means daring to think that your vision can break the bounds of what you, in your present mode of thinking, can allow or imagine.

All of this may make intention sound abstract and mysterious, but on another level, intention is nothing more than what you pay attention to. It's a variation of Aligning with the Inside. In this case, you're aligning your thoughts and feelings toward what you desire and away from anything that takes you away from it. By doing this, you water the flowers, not the weeds. You add energy in the direction of the vision you are holding. You turn up the volume. At the same time, you begin to withdraw energy, both physical and mental, from those areas of life you plan to leave behind.

"I'm planting my flag on the ground," Maxine concluded. She started working more consistently on her play after that experience. She felt certain that she was meant to work in a very different way, although she couldn't say how. She was getting ready to make a change.

Change found her first. A month after the workshop, her closest friend and colleague told her that she and two other attorneys at the law firm were planning to open their own firm, and asked Maxine if she wanted to join them. As a group, they marketed their services to small businesses and startups, which Maxine found more personal and enjoyable than the corporate work she'd been doing. She also made a decision to work thirty hours a week. She started living exactly the life she had envisioned.

Getting Your Inner Fire Going

I'm allowing myself to hope and dream again. I'm allowing myself to say, "Maybe I will, and maybe I won't. But maybe I will."
—Nina, thirty-three

But you may not feel all of this great intention yet. To go from a vision to a firm intention may be the hugest shift of all. Everyone can think of a time when they got all excited about a vision, only to find that a day or a week later the feeling was totally gone.

This is because a vision, since it originates in the realm of feelings, is by its nature ephemeral. It's not yet anchored in reality. Indeed, it may be a radical departure from the reality surrounding you.

In effect, by claiming a vision, what you've done is to collect the sparks of your inner nature, add paper and dry leaves, and blow on them to make a fire. But a paper fire, no matter how huge, goes out quickly. It needs wood.

But not logs. If you throw logs on a paper fire, it probably won't catch. What's needed first is kindling and thin sticks. In the same way, throwing a log on your inner fire by immediately making up your mind to take an action step that feels intimidating to you can very easily put the whole flame out. Your very first goal, for most visions, is simply to get your inner fire well-established.

While you are excited about your vision, write it down or record the reasons you feel this vision is meant for you, and everything that has led you to choose this dream. Name the outside voices that you know are going to come up for you later and then answer them. State your major intention in the form of "I'm going to," as Maxine did when she said, "I'm going to write my play and see it performed."

A very important step is to start a journal or a folder on your computer for your vision and begin writing down anything you think or feel about it, any new information you have about it, and any ideas for actions you can take to pursue it. You don't have to make it very formal at first. You don't need a list of twenty action steps. You just need to start regularly thinking about it.

Share your vision with someone supportive. Once a vision is shared, it has a toehold in reality. As Sabrina, who wanted to market a line of greeting cards, said,

> In the past, I never shared with anyone any idea I had about what I wanted to do. I felt too embarrassed, like no one would believe me. I thought I had to have something to show first. And I never got very far. Just sharing my dream of starting a business has made a tremendous difference. For one thing, it's a lot harder to quit when you know someone's hoping you'll follow your dreams.

I've found it very helpful for myself and many others to have a "dream buddy" or group with a regularly scheduled phone call. Again, at first it's not so important to set stringent goals and action steps. Just talk about your vision, the steps you want to make or are making toward it, and any feelings you are having about it. Support the other person's vision. And let your vision be refined and honed. Over time, as you become more intent and active in pursuing your dreams, you can help each other stay on track and keep going. Just knowing that you're going to have to talk about what you've done or haven't done can help you keep your intention alive and work through the blocks.

As time goes on, a dream buddy or group can become some of the most supportive relationships in your entire life. Nina, a thirty-three-year-old mother of two with a dream of becoming a singer, described a recent conversation she had with her friend.

> I said to my friend Gail, maybe I should start a school. "You don't want to start a school, Nina, you want to sing." Well maybe I should start my own business. "You don't want to start a business. You want to sing and perform." Well maybe I should do something else. "HELLO, you need to go toward the thing you love, music." I tell her I don't want to, it's a curse, let other people do it. She says to me, "But they can't, Nina. They don't have the talent you have."

It's very tempting to believe that you should move as fast as you can toward your vision. But if you're finding it difficult to move forward, take the safest, most enjoyable ten-degree steps you can. Build the *internal* reality of your vision first, by clarifying it, learning about it, desiring it and feeling it inside you. Sometimes this can take many months, or even longer. In the children's book, *The Velveteen Rabbit*, a little boy loves and plays with his stuffed rabbit so much that it becomes real. The more you love and *play with* your vision at first, the more chance you'll have of overcoming obstacles later and making your vision a reality.

Another way to choose action steps is to get your Future Self to mentor you. In the following innercize, you imagine yourself twenty years in the future and let your future self advise you about what to do next.

"I can see myself selling paintings," Nikki said after calling upon her future self. "The image of myself older looks very happy, very much at peace."

"If you think backwards from then until now, what would you do next, to become the woman you saw?"

INNERCIZE 26
Your Future Self as Mentor

Let's move a little forward in time. You'll be amazed at your ability to call upon all the wonderful wisdom you have "learned" in the next twenty years.

Take a moment and begin to imagine yourself twenty or so years in the future. Picture yourself as that person. What does she look like, how is she feeling, what is she doing in her life? Connect with this future version of you inside.

Then, ask your future self what advice she has for you. If she is doing what you hope for, ask her what you need to do right now to start becoming her. If you wish, write down or tell someone what you received.

"I need to go back to school and learn technique. Not just landscape and still lifes, but figure drawing and portraiture. That's very challenging, but I want to do it all, or at least try to.

"Also, I need to make the time to do my art. I want to develop a series of paintings, and create a collection."

Intention goes beyond temporal feelings. Sometimes you need to follow your intentions *even when you don't feel them.* Sometimes you lose the feeling, or you have to table a vision you're working on to take care of some other matter in your life. When you're able to come back, you might not immediately feel the "juice." But the action brings the feeling. Taking even a small step in its direction will frequently reignite a vision. It's like losing touch with an old friend. The instant you get back together, the feeling comes back.

Outside Voices and the Hijacking of Your Dream

Once you truly decide that you want to bring a vision to life, you're setting a course for change, which can be very threatening. That's when the outside voices are likely to lease a twelve-room suite in your head and call you up every day to yell in your ear. *I can't do that. It's not real. It's too late. It's impossible. It's selfish. It's just a pipe dream. Maybe when the kids are grown. I have everything I've ever wanted. Why shouldn't I feel fulfilled?*

Or something else very interesting may happen. Suddenly, all of your enthusiasm and desire to pursue your dream utterly disappears, and you wonder how you ever wanted to do it in the first place. The slightest step in the direction of your dream feels like scaling a mountain.

What's happened is that your vision has been hijacked. For twenty, thirty, forty years or more, you've kept your dreams and visions hidden and locked away near your heart, where they couldn't grow—*but they couldn't die, either.* But now you've tentatively allowed some inner vision to step out into the big, dangerous world. This has set off a loud alarm in the security headquarters of your brain. Faster than you can say, "I have a dream," those parts of your psyche responsible for keeping you and your dreams safe and protected have rounded up your vision and put it back in its padded cell.

The first thing to do is to realize what's happened. This can be difficult to do, because a dream can be hijacked so fast that you don't even get a chance to notice that you got scared. Also, what triggered the fear may have been either nothing at all, or an action so tiny, it's embarrassing to think you were frightened by it. "I'm not scared to bring my résumé file up on my computer and look at it. I'm just not in the mood right now. I'll do it next week. Unless I get too busy. . . ."

Take it on faith that there must have been *some* part of you that got very scared. Then, placing yourself in the reflective stance, invite it to reveal itself, and let it tell you its story. Listen to what it's afraid of. Thank it for wanting to protect you. And ask it, after you've heard its point of view for a while, if there is something you can do to make following your dream safer and less threatening.

Sabrina traced her "hijacker" to this outside voice:

It's saying, What's the point, what's this going to amount to? What if I'm as wrong about this as I've been about other things that I've tried and done and that haven't worked out? What will I have left?

For Sabrina, simply identifying it and saying out loud what it was telling her took away most of its power to stop her.

A second major reason for outside voices is that, if you're married or a mother, you're painfully aware that any change in your available time or energy changes the balance of your entire family. Causing that change is in itself stressful, because you'll have to deal with the fallout. Also, it arouses guilt. As Barbara Sher points out in her book, *I Could Do Anything If I Only Knew What It Was*, when men pursue a career, they feel like they're fulfilling their family obligations, but when women pursue their careers, they can still feel as if they're shirking them.

It helps to remember that going after your dreams is a very good thing to do for your kids, even though it causes some turmoil. You're training your sons to see that the women in their lives, including the ones they will someday marry, have hopes and dreams of their own and do not exist to service their needs. And your daughters will soak up with every pore of their being the process you follow to reach your dream, and will adapt it to themselves later on in their lives. Simply by following your dream, you're teaching them that a woman has a right to follow her own spirit throughout her entire life. You may even positively affect your nieces and nephews.

You can also notice when the outside voices are taking over, and turn them around by aligning with your inside. Julianne did this one day when she hired an experienced baby-sitter to care for her one-year-old while she worked on her master's thesis. After a few hours she needed a break, and decided to go bicycling.

I was bicycling, but I noticed that I wasn't enjoying it at all. How could I go biking while someone else watches my baby? I was sure the baby-sitter had looked at me disapprovingly. I felt surrounded by the glaring eyes and disapproving voices of all the mothers and mothers-in-law and older sisters in the world saying *you can't do this. If you're going to neglect your child to finish your degree, at least you'd better stay busy.*

I asked myself, What do I know to be true here? Let's see . . . I know my baby's okay. I love feeling the wind on my back. And then it welled up in me, a fierce, bottom-line, bedrock feeling. I had no intention of giving up my dream. I had no intention of turning back. I felt hard inside, like hard muscle. Resolute. The strength emanated down my arms and legs. I started biking very fast, and with each pumping motion I found myself thinking *I have an obligation to myself, an obligation to myself, an obligation to myself.*

Sometimes your intention disappears because you haven't pinpointed your true vision. Jana realized that she didn't just want to *look* at blueprints, she wanted to create them. In fact, she had been drawn to the construction and engineering business because she loved the idea of building things.

But she'd never thought she wanted architecture, because it struck her as too structured and "dry." On the other hand, gardening didn't appeal to the more intellectual side of her nature, and the only way she thought people could do it professionally was to create personal gardens for affluent clients, which didn't appeal to her. After beginning to look into programs to learn architecture or landscape design, she gave up on both of them.

When I hadn't heard anything about her career search for a while, I asked her about it. Exploring her feelings further, she realized that she didn't want either one—she wanted *both.* Also, that she loved horticulture, but to do it for a career, she needed to use it for a more social, public purpose.

She came back the next week very excited. She'd spent every available free moment learning about "green," environmentally friendly architecture and, through the Internet, making contacts with people involved with it all around the world. She also learned how gardens were being used along with "green" buildings to improve the environment. "Did you know that you could put gardens on the rooftops of city buildings to provide vegetables and flowers for the whole city, *and* improve air quality and make the city cooler in the summer?" she asked me. She'd found her calling: to use her love of both architecture and horticulture to improve the environment and create more harmonious surroundings.

She returned to school for a double master's in both architectural design and landscape design, and is currently working hard and living the life of a student again. Her vision still excites her.

Action

All the flowers of all the tomorrows are in the seeds of today.
  —Chinese proverb

If you've spent whatever time you needed talking about your vision, getting support for it, learning about it and taking small exploratory steps toward it, there comes a point when it becomes a fairly stable part of your being. At this point, the focus of pursuing your vision shifts from tending it and keeping it going to directly engaging with the world.

This is exciting and scary and challenging, because you have this wonderful vision in your heart, but now you've got to make that larger world around you go along with your good idea. And generally speaking, this doesn't happen easily! Sometimes women give up on their visions far too soon, thinking that if they meet a lot of difficulties and resistance, it must mean that what they desire is not "meant to be." Some popular books have made it sound as if, when you're fully aligned with the Universe, you manifest your visions almost effortlessly. But if that were true, why did it take seventy-two years of continual political effort for women to secure the right to vote? Perhaps the greatest dreams encounter the greatest difficulties.

Whole books have been written on the topic of taking action toward your goals and visions. Here I can cover just a few points that I think are important, some of which frequently get overlooked.

The greatest gifts you can give yourself are patience—with yourself, and with the process—and persistence, and to stay true to yourself. Like beginning any important new relationship, only more so, you have a *lot* of "working things out" to do. Some visions, like some partners, look great from afar, but the moment you start to get to know them you realize they're not right for you. But others require a continual process of revision and negotiation, revision and negotiation. In this extended conversation you are having with the world, paying attention to the reaction you get back from the world and deciding how to respond to it becomes very important, because this becomes your *strategy*. People frequently give up on their visions when they fail, when in fact their visions were attainable. They just needed to approach them more strategically.

If you're working on pursuing your vision, taking steps toward it and adjusting your course when you need to, that's wonderful! It's like being in love. You have a passionate focus for your life. But if your vision is stuck, if you're neither moving forward with it nor giving it up, and it's giving you no sense of mastery or satisfaction, then it's time to look at what's going on.

Working with the Emotions of Change

"I'm not emotionally ready," Connie said about taking a photography assignment.

"Tell me more about what that means, 'emotionally ready.' "

"I keep telling myself I'm not. I don't have the confidence in myself that I can do it. Even though I can see myself doing it."

The seeds of Connie's business that she had sown were beginning to bear fruit. People were calling and asking her to do weddings. A tour guide company and a maker of wrought-iron garden ornaments wanted her to do photographs for their brochures. So what did she do? She didn't call back the tour guide company and lost the ornament company owner's business card. The Universe had answered her call to become a photographer, and she was doing everything she could to hang up the phone.

"Can you be with the feeling that comes up, when you think of doing these assignments?"

"Oh, I don't know. My chest tightens up. I can't breathe. There's a startled, panicky feeling running down my arms. I don't know how much to charge. It's just too overwhelming. I don't want to mess up my home life, going off and doing this business. It's like a black wall. . . ."

Connie was up against *intimidation*. Anything that in*timid*ates you makes you feel timid, small, like you can't handle it. Usually, there are many steps in the process of manifesting a vision that you can feel too "small" to handle. Having made the transition to seeing herself as a photographer, she was being called upon to take her work to a new level, seeing herself as a professional and giving her work value. And that was a different story.

There are some fears that you know you can get through, and then there are some fears that you tell yourself you *should* get through, you *should* have the courage to overcome. A week goes by. Two weeks. A month, then two, then three. You berate yourself for being such a wimp. If you had to, if you would *starve* if you didn't pursue your vision, you'd take that step. So why don't you just do it, like the Nike ads say?

If intimidation has truly stopped you, denying it isn't going to help. It's time to listen to that fear. Look to see if the step you wish to take can be changed in some way to make it less intimidating. Or see if you've jumped too far ahead and need to do several other steps first.

To accomplish any vision, you sometimes have to do things that feel scary. But if you feel like you have to completely "white-knuckle" it to get where you want to be, something is a little off-kilter. To be true to yourself, you may need to revise your vision to make it more doable at least for now. This can be a huge step in the direction of your dreams. Learning what you can't do is as important as knowing what you can.

Not all fear is the kind that totally stops you. The further you go toward a certain vision, the more opportunities you have to feel a whole host of not usually welcomed feelings. Besides fear, there is nervousness, embarrassment, awkwardness, vulnerability and uncertainty. If you're feeling this crummy, can you really be doing the right thing? The answer, most likely, is yes. If you're experiencing these feelings, chances are you're on the right track. You might think that you should feel good and confident, now that you're doing what you should have been doing all of your life. But you've got it backwards. You feel confident when you do the same thing for years and years. When you take the risk to do something completely new, you don't feel confident at all at first. But eventually you will. You'll also feel thrilled, joyful, even ecstatic at times, each time you get closer to your dream.

As for fear, it's helpful to remember that fear and excitement travel together. Physiologically they're very similar. I've noticed that many women learn early in their lives to turn much of their excitement into fear. When they were young, they wanted to pump their swing higher, explore further, stay out later. But they heard, "Don't swing so high, you'll fall." They learned too well that the "juice" of life can lead to danger. But you can reclaim the feeling of excitement if you can ask yourself, when you're feeling afraid, if there is a *part* of you that is also excited. If there is, welcome it and start including it. You can begin to stretch yourself beyond the bounds of safety.

Finally, stay clear about your desire. The best solution to outside voices and difficult emotions is to not to combat them directly, but to align with the vision within you.

At the Edge of Knowing

Connie's fears were understandable. She was suddenly going from being a full-time homemaker practically her entire adult life to being in business by herself. She actually knew little about the business of photography.

Connie was at the edge of her knowing. She needed to look at what she knew, and what she knew she didn't know yet and needed to know.

The next step, of course, is to figure out what you need to *do* to find out what you need to *know*. When Connie realized what a stumbling block the financial aspects were to her, she met with her accountant, who showed her that setting up books for her business was much easier than she imagined it was. Taking that one simple action seemed to uncork

⅔ INNERCIZE 27 ⅇ
The Edge of Knowing

Write your vision at the top of a page. Divide the page into two columns. On one side, write everything you already know about reaching your vision. On the other side, write, "What I know that I don't know yet, that I need to find out."

something inside her. She tracked down the phone number of the ornament company owner, got the job, and then lined up three more jobs in rapid succession. Now that she felt "legitimate," she called several professional photographers to ask them how they set their prices.

Incidentally, Connie finally did this after spending weeks wanting to deal with every other problem in her life rather than take a step toward becoming a photographer. But, by keeping her intention and saying out loud a thousand different doubts and fears, she got over the hump.

This is how it happens sometimes. You can feel your absolute worst right before you take a major step forward. I remember in graduate school having to write very long term papers. When they were almost finished, I would feel as though there were a hundred things wrong with my life. I'd tell my husband, and he knew me well enough to say, "Don't worry. Just finish the paper and you'll feel totally different." And he was right.

I'm a strong proponent of learning as much as you can about a particular goal or vision. It makes you both more effective and less intimidated. Sometimes people avoid learning much about what they've envisioned because they fear they'll get too discouraged about its difficulty. It's true that you're likely to get information that's going to be discouraging. A certain measure of blind naïveté must be part of the Divine plan, because, as my father once told me, if people knew ahead of time what they were getting into, they wouldn't do half the things they do. Yet there are many rich sources of information, such as books, courses and mentors, that are encouraging yet don't hide the pitfalls, and may even give you a step-by-step guide for you to follow. This is invaluable.

You don't have to do it alone. In fact, the exact opposite is true. One of the most important secrets to manifesting a vision is the ability to get help when needed. People who are truly grounded in their vision are very open to support and input from every source in whatever form it takes. It's vulnerable to be a novice, but if you look around, there's always someone willing to help people who are just beginning. If there's one thing we women know about, it's that we don't have to be islands.

Making Time Your Ally

After lack of money, lack of time is the biggest impediment people name to following their dreams. Of course there's a reality to this. Yet at the same time, we all know that under pressure we can accomplish amazing things. On the other hand, you don't want to spend every minute being a taskmaster to yourself.

There are shelves of books, many of them excellent, on time management. But before people begin opening their Day-Timers or pulling their PDAs from their purses, I ask them to ask their inner selves to work with the resource of time. When your intention becomes strong, your inner self has a way of knowing how to make time your ally, rather than your enemy. Nikki found that designating a day a week as her painting day worked for her. For Jana, it was designating a set time to begin, since switching gears from her stressful day job was difficult for her. Once she got started, her work took on a life of its own. What works is what most matches your own inner way of being.

Maxine had begun to live the lifestyle she had hoped for, with more time to herself than she had in twenty years—and was writing less on her play than when she had absolutely no time at all! For a while, she gave herself a break, realizing that she was taking a much-deserved breather. But then she began to be dissatisfied with her lack of progress.

"What can I do about this?" she asked. "I never feel like writing anymore."

"How about sensing inside what you need," I answered.

Quickly she received an answer. "Short time bursts work best for me. I need a tight deadline. It gets my competitive fires burning."

She gave herself just three weeks to write the first draft of her play that was less than half done. "That's the way I do things," she said. "Watch. I'm going to beat this deadline." She decided that when she worked on her play, she was going to work in the library of the local university, telling her husband that she was unreachable except for a dire emergency.

Crossing the Narrow Bridges

All the world is like a narrow bridge. But above all, do not fear.
— Rabbi Nachman of Breslov

Kaye had left an extremely stressful job as a manager an hour's commute away for a more technical job closer to home that paid less. She had made the switch thinking it would give her more time and make her life better, but she hated her new job. She was going into a tailspin, berating herself for making the "wrong" decision, thinking about all the money she wasn't going to make and considering calling her old boss to see if she could get her old job back.

Rarely does change go smoothly. Kaye was crossing a "narrow bridge," those times when you're no longer in your old life—either because you've left it or your life has changed—but neither has what you've desired and envisioned come true. Instead, everything looks like it's gone completely *wrong*.

The present is uncomfortable and the future is uncertain, so every animal instinct is to find something that is certain and safe as quickly as possible. It's very tempting to attack yourself for causing these new circumstances to come about, and to grab onto something solid, even if it means going back to a bad old situation or giving up on your dream.

Reflexively reacting out of fear or anger are ways to get back to solid ground quickly, but they stop you from moving forward. This leads to my "toothpaste tube" theory of personal growth: You never know what you're capable of until you're being squeezed.

Experiencing pain and turmoil does not mean that your vision won't happen. This is the time to remember the ABCs of Acknowledging, Being With and Compassion, because you want to slow your reactions down and have compassion for yourself. You're experiencing pain and turmoil precisely because you are going for what you most want in life.

When you're crossing a narrow bridge, life can feel confusing, even chaotic. You may tense up and try to force events to come out the way you want. See if instead, you can stay open to receiving help from others, and open yourself to the feeling that some force larger than yourself is behind you. You don't have the total picture yet, but if you take it slowly and treat each obstacle as something that is leading you to where you want to go, you will get through.

"I've decided that establishing a charter school is a lot like having children," said Leslie, one of the founders and the prime force behind the charter school my daughter goes to. It's the first and so far only charter school in the state. "There are challenges at every stage, but getting through one stage gives you some confidence that you can get through the next. And, as you work on the present challenge, the previous challenges don't look so bad—it wasn't so hard back then, compared to how it is now!"

The school went through several heart-stopping "narrow bridges" before it opened. The founders had already been working hard on it for more than two years just to get to where they could submit an application to the local school board. When they submitted it and got back the school board's first response,

> We thought we were sunk. They had recalculated our finances, and we were totally in the red. We had to make a tough choice, deciding that it was better to increase the class size from twenty-four to thirty than not to open a school.

They were kept for five months in the classic chicken-and-egg situation. The school board wouldn't approve their revised application if they didn't have a space and teachers, but prospective teachers and landlords wouldn't even *talk* to them without that approval. Finding a suitable yet affordable space for a school, hard enough under any circumstances, was made much harder by a drought, which meant that they had to find a space with enough bathroom fixtures for a school, because the city wasn't granting any permits to add them. Just then a commercial developer called Leslie and volunteered his time to find the school a space.

> That's the way it worked. We'd get to these spots where we couldn't go any further and then something good would happen, and we'd say, "Wow! That's a sign! Let's keep going!"

Finally a few teachers risked to commit to teaching in a school that had a good chance of not opening, and in June the board gave them provisional approval. They signed a lease, and then had only two months to turn a warehouse into a school with a tiny budget to do so. Again help appeared out of nowhere to make the impossible possible. A contractor who didn't even have young children worked all summer for free to get the job done.

> There were plenty of times when things looked very bleak, and other people needed me to be the one to say that we'd get through. What kept me going was a women's group at the church I belong to. Sometimes I'd call them and say, I need some support here! This is one public school that's been prayed for quite a bit. I hope that doesn't break any church-state separation rules!

"I've done it! I finished my first draft!" Maxine said, waving a thick stack of pages in her hand like a trophy. She'd broken her deadline with two days to spare.

We took a few minutes just to celebrate. Then she grew more serious. "My entire life I've done the practical thing. And I've done it well," she reflected, "but that's all I felt like I could do. For the first time I have a mission, a purpose besides my family."

Ultimately, living from your inner voice goes beyond bringing any particular vision or goal into fruition. It's about following "the soft animal of yourself," in poet Mary Oliver's words. Each day, week, month, and year are new creations. It's all a question of how much you let your inner self unfold.

None of us can know what our future holds for us. The universe seems to have its own intentions. But the inner voice doesn't tell you that you've lived your life wrongly, nor does it label as "hopeless" any present circumstance. Instead it gently whispers to you your next possible step from your present circumstance toward the fulfillment of your own spirit in the hope that you will hear it, and take it.

Whenever you follow an urge or impulse that comes from your inner self, whether it's a new career or something small, like taking up a hobby you've been considering, you not only make your life more pleasurable, but more meaningful. You alone determine what gives or can give meaning to your life. What's most important is manifesting what gives you meaning and joy.

The Larger Picture

It is time to apply in the arena of the world the wisdom and experience that women have gained over so many thousands of years.

—Aung San Suu Kyi, Nobel Laureate

We are living today through one of the most profound changes in human behavior in all of recorded history: Women are finding their voices. For thousands of years women were considered inferior to men, intellectually, emotionally, spiritually and even morally. We weren't given the same education as men, we were told we couldn't be anything but mothers, secretaries, nurses and teachers, and our husbands had vast legal rights to dominate us and control our lives.

In our country and the rest of the Western world, this for the most part is *gone*. Women have freedoms and opportunities unimaginable sixty years ago. Our daughters hear from all around them that they are as smart and capable as boys. These changes seem so self-evident to us, so much a matter of simple and obvious fairness, that we can be tempted to overlook how radical a transformation this really is.

But the transformation is not yet complete, and won't be for some time. There are many non-Western nations where the battle for women's equality has barely begun. And in our own and other Western countries, men still fill most of the positions of power, and women are discriminated against in many ways. And in a broader sense, the vast genius of women—our ability to form connections and respond to the cries in the night—does not yet influence the larger world to the degree to which it should and must. Our inner voices are only beginning to be heard. My hope and goal for women is that their inner voices become so irrepressible that they can't help but spill over into every aspect of their lives: from their inner selves, to all of their relationships, into their work and the ways they play, and in how they see themselves politically.

One of the greatest distractions keeping women from following their true inner voice is perfectionism. Perfectionism misdirects the great power of your inner voice against yourself. Daily I see the damaging effects of women always trying to look better, do more and be more perfect products, rather than imperfect but perfectly wonderful human beings. Women tell me that they feel more isolated than they used to, that everyone they know is working harder and feeling more stressed, and that there's far less time for simply being. While there are things you personally can do to help your own life be more sane, the problem is not just in yourself. A society where it seems the majority of people feel stressed, harried and inadequate is not working the way it should.

What would the world look like if women's inner voices had a strong influence upon society? I am sure it would look quite different. See if you can trust your inner self to speak to you about the way the world is today. What do you know to be true? What do you sense is going on? What do you want for the future, for your children?

Simply asking these questions may bring up feelings that deserve to be acknowledged. One is the fear that you don't "know enough," or you don't have the facts. Another is the powerlessness about affecting the larger world that almost all of us feel. Those feelings are shared by so many women that they may be the places where we all must start. I wonder what would happen if all the women who never once thought of themselves as "political" before came together and talked from their hearts, freely acknowledging to each other their fears and doubts, and also their hopes and visions for the world.

Maybe it's no accident that women's voices are coming out now at this time in human history. By insisting on dominating nature rather than listening to it, we are destroying the fragile balance of life on Earth. And with all of humanity's knowledge comes even greater power to hurt ourselves and each other. Less and less will we be able to conquer one another, barricade ourselves against one another, and pretend not to *hear* or *see* each other.

Maybe whatever divine Spirit is watching over this fragile planet is counting on women—counting on *us*—to awaken to our own strength and authority. Then we will unleash and channel the power of our inner voices into the greatest force the world has ever known. We will come together and declare that compassion, empathy for one another and the honoring of life are truly the grandest traits that human beings are capable of. I pray that this century will be one where the journeys to the edges of outer knowledge will be matched, if not surpassed, by a great mass expedition into the human heart.

Recently, I joined more than 900 women at the Washington National Cathedral for "A Celebration of Women's Spirituality." The women spiritual leaders came from Christianity, Judaism, Islam, Buddhism and many other faiths, but they were joined in the belief that the great truth taught by all religion is to love and honor all people as one. It seemed so easy and natural for women to agree on this. On this day I felt the power of women collectively imagining a world of strength without violence, a world devoted to caring for and encouraging the inner voices of all people and protecting the Earth.

Let me leave you with a few more thoughts. Living from your inner voice does not mean having a perfect life or always feeling good. It means feeling a spaciousness in your soul. It means going from living from what seem to be your only choices, to living from what's truly possible.

You have the right to need validation. You don't have to do it alone. It's very hard to hold on to trusting your inner voice when everyone around you is avoiding theirs. Look for other women or men who are trying to follow their inner voice, and make a pact to cheer each other on. My hope for all women is that we align with ourselves and still have all the alliances we want, because it is our gift for alliance that makes women so wonderful and gives us so much joy. Yet remember as well that you also have the right to disconnect, and you can choose to disconnect, from people who don't validate your inner self.

Remember to treat your daughters, nieces and granddaughters as though their opinions and feelings matter, even when you disagree or it's inconvenient for you. Start as early in their lives as you can. There are so many forces that will press upon them to forget themselves and give themselves up. The best way you can help them grow up to know and value themselves is for you to get to know them and to value their strong, independent spirits.

When you follow your inner voice, you no longer are just a responder and reactor to life—you are a creator. Reactor and creator use the exact same letters—they're just arranged a little differently. The world needs women who are creators, millions upon millions of them; women who believe in the power of compassion, who don't give up on their dreams and who trust what they know to be true in their bodies, minds and hearts.

I hope that you have enjoyed taking this journey with me. Know that when you grow toward your true self, your growth ripples outward, reverberating along the strands of the many interconnected webs of relationship, touching the lives of many women. I hope that you take what you've gleaned from this book into both your inner and outer lives, and that you come back and share what you've discovered with me and with other women, and with men of heart as well. Perhaps together we can build a path to the inner self that even more women can follow.

Recommended Reading

Ban Breathnach, Sarah. *A Daybook of Comfort and Joy*. New York: Warner Books, 1995.

Bateson, Mary Catherine. *Composing A Life*. New York: Grove Atlantic, 1989.

Belenky, Mary, Blythe Clinchy, Nancy Goldberger, and Jill Tarule. *Women's Ways of Knowing*. New York: Basic Books, 1986.

Bingham, Mindy and Sandy Stryker. *Things Will Be Different for My Daughter: A Practical Guide to Building Her Self-Esteem and Self-Reliance*. New York: Penguin Putnam, 1995.

Borysenko, Joan. *A Woman's Book of Life: The Biology, Psychology, and Spirituality of the Feminine Life Cycle*. New York: Riverhead Books, 1997.

Brown, Lyn Mikel and Carol Gilligan. *Meeting at the Crossroads: Women's Psychology and Girls' Development*. New York: Ballantine Books, 1992.

Cameron, Julia. *The Artist's Way: A Spiritual Path to Higher Creativity*. New York: Putnam, 1992.

Cantor, Dorothy W. and Toni Bernay. *Women in Power: The Secrets of Leadership*. New York: Houghton Mifflin Company, 1992.

Cornell, Ann Weiser. *The Power of Focusing: A Practical Guide to Emotional Self-Healing*. Oakland, Calif.: New Harbinger, 1996.

Cornell, Ann Weiser and Barbara McGavin. *The Focusing Student's and Companion's Manual—Parts One and Two*. Calluna Press, 2002.

De Becker, Gavin. *The Gift of Fear*. New York: Little, Brown and Co., 1997.

Estes, Clarissa Pinkola. *Women Who Run With the Wolves*. New York: Ballantine Books, 1992.

Gendlin, Eugene T. *Focusing*. New York: Bantam Books, 1981.

Gendlin, Eugene T., Carl Gustav Jung. *Let Your Body Interpret Your Dreams*. Willmette, Illinois: Chiron Publications, 1986

Gilligan, Carol. *In a Different Voice: Psychological Theory and Women's Development*. Cambridge, Mass.: Harvard University Press, 1982.

Godfrey, Jolene. *No More Frogs to Kiss: 99 Ways to Give Economic Power to Girls.* New York: HarperCollins, 1995.

Hollander, Dory, Ph.D. *101 Lies Men Tell Women and Why Women Believe Them.* New York: HarperCollins, 1995.

Jack, Dana Crowley. *Silencing the Self: Depression and Women.* Cambridge, Mass.: Harvard University Press, 1991.

Johnson, Susan M., Ed. D. *Creating Connection: The Practice of Emotionally Focused Marital Therapy.* New York: Bruner Mazel, 1996.

Jordan, Judith, Alexandra Kaplan, Jean Baker Miller, Irene Stiver and Janet Surrey. *Women's Growth in Connection.* New York: Guilford Press, 1991.

Kelly, Thomas. *A Testament of Devotion.* New York: Harper & Brothers, 1941.

Klauser, Henriette Anne. *Write it Down, Make It Happen.* New York: Simon & Schuster, 2000.

Lerner, Harriet Goldhor, Ph.D. *The Dance of Anger.* New York: Harper-Collins, 1997.

Maddox, Rebecca. *Inc. Your Dreams: For any Woman Who is Thinking About Her Own Business.* New York: Viking, 1995.

Michaelson, Maureen. *Women and Work: In Their Own Words.* Troudale, Ore.: Newsage Press, 1994.

Miller, Jean Baker. *Toward a New Psychology of Women.* Boston: Beacon Press, 1988.

Ms. Foundation for Women. *Girls Seen and Heard: 52 Life Lessons for Our Daughters.* New York: Jeremy P. Tarcher/Putnam, 1998.

Northrup, Christiane. *The Wisdom of Menopause: Creating Physical and Emotional Health and Healing During the Change.* New York: Bantam Doubleday, 2003.

———. *Women's Bodies, Women's Wisdom: Creating Physical and Emotional Health and Healing.* New York: Bantam Doubleday Dell, reprint edition, 2002.

Pipher, Mary. *Reviving Opehilia: Saving the Selves of Adolescent Girls.* New York: Ballantine Books, 1994.

Pittman, Frank. *Man Enough: Fathers, Sons and the Search for Masculinity.* Berkley Publishing Group, 1994.

Rosenberg, Marshall B. *Nonviolent Communication: A Language of Compassion.* PuddleDancer Press; March 1999.

Sark. *Transformation Soup: Healing for the Splendidly Imperfect.* New York: Simon & Schuster, 2000.

Sher, Barbara. *I Could Do Anything If I Only Knew What It Was.* New York: Dell, 1994.

Sher, Barbara with Barbara Annie Gottlieb. *Wishcraft: How to Get What You Really Want.* New York: Ballantine Books, 1979.

Tannen, Deborah. *You Just Don't Understand: Women and Men in Conversation.* New York: Ballantine Books, 1990.

Taylor, Shelley. *The Tending Instinct: How Nurturing Is Essential to Who We Are and How We Live.* New York: Times Books, 2002.